Upon that Mountain

Upon that Mountain

ERIC SHIPTON

Vertebrate Publishing, Sheffield
www.v-publishing.co.uk

Upon that Mountain

Eric Shipton

 Vertebrate Publishing
Omega Court, 352 Cemetery Road, Sheffield S11 8FT, United Kingdom.
www.v-publishing.co.uk

First published by Hodder and Stoughton Limited, 1943.
This edition first published in 2019 by Vertebrate Publishing.

Vertebrate Publishing
Omega Court, 352 Cemetery Road, Sheffield S11 8FT, UK

ISBN 978-1-912560-08-0 (Paperback)
ISBN 978-1-910240-26-7 (Ebook)

Produced by Vertebrate Publishing.

Contents

Shipton's Legacy for Mountaineers
by Stephen Venables

Eric Shipton was one of the great mountain explorers of the twentieth century. As a young climber he was brave and skilful, with a prodigious flair for pioneering new routes on remote peaks, far from any hope of rescue. During the course of his life that bold vision broadened to encompass immense landscapes and he was drawn increasingly to the wide canvas of exploration, with the result that we sometimes forget what a brilliant natural climber he was. However, whether we view him as an explorer, or climber, or both, his greatest achievement was to unlock the secrets of so many mountain ranges. The mountains he discovered – and the manner in which he discovered them – remain an inspiration to all who have attempted to follow in his steps.

I first came across his name in 1972. I had just started climbing, I was filled with dreams of far off mountains and was devouring everything I could on the subject. One book in particular seemed to enshrine all my half-formed aspirations. It was Shipton's autobiography, *That Untravelled World*. Here was a man who had dared to follow his dreams and whose sense of enchantment sparkled from every page of unadorned prose.

Soon I got to know all the other books and followed Shipton's travels in more detail, discovering the intricacies of the Nanda Devi adventure, the repeated attempts on Everest and the breathtaking scope of the great Karakoram explorations told in my favourite of all, *Blank on the Map*. I couldn't afford to buy first editions and had to rely on borrowed library copies. So I was delighted when a new *omnibus Eric Shipton: The Six Mountain-Travel Books* assembled all his early narratives into a single affordable volume, complete with well-captioned photos, additional articles, clear maps, pertinent appendices and an eloquent Introduction by Jim Perrin. It remains a treasured and constantly rejuvenating source of inspiration.

Since first reading Shipton's books, I have got to know some of the people who actually climbed with him – Scott Russell in the Karakoram, George Lowe and Charles Wylie in Nepal, John Earle in Patagonia. They all found him a delightful companion, a great conversationalist, an enthusiast but also a gently provocative rocker of the establishment. And it's that same engaging personality that speaks through the books; they are immensely readable.

As Jim Perrin points out, the writings would be remarkable if only for their sheer geographical scope. From his astonishingly bold, assured, pioneering debut on Mount Kenya, to Everest, to Garhwal and the Karakoram, to Turkestan, to Patagonia, Shipton's explorations covered immense areas of wilderness. But it was the manner of those explorations that made them such a continuing inspiration to modern mountaineers. Few of us cover as much ground; none of us has equalled the record of the 1935 Everest reconnaissance expedition that made first ascents of twenty-two peaks over 20,000 feet; most of us would baulk at the frugality espoused by Shipton and his famously austere companion, Bill Tilman; but the ideal – of achieving more with less, travelling uncluttered, attuned to the landscape – remains an aspiration.

As Harold Evans famously pointed out, a picture can be worth a thousand words. It was Eric Shipton's 1937 photos of the Latok peaks, the Ogre and Uli Biaho that inspired the next generation. In a sense he threw down the gauntlet for John Roskelley, Doug Scott, Jim Donini and all those others who brought modern techniques to the soaring granite towers in what is now northern Pakistan. More recently the spire that bears Shipton's name has been a recurring magnet for modern American climbers like Greg Child, Mark Synott and Steph Davis. Shipton had the grand vision to reveal vast tracts of previously unexplored mountain country; his modern followers are enjoying the fruits – whether it is the fine detail of a vertical rock tower or the broader sweep of the great Karakoram ski tours carried out by people like Ned Gillete, David Hamilton and the Odier brothers. For myself, with Phil Bartlett and Duncan Tunstall, it was thrilling, in 1987, to try and emulate Shipton, making a serendipitous first ascent above the Biafo Glacier, before continuing over Snow Lake to the same Khurdopin Pass he had reached with Scott Russell 48 years earlier, at the outbreak of the Second World War.

That war saw Russell incarcerated in the infamous Changi jail in Singapore, while Shipton languished more comfortably in one of the few proper jobs he ever had – as British Consul in Kashgar. There he wrote his first volume of autobiography, *Upon That Mountain*. He ends the book on an elegiac note, describing his last evening on Snow Lake before returning to a 'civilisation' embarked on a cataclysmic war. 'The great granite spires of the Biafo stood black against a deep blue sky. At least this mountain world, to which I owed so much of life and happiness, would stand above the ruin of human hopes, the heritage of a saner generation of men.'

Elegant prose from a man who, as Peter Steele's excellent 1998 biography revealed, was dyslexic and relied heavily on editorial help from some of his many girlfriends. If only some of today's celebrity adventurer authors could be given similar help. But it's not just down to writing style. All too often the authors are simply ticking lists, notching up goals. With Shipton the journey was everything, the tantalising view into an unknown cirque more important than the prestigious summit. Despite his obvious natural flair as a climber, he became increasingly drawn to the bigger picture, the far horizon. And by all accounts he could be hazy about logistical details. Hence the Everest putsch of 1952, when he lost the leadership of what was likely to be, finally, the successful expedition. The irony was that Shipton had taken part in more Everest expeditions than anyone else alive. As an outraged Charles Wylie pointed out, 'he was *the* man, he was Mr Everest.' Of course, the replacement leader, John Hunt, was in his very different way just as charming and charismatic as Shipton, and he ran a brilliant show. But, as Hunt was the first to acknowledge, it was Shipton who had assembled his crack team, including the two New Zealanders, George Lowe and Ed Hillary, who both played such key roles in 1953. And it was Shipton who had, in 1935, first employed the aspiring young Tibetan, Tenzing Norgay.

Even the most selfless, unworldly saint would be aggrieved at losing his chance of global fame. Shipton had obviously thrilled to the opportunity, in 1951 and 1952, to be first into untouched country along the Nepal-Tibet border, all the way from Makalu to Menlungtse, but for a jobbing mountain lecturer and writer, success on Everest itself would have brought useful kudos. The sense of missed opportunity cannot have been helped by the subsequent break-up of his marriage. For a while he began to resemble a character from a Benjamin Britten opera – an outcast, an oddball, a penniless misfit.

There the story might have ended, had it not been for the redemptive solace of mountain wilderness and the realisation of new challenges. Like his former climbing partner Tilman, Shipton began a whole new career of exploration in the far south, rejuvenated by the stark empty spaces of Patagonia and Tierra del Fuego. And here again the world he explored has become a magnet for modern climbers. His gruelling first crossings of the great southern icecaps remain a template for today's sledge-haulers, including his younger son, John Shipton, who is increasingly following in his father's steps. Likewise on Tierra del Fuego, where one of today's most imaginative and ascetic mountaineers, Andy Parkin – and his frequent companion Simon Yates – is drawn repeatedly to the mountain ranges Shipton first unravelled. And on the great spires of Cerro Torre and FitzRoy, virtuosos like Rolando Garibotti, Ermanno Salvaterra, Kelly Cordes and Colin Haley still exemplify the Shipton ideal of travelling light, paring down, achieving more with less.

As for that most vulgarised of all mountains – Everest; there too, during a golden age of new possibilities in the seventies and eighties, Shipton's ideals were finally realised. The Australian route up the Great Couloir and the Anglo-American-Canadian route up the East Face, which I was lucky enough to join, were both pulled off by a handful of climbers, without oxygen equipment, and without the help of high altitude porters. As for Reinhold Messner's audacious solo ascent of the North Face – or the remarkable forty-one-hour dash up and down the Japanese-Hornbein Couloir by Erhard Loretan and Jean Troillet – they probably exceeded Shipton's wildest imaginings.

There is one other quality – seemingly modern but actually timeless – that many modern climbers share with Eric Shipton, and that is the decision to follow the path of their own choosing. There was a wonderful moment in the early thirties when Shipton realised that expeditioning really could become his life, that he could continue to play this endlessly fascinating game, in his case never losing that vital sense of curiosity. That is what makes these books so compelling to every generation that follows. As he wrote in his coda to *Upon That Mountain:*

> There are few treasures of more lasting worth than the experiences of a way of life that is in itself wholly satisfying. Such, after all, are the only possessions of which no fate, no cosmic catastrophe can deprive us; nothing can alter the fact if for one moment in eternity we have really lived.

Stephen Venables
June 2010

Introduction:
Eric Shipton by Jim Perrin

Early in 1930 a young planter in Kenya unexpectedly received a letter from an ex-soldier ten years his senior, who had settled in the colony after the Great War. The letter mentioned that its writer had done some climbing in the English Lake District on his last home leave, and asked advice about visiting the East African mountains. Its immediate results were a meeting between the two men, an initial jaunt up Kilimanjaro together, and the first ascent, later that year, of the West Ridge of Mount Kenya – one of the major pre-war achievements of British alpinism.

The two men were, of course, Eric Shipton and H.W. Tilman, and their chance meeting, out in the colonies at the very beginning of the decade, led to one of the most fruitful partnerships and entrancing sagas in the history of mountain exploration. Indeed, the centrality of their role in that history throughout one of its vital phases is unarguable. The chance of their acquaintance and the magnitude of their travels aside, there is another aspect of these two men which is perhaps even more remarkable. For they were both inveterate chroniclers of their climbs and journeys, and the quality of the writings so produced places them absolutely in the forefront of mountaineering and travel literature.

For the span of their contents alone, Shipton's books are noteworthy: *Nanda Devi* (1936), his first, deals with the 1934 penetration up the Rishi Gorge into the Nanda Devi sanctuary in company with Tilman, as well as the two traverses of the Badrinath-Kedamath and Badrinath-Gangotri watersheds. From the moment of its first publication, for reasons to be examined below, it was regarded as one of the revolutionary texts of mountain literature, and it remains an enthralling story of hazardous and uncertain journeying with minimal resources through unknown country. *Blank on the Map* (1938) describes the 1937 Shaksgam survey expedition undertaken with Michael Spender, John Auden, (brothers to the poets) and Tilman – an important venture into a little-known region of the Himalayas which provided a basis for much subsequent mountaineering activity in the Karakoram. (First editions of this very rare title now command fabulous prices amongst collectors.)

From 1940 to 1942 Shipton served as British Consul-General at Kashgar, in the Chinese Province of Sinkiang. During this period he completed a first volume of memoirs, entitled *Upon that Mountain*, published in 1943. This frank, vivid polemic set out his basic mountaineering creed, whilst also describing his early Alpine and Himalayan seasons, the series of climbs on Mount Kenya, and the four attempts on Everest and two survey-trips to the Karakoram in which he took part during the thirties. His next book was very different in tone. *Mountains of Tartary* (1950) is a series of light-hearted sketches of weeks or weekends seized from official consular work – in the main during his second spell of office in Kashgar – and spent on Bogdo Ola, Mustagh Ata, Chakragil (mountains which are again coming into vogue in the eighties since China's relaxation of restrictions on travel). The *Mount Everest Reconnaissance Expedition 1951* (1952) was basically a photographic volume, prefaced by a succinct and entertaining narrative about this vital piece of mountain exploration, which cleared the path for John Hunt's successful expedition to the mountain in 1953. The final book in this series, *Land of Tempest*, written in 1963, takes for theme the period of Shipton's life from 1958 to 1962 and includes accounts of three trips to Patagonia – on the last of which he made the first crossing of the main Patagonian ice-cap – and one to Tierra del Fuego.

The above bald catalogue suggests the range, but captures little of the flavour, of this extraordinary man's life, the brief outline of which is as follows. He was born in Ceylon in 1907, his father a tea-planter who died before his son was three. Thereafter, Shipton, his sister and mother travelled extensively between Ceylon, India, France and England, before the family finally settled in the latter country for purposes of the children's schooling. Shipton's mountaineering career began in 1924 with holidays in Norway and Switzerland and was consolidated through four successive alpine seasons in 1925–1928. His first ascent of Nelion, the unclimbed twin summit of Mount Kenya, with Wyn Harris in 1929, and of the same mountain's West Ridge with Tilman the following year, brought him to the notice of the mountaineering establishment of the day and elicited an invitation to join the expedition led by Frank Smythe to Kamet, in the Garhwal region, in 1931. Shipton distinguished himself on this trip, being in the summit party on eleven of the twelve peaks climbed by the expedition, including that of Kamet itself, which at 25,447ft was the highest summit then attained. His performance in 1931 led to an invitation to join Ruttledge's 1933 Everest expedition. Thereafter the milestones slip by: Rishi Gorge 1934; Everest Reconnaissance 1935, which he led; Everest and Nanda Devi 1936; Shaksgam 1937; Everest 1938; Karakoram 1939 are the main ones amongst them, but virtually the whole decade was spent in Himalayan travel, and the extent of his exploratory achievement perhaps even now lacks full recognition.

He spent the Second World War in Government service in Sinkiang, Persia and Hungary, went back for a further spell in Kashgar from 1946 to 1948, accompanied by his wife Diana, and was Consul-General at Kunming, in

Southern China, from 1949 to 1951. On his return to England he was asked to lead an expedition to reconnoitre the Southern approaches to Everest, in the course of which he and Ed Hillary first espied the eventual line of ascent up the Western Cwm to the South Col, from a vantage point on the slopes of Pumori. The following year he led a rather unsatisfactory training expedition to Cho Oyu. In the late summer of 1952, Shipton having been urged to lead a further expedition to Everest in 1953 and having accepted, the joint Himalayan Committee of the Alpine Club and the Royal Geographical Society performed an astonishing volte-face, appointing the competent and experienced but at that time virtually unknown Colonel John Hunt as leader, and accepting Shipton's consequent resignation.

This sorry episode effectively formed a watershed in Shipton's life. After the break-up of his marriage and loss of his post as Warden of the Outward Bound School at Eskdale, which occurred shortly after the events of 1952-53, he lived for a time in the rural seclusion of Shropshire, working as a forestry labourer. He was enticed back for a last trip to the Karakoram in 1957, and thereafter developed a new grand obsession with travel in the southernmost regions of South America, which absorbed most of the next decade in his life. Finally, in his sixties, he was a popular lecturer on cruises to such places as the Galapagos Islands, and leader of mild Himalayan treks. He died of liver cancer at the home of a friend in Wiltshire during the spring of 1977.

This, then, is the bare outline of an outstanding life. The man who lived it, through his involvement in the 1931 Kamet and 1933 Everest expeditions, had attained a considerable degree of national celebrity by the early thirties, yet at that time he was to all intents and purposes a professionless pauper and a kind of international tramp, whose possessions amounted to little more than the clothes in which he stood. There is an admirable passage in Upon That Mountain where Shipton recounts the dawning of a realisation that the way of life which most appealed to him perhaps presented a practical possibility. It happened on the way back to India from the North Side of Everest in 1933. In company with the geologist Lawrence Wager, he had made his way across a strip of unexplored country and over a new pass into Sikkim. Wager's influence shifted the emphasis of Shipton's interest away from the climbing of peaks to enthusiasm for a general mode of exploration – a fascination with geography itself. Twenty years later, this shift was to provide his detractors with an easy target. For the moment, his mind works over the ground thus:

> 'Why not spend the rest of my life doing this sort of thing?' There was no way of life that I liked more, the scope appeared to be unlimited, others had done it, vague plans had already begun to take shape, why not put some of them into practice? ... The

most obvious snag, of course, was lack of private means; but surely such a mundane consideration could not be decisive. In the first place I was convinced that expeditions could be run for a tithe of the cost generally considered necessary. Secondly if one could produce useful or interesting results one would surely find support ... '

When he took into account his reactions to the milieu of the large expedition, ('The small town of tents that sprung up each evening, the noise and racket of each fresh start, the sight of a huge army invading the peaceful valleys, it was all so far removed from the light, free spirit with which we were wont to approach our peaks'), then the virtue to be made of necessity was obvious, and of it was born what came to be known as the 'Shipton/Tilman style of lightweight expedition'. I referred above to Shipton's *Nanda Devi* as a revolutionary text, and it was just that. I doubt if there has ever been a less formulaic account of an expedition. It has a magical, fresh quality, a get-through-by-the-skin-of-your-teeth spontaneity, a candour, a clear rationale, an excited commitment, an elation about the enterprise undertaken, which no previous mountaineering book had approached. From the outset the terms are made clear: five months in the Garhwal Himalaya to tackle some of its outstanding topographical problems, 'climbing peaks when opportunity occurred', on a budget of £150 each for himself and Tilman (some of Shipton's share of which is advanced by Tilman 'against uncertain security'). The scenes throughout, from the broken-toed, frock-coated setting-out from Ranikhet to the final descent from the Sunderdhunga Col to Maiktoli, are evoked in a clear and economical style. But it is the message – the simple moral that it is possible, and in terms of response to the landscape and its peoples even desirable, to travel cheap and light, to move fast and live off the land – which is the book's revolutionary charge, and which was to make Shipton and Tilman, in the words of the American writer David Roberts, 'retroactive heroes of the avant-garde'.

Two major characteristics distinguish *Nanda Devi* and were to become hallmarks of Shipton's writing. The first of these is an intense curiosity-which remains with him, his conclusions growing more authoritative with increase of experience – about natural landforms, whether they be mountains, valleys, rivers, volcanoes or glaciers. This curiosity acts as a stimulus, a fund of energy, in his explorations, continually used as a basis, a point of reference: 'It was enthralling to disentangle the geography of the region ... for me, the basic reason for mountaineering'.

Alongside this drive to understand the physical make-up of a landscape there operates a more reflective principle, very close to traditional nature-mysticism, which Shipton almost invariably carries off with great poise and delicacy, sure-footedly avoiding the obvious pitfalls of bathos or inflation.

> We settled down on a comfortable bed of sand, and watched the approach of night transform the wild desert mountains into phantoms of soft unreality. How satisfying it was to be travelling with such simplicity. I lay awaiting the approach of sleep, watching the constellations swing across the sky. Did I sleep that night – or was I caught up for a moment into the ceaseless rhythm of space?
> *Blank on the Map*

A very satisfying irony lies in suggesting an affinity with mysticism of a man who claimed througout his adult life to be an agnostic, and who would probably, even if only for the sheer joy of argument, have vigorously rejected the intimation. Perhaps his disclaimer of religious belief was like that of Simone Weill, and masked a genuine sense of divine mystery within the universe. Certainly much of the interest in Shipton's writings derives from a tension between the very practical preoccupations with physical phenomena, and a frequent lapsing into a more quietistic mode of thought. (To compound the mischief, I have to say that *Nanda Devi* puts me in mind of no other text so much as one of the late poems of that most ascetic of saints, St John of the Cross, quoted here in the translation by Roy Campbell:

> The generous heart upon its quest
> Will never falter, nor go slow,
> But pushes on, and scorns to rest,
> Wherever it's most hard to go.
> It runs ahead and wearies not
> But upward hurls its fierce advance
> For it enjoys I know not what
> That is achieved by lucky chance.

Those who knew Shipton well sound a recurrent note in their reminiscences which supports the contention that there was a mystical element to his character. It concerns a quality of detachment he possessed, and invariably fastens on a specific physical detail. The following is typical:

> He had the most marvellous blue eyes, very kindly, very amused, and very wise. But there was always a sense, when you talked

with him, that somehow he was not with you, was looking right through you, searching out farther and farther horizons.

In the course of researching Shipton's biography, it was remarkable and eventually almost comical how often that impression, almost word-for-word, was repeated. Without the evidence of the text it could be taken as a mannerism, but in his books there recur time and again passages which define his response to landscape as one striving towards a mystical awareness.

In this he is very different to Tilman, his most frequent companion of the thirties, and it is interesting to compare the two men. The ten-year difference in age is for once significant, for Tilman's seniority ensured that he underwent the determining influence on his character of the First World War, and it affected him profoundly. It is what made him a master of that most serious of all forms of writing, comic irony, and it is what causes him to veer dangerously close at times to a distinct misanthropy. It explains the prelapsarian vitality with which he imbues his native characters, the neglectful portrayal of his compatriots, and the isolation which identifies his authorial persona. In his personal conduct, it provides the reason for his taciturnity, his phlegmatism and unemotional responses to situations. The vulnerability of youth, its lack of circumspection and eager commitment to affection or cause were in Tilman's case the victims of war, and the survivor, psychic and physical, of that particularly obscene war had need to be encased in adamantine.

Shipton's enthusiasms, on the other hand, operate under no such constraint. He can indulge his feelings as freely as he will, the zest and gaiety of the twenties glitters around his early activities. He commits himself freely, and as equally with a climb as a journey of exploration or to one of the many women who shared his life. A couple of comments upon him from 1931 by Frank Smythe capture the temperament of the man:

> No one who climbs with Shipton can remain pessimistic, for he imparts an imperturbability and confidence into a day's work which are in themselves a guarantee of success.

Or again, about his climbing:

> I saw Shipton's eye light up, and next instant he went at the slope with the energy of a boxer who, after months of training, sees his opponent before him.

The differences in their characters probably acted as a bond between Shipton and Tilman, and account for their sharing of some of the most ambitious undertakings of their lives. For Tilman, his own youth lost, Shipton's enthusiasm and boundless energy must have been inspiriting and invigorating, whilst the fatherless Shipton may well have found that Tilman's wry, benevolent maturity fulfilled a need in him at a certain stage of his life. In mountaineering terms, the roles were reversed, and the more experienced Shipton was the leader. One very telling indication of this occurs in Tilman's diary for 30 May, 1934. After reconnoitring one of the crucial – and very tortuous – passages of the route up the Rishi Gorge, they have to hurry back to camp. The subsequent diary entry briefly states, 'Shipton's route-memory invaluable as usual, self hopeless.'

It has to be said, though, that a change occurs in Shipton's outlook, especially with regard to mountaineering, during the mid-thirties. It seems to me complex and cumulative rather than associated with specific circumstances. The influence of older companions such as Tilman and Wager would have played a part. So too, perhaps, did the relationship upon which he had embarked with Pamela Freston. But two related events could be seen as decisive in the transition from joyful mountaineering innocence to prudent experience. These were the two avalanches which Shipton witnessed on the slopes leading to the North Col of Everest during successive expeditions in 1935 and 1936. Of the first one, he had to say 'I am sure that no one could have escaped from an avalanche such as that which broke away below us while we were lying peacefully on the North Col'. The following year, as he and Wyn Harris were climbing up the same slope, this is what happened:

> We climbed quickly over a lovely hard surface in which one sharp kick produced a perfect foothold. About half-way up to the col we started traversing to the left. Wyn anchored himself firmly on the lower lip of a crevasse while I led across the slope. I had almost reached the end of the rope and Wyn was starting to follow when there was a rending sound … a short way above me, and the whole surface of the slope I was standing on started to move slowly down towards the brink of an ice-cliff a couple of hundred feet below …

Wyn Harris managed to jump back into the crevasse and re-establish the belay, the snow failed to gather momentum, and Shipton survived. It was the last attempt on the mountain that year. The point is, that Shipton's faith in the material he was climbing had been undermined – just as in personal relationships, when the trust has gone the commitment is withdrawn. Shipton's heyday as a climber is delimited by these events. Though there are inevitably some exciting and perilous escapades after 1936 – the climb on the Dent Blanche-like peak above the Bostan Terek valley is a striking example

– henceforwards, reading these books, we keep company with a much more circumspect mountaineer.

This line of reasoning inevitably leads us towards a consideration of what is generally and I think rightly regarded as one of the cruces of Shipton's life – the circumstances surrounding the choice of leadership for the 1953 expedition to Everest. It is very difficult to summarise in brief the main points of what is still a controversial topic. Even Walt Unsworth's Everest book, which comes nearest to being an authoritative history of the mountain, overlooked important material in its researches which throws a clearer light on some aspects of this vital area. What emerges, from close examination of relevant Himalayan Committee minutes and written submissions from its surviving members, is a bizarre tale of fudging and mudging, falsification of official minutes, unauthorised invitations, and opportunistic and desperate last-minute seizures of initiative by a particular faction. It is a perfect illustration of the cock-up rather than the conspiracy theory of history, from which little credit redounds upon the British mountaineering establishment of the time. The saddest fact about the whole sorry tale is that it appeared to place in conflict two honourable and quite innocent men – Shipton and John Hunt.

There are two basic themes to be considered. The first of these is the general climate of feeling surrounding Shipton's attitude for, and interest in, the leadership of an expedition which, even in the early stages of its planning, was subject to a jingoistic insistence that Everest must be climbed by a British party. (That this was not to be achieved for a further 22 years scarcely mattered in the event, the national attachments of the first summiteers being clearly turned to the Commonwealth's greater glory.) This climate of feeling, accepting some of Shipton's own statements at face value, and drawing in other rather more questionable evidence, particularly that relating to the 1952 Cho Oyu expedition, where peculiar circumstances undoubtedly affected Shipton's leadership, had drifted towards the view that Shipton lacked the urgency, the thrust, the killer instinct which would be necessary to 'conquer' Everest.[1] It was immeasurably strengthened by Shipton's own submission to the Himalayan Committee meeting of 28 July, 1952, in which he expressed doubts about his suitability for the job on the following grounds: he had to consider his own career – with a wife and two young children to support, he was out of a job and needed to get one; he felt that new blood was needed to undertake the task; his strong preference was for smaller parties, lightly equipped.

At this juncture we need to pass over to a consideration of the second basic theme – the conduct of members of the Himalayan Committee over the

---

1 In *Upon That Mountain*, for example, he had written that 'there are some, even among those who have themselves attempted to reach the summit, who nurse a secret hope that Mount Everest will never be climbed. I must confess to such feelings myself.'

matter of the leadership. The first point to be made is that the Committee was very weakly chaired. Because of this, the pro-Shipton faction carried the day at the meeting of July 28 and, chiefly through the efforts of Laurence Kirwan, Shipton was strongly prevailed upon to accept the leadership, the contention then resting with the matter of deputy leadership.

However, there also existed a pro-Hunt faction, headed by Basil Goodfellow and Colonel Tobin, who had both been absent from the July 28 meeting. These two men lobbied forcefully that the deputy – or assault – leadership should fall to Hunt, which would inevitably compromise Shipton, whose choice had been Charles Evans and to whom Hunt was therefore unacceptable in that role. The crucial committee meeting took place on 11 September. The pro-Hunt faction was present in force, determined to reverse the decision of the previous meeting. The more ardent Shiptonians – most notably Kirwan and Shipton's old friend Wager – were absent. Shipton was morally compelled to offer his resignation. The rest is history, apart from a few squalid diversions, such as the subsequent falsification of this meeting's minutes by Claude Elliott, the chairman – in the words of one contemporary observer, 'as bad a chairman of committees as one could find; he was hopelessly indecisive and hesitant and was too easily swayed by anyone (like Kirwan) who held firm opinions, however wrong these might be'.

What the effect would have been upon Shipton had he led the successful expedition to Everest is a matter for conjecture. John Hunt was patently well-equipped to cope with the ensuing celebrity, and used it tirelessly in the public good. It could perhaps be thought doubtful that Shipton would have enjoyed, and responded so positively, to the inevitably massive public acclaim.

After 1953, his life went through a difficult period, but it emerged into a golden late summer of exploration in an area completely fresh to him. His Patagonian journeys of the late fifties and sixties were a harking-back in many ways to his great Karakoram travels of the thirties. They would have been rendered immensely more public and difficult and perhaps thus less satisfying to him, by the burden of international fame. Instead, he was able to slip quietly away, pursue his own bent amongst the unknown mountains and glaciers of a new wilderness. It is a myth fulfilled, a proper consummation in the life of this explorer-mystic, whose outlook and progress resonate so closely with those of Tennyson's 'Ulysses', from which poem he took the motto for the first part of Blank on the Map, and the title for his magnificent second autobiography, *That Untravelled World*.

There is a phrase of Shipton's from this latter book which gives perfect expression to one of the great lives of our century – 'a random harvest of delight'. That is exactly what the books collected together between these covers are, in general terms. But they are also an opportunity for a new generation of readers to engage with one of the most attractive personalities the sport of mountaineering has ever produced, to keep company with his spare, lithe figure loping off into the ranges, seeking out the undiscovered country, his distant blue eyes lingering on the form of a particular peak, the passage over to an unexplored glacier. If curiosity, appreciation, aspiration and delight are a form of praise – as assuredly they are – then here is one man's testament of a lifetime spent in worship of the great world around him.

I am a part of all that I have met;

Yet all experience is an arch wherethrough Gleams that untravelled world, whose margin fades For ever and for ever when I move.

It is the epitaph Shipton would have chosen for himself. No man lived out its theme more fully, nor finally more deserved its implicit tribute.

Jim Perrin
January 1985

Foreword
by Geoffrey Winthrop Young

The outbreak of war overtook Eric Shipton beyond the frontiers of India. His long and self-reliant experience of peoples, places and tongues qualified him for war work of a responsible kind. He returned last winter for a few weeks, writing this book upon the journey; he married, surveyed the home field, left to his wife the publication of the book in the intervals of her own work in the ATS, and again disappeared, upon a distant, responsible charge. The adventures, and this their fashion of issue, seem to me equally characteristic of the man; and it is a peculiar pleasure that their richness of suggestion for the future of mountain exploration should be appearing during my own presidency of the Alpine Club, the parent of all mountain associations. For, as it has been the nursery of the finest of adventurous traditions, so also the Club should continue to show itself the guardian of the new training for fitness of body and spirit which our own hills, no less than distant ranges, will be offering to on-coming generations.

Twice in a lifetime we have seen war – indefensible in itself – eliciting from commonplace or uncultivated men and boys and girls qualities of heroism and acts of supreme self-sacrifice, and educating in the majority of those who by chance survived its dangers a new and finer moral and social conscience. And twice we have had to face the realisation – not agreeable to the educational minded – that our accepted ways of training the young in peace years have been defective; and that they will go on being so, until we have discovered how to stress qualities of chivalry, self-reliance and generosity, and how to soft-pedal their opposites, without having to wait for some periodic purge of war to educate those whom it does not destroy.

Only a contact with realities, realities of endurance, of uncertainty and of service, can train character; and in our early years they must be realities so modified as to test but not overtest immaturity. There is no such reality in the competition of games, or of examination. It can be found only in contests of uncertain issue, and progressive severity, with opposing natural forces: either with other human beings in destructive warfare, or with the elements, waves and winds and height and space. Even during this war we have reflected; and we have begun to retrace our steps in the revival of our one-time splendid sea training. Sea schools, and not only for the future sailors, are one answer to our problem. Another is to be found in this book, in the story of the discipline and spiritual self-realisation which are to be found on the ascent of the Hill Difficulty and in the sojourn among hostile spaces.

Eric Shipton stands in the forefront of our present-day explorers. Since boyhood he has been an adventurer, and since boyhood a rebellious intelligence has held him back from all conventional openings and steered him inevitably into the single positive alternative – the life of a pioneer. He has refused to accept traditional methods even in exploration, and he has gone far towards perfecting a new technique of toughening by travel. Happily, he is also an illuminating writer, and I have for long placed his 'Nanda Devi', the first penetration into the sanctuary of that glorious mountain, among the best books of adventure known to me. In the present volume he relates his whole Odyssey from a fortunate boyhood, when even in school holidays he was free to wander far afield, to the week when news of the war found him in the Shaksgam valleys.

In each of his chapters, or stages, we can now see that he set himself to solve some special explorer's problem: how, for instance, to mountaineer for long and far at little cost, and without the majestic cumbrousness of preceding Himalayan tradition; how to inure the human body to hardship and perpetual rains under tropical conditions, until an absolute fitness is attained, at which point the capacity to enjoy beauty or strangeness begins to function again independently of physical discomfort; how, without large provisioning, to live off a barren or glacial land, even if it means competing with the local bears for the seasonal bamboo-shoot to avert starvation; how again, where even bamboo-shoots are wanting, to carry provisioning enough oneself, even though it meant a schism between the Shipton and the Tilman schools – whether a second shirt is or is not a superfluity for a three months' rude travel; how again to evade the restrictions of time hitherto imposed by the coming of the monsoon; and again how – but the solution in this case was postponed by the war – to fortify an explorer so that he may be able to continue his work irrespective of the coming of winter and its additional severities among glacial ranges. He traverses new ground, also, when he is treating of the management of temper and mood under primitive conditions; a vital but formerly unmentionable condition of success, which I ventured first to approach, in writing of mountaineering, after the last world war had dissipated some little of our dangerous Victorian reticence.

Eric Shipton is picturing for us, in effect, a transition to which he has been contributing: the ending of one epoch in mountain exploration and the beginning of a new epoch, in which such venturing may well be within reach of all, regardless of the size of a bank balance, and in which such determined courses may even be insisted upon as essential to a training for any form of leadership. He gives us also the answer to another question, of how a post-war generation will be able to accumulate even the lesser funds needed for the new method of exploration. For the principles governing all such adventure, and directing the process of preparing for it, are the same, whether we are setting out as experienced travellers without hoarded pounds for Turkestan, or tramping as boys, upon our hoarded shillings, into the – to us – equally unknown and wonderful hill spaces of Wales or Cumberland or Scotland. Weather, hunger, weariness, loss of route or of temper or of nerve, are to be our opponents in either case, and our own spirit is to become the disciplined ally, whose measure we have first to take and then to mend, until it can serve us as a fit and happy leader.

Like most of us, Eric Shipton started his adventure from two impulses: the one, the urge to try himself out against the unknown; the other, the passion to reach 'neverendingness', to be free of that inevitable 'other side' which bore so heavily upon Richard Jefferies' Bevis. Like many of us, too, he was first inspired by Whymper's writings to look for this realisation among mountains; and like R. L. Stevenson – and again like a number of us – he began with a solitary wandering in France. We can follow his expeditions, almost unaware of the twofold progress we are sharing, until we find ourselves echoing his own dictum, that 'it is not the approach that matters, but the attitude of mind', and we realise suddenly the inner meaning and the true end of his – as of all – good physical adventuring. It is not long since the restless spirit of a disillusioned younger Europe was acclaiming the frantic feats of young Fascists and Nazis upon northern Alpine rock walls and in contempt of all known Himalayan risks. It would be hard to imagine a wider divergence, in the method and nature of the undertaking, in the spirit of the doing and in the ultimate effect upon the performer, than that between the stories of those single despairing stunts, to force some self-reassurance from death or from notoriety, and these memories of austere and perilous journeys, pursued in seclusion, and achieving as between the adventurer and his surroundings an always heightened sense of the humour, the beauty and the deeper, harder values of a life lived under natural conditions. I remember Gino Watkins, a forerunner in the art of exploration as a higher art of living, saying that he would prefer to live among Eskimos in the Arctic, but that returns to civilised ways were necessary, as contrast, in order to be able to retain a detached judgment and to renew a deliberate choice. Eric Shipton reinforces this view. Culture and our civilised arts are there to discover to us the apparent values of this or that fashion of living. But, in order to be able to live, in actual conduct, up to these standards, and to develop in accordance with them, we have to undergo real and hard experience. The outcome for us, whether we match our forces with nearer hill and lake and coast, or further glacier, desert and ocean, is to be our escape from hearsay, from wishful book worlds and from wilful creeds, and our achievement of a lively and ennobling inward adventure, by means of a series of inspiriting outward conflicts and travels.

Geoffrey Winthrop Young

1 The Approach

> 'In the calm darkness of the moonless nights,
> In the lone glare of day,
> the snows descend
> Upon that mountain;
> none beholds them there,
> Nor when the flakes burn in the sinking sun
> Or the star beams dart through them.'
>
> Shelley (Lines from *Mont Blanc*, 1816.)

Every child, I suppose, spends a large proportion of its time in a day-dream about trees, or engines, or the sea, or horses, or Central Africa, or some other subject that has captured its imagination. Unfortunately these longings are seldom expressed and are generally submerged by the weight of conventional upbringing and education, but sometimes sufficient remains to have a decisive effect upon later life.

My earliest recollections are of day-dreams about strange countries. My adventures in these places were not very startling, but everything had a quality of endlessness – the rivers went on for ever, the mountains were infinitely high, and the country always changing. My great delight at the seaside was to put a bottle or a piece of pumice into the sea and watch it float away, or on a windy day to throw a rag into the air to be blown away. I used to imagine these objects travelling on for ever, and I went with them. I am glad that nobody pointed out that my bottles and pumice would be washed up a few hundred yards farther along the beach, or that my rags would soon be swept into a dustbin.

I was lucky, as I had plenty to stimulate my imagination, for I was never in one place for long, and spent much of my time travelling about in Ceylon and Southern India with frequent voyages between Europe and the East. To an adult these journeys measured in an exact number of geographical miles, or in days and hours, become rather monotonous. I found them immensely exciting, and often finished them in a state of exhaustion. Having no precise conception of time and distance, they confirmed my notion of a boundless world. The train winding towards the sandy tip of India at Dhanushkodi, and chugging noisily through the jungle clad gorges of up-country Ceylon and the

Nilgiris; an early morning of strange scents, travelling swiftly by coconut palms and paddy fields; Stromboli belching fire and smoke; a whale spouting far in the wake of the ship – these were some of the impressions that kept alive the blissful day-dreams during the later dreary years of preparatory school routine, and successfully removed all chance of mastering Latin syntax.

Then came those old-fashioned books of natural history that dealt courageously with The Universe, illustrating it with quaint engravings of strange rock formations in the Hartz Mountains, the Mammoth Caves in Kentucky, the Aurora Borealis, and eruption of Mount Etna; always with little men, armed with long staves, looking on as though they themselves were responsible for the phenomena. But none of these things was a part of the school curriculum. They could find no expression; and never for a moment did it occur to me that interest in such things might suggest a line of approach when considering the awful question, 'What will I do when I grow up?' The choice of a profession seemed to be limited to the Army, the Church, Doctoring, or an office (whatever that meant). At the time none of these seemed very attractive, but seeing no alternatives I avoided the question as much as possible. Explorers were only mythical beings that one read about, and scientists were men of vast intellect who would certainly have had no difficulty in learning Kennedy's Latin Primer by heart. So my all absorbing interests were relegated to the classification of 'a hobby' – hardly even that since I could do nothing about it.

Any particular set of tastes can find expression in a variety of ways, and most people who know what they want have a large choice of routes along which they can pursue the same objective. If at an early age I had been taught to handle and navigate a small boat, I think I should have derived as much satisfaction from sailing as I have from climbing; the sea would have absorbed my interest and enthusiasm in the same way that mountains have done. The two pursuits offer the same opportunities for personal identification with natural phenomena – both demand a thorough knowledge of the elements concerned and skill in dealing with them; both provide an unlimited outlet for physical energy and a capacity for aesthetic enjoyment; both open up a vast field of possibility, each has its great tradition of adventure, each has its history, though while the history of sailing is as old as that of the human race, the history of mountaineering covers only the last 150 years.

But instead of learning to sail, I read Edward *Whymper's Travels Among the Great Andes of the Equator*. The author is better known for his 'Scrambles Amongst the Alps', but this came later in my education. On his Andes trip Whymper set out, with two Alpine guides, to study natural phenomena at high altitudes. He approached his task with that extraordinary diversity of interest which was a quality of travellers of the nineteenth century. He described his adventures with delightful simplicity, and illustrated them with countless engravings. How much more satisfactory are those engravings than the modern photograph! I have not read the book again, but I still have the most vivid impressions of it: the climbing of Chimborazo; the illustration of the be-goggled climbers, with enormous mercurial barometers on their backs, flogging their way through deep snow towards the summit, while below was the dramatic caption, 'We were then 20,000 feet high' – to reach 20,000 feet on a mountain seemed to me an achievement with which I would die happily; the night spent on the summit of Cotopaxi, looking down into the inferno of the active crater; the yarn about thousands of tons of eyeless fish erupted by the volcano from subterranean rivers that never saw the light; the frontispiece depicting the party struggling to erect their tent in a blizzard – 'The whirling snow mocked our efforts.' This book focused my attention upon mountains and my dreams upon mountain travel. It was obviously a field with unlimited scope for adventure and strange experience. I read everything I could lay my hands on about mountains.

Soon after this I spent an Easter holiday with my mother and sister in the Pyrenees. It was thrilling to see that the things I had read about really did exist: the thundering torrents, the great rock gorges with glistening, sweating flanks, the dark pine forests that guarded the approaches to the wonderland of ever-lasting ice and snow beyond, the great peaks infinitely remote and inaccessible and with all the strange feeling of mystery and hidden treasure. One wonderful day we went to some caves and sailed in a boat down a subterranean river overhung by fantastic stalactites. The journey took about two hours, as far as I can remember, and carried us clean through a mountain. On another occasion we went to see the Cirque de Gavarnie, which had been the subject of an illustration in one of my Universe books.

Yes, there was no question about it, mountains offered all that the heart could desire. Once I saw a party of climbers with ice-axes and rope. I regarded them with reverence and awe. I was a bit worried about this climbing business. Obviously, it seemed, one must climb if one were to have anything to do with mountains. I had experienced a tremendous thrill scrambling up a rough mountain slope, which suffered little by the disillusionment of my rapid exhaustion. But real climbing involved hanging by finger nails over giddy drops. I was frightened of drops, and could not bear to look over the edge of a high building or even to stand on a high balcony with only a flimsy iron railing between me and the street below. But the attraction of mountains was so strong that even this fear assumed a kind of fascination.

But how did one set about climbing? I had met no one who was remotely interested in that sort of thing. Mountaineering obviously did not form part of the more serious life, in preparation for which I was spending so many dreary hours and days trying to get some sense out of meaningless Latin text books. Whymper had gone to the Alps as an artist for some London newspaper,

Tyndall as a scientific professor, but I was just an inky-fingered schoolboy. My holidays had all been arranged for me, and I did not conceive the notion of going off to the mountains on my own. It is curious at that age how shy one is of talking about one's passions, particularly when those passions are evidently outlandish and not shared by normal people. It was particularly strange in my case, for I would certainly have received a sympathetic hearing at home. But the set formulae of examination and athletic education did nothing to encourage originality of interest and outlook.

However, Providence was remarkably kind, and sent a Norwegian lad named Gustav Sommerfelt of about my own age, to my school. He came in the Easter term preceding my visit to the Pyrenees, and was due to go back to Norway after the summer term. Early in the summer term he proposed that I should go to Norway with him to spend as much of the holidays as we could afford in the Jotunheimen, the highest mountains in Norway, and the rest of the time in a hut that his parents owned in the forests farther to the south. The proposal took my breath away and it was a long time before I could bring myself to believe in its possibility. There must be a snag somewhere. Such a thing was just too good to be true. What about the passage to Norway, surely that must cost the Earth? But no, the father of my remarkable friend knew a man who had something to do with shipping, and he could easily fix us up with a free passage on a cargo boat.

The weeks of that term were the longest I have ever known. I could talk and think of nothing else but the Jotunheimen, and day by day Gustav's descriptions of the country increased my excitement. It appeared that we were to carry everything on our backs and just push off by ourselves into the mountains with nothing to govern our movements except a map and compass and our own fancy. It was going to be the most wonderful thing that had ever happened. But behind all this exultation was an awful dread. Would something happen to crush with one blow all these heavenly plans? A broken limb, the measles, a decision to keep Gustav in England for another term; it seemed impossible that all those weeks could go by without providing some such disaster. But these fearful speculations were confined to the hours of 'work'. Leisure hours were devoted to blissful discussion of plans, when nothing but the one glorious certainty of our project was allowed to obtrude. Then suddenly everything crashed. Gustav came to me with a long face and announced that he had strained his heart, and had been ordered to rest for an indefinite period. Of course it had to be like that. I had known all along that such castles in the air could not really turn out to be built on solid foundations. The bitterness of the disappointment swamped me, and it never occurred to me that the idea was still there and could surely be put into practice somehow. However, the diagnosis had either been wrong or Gustav's heart made a remarkable recovery, for he was soon pronounced fit again.

The sailings of Norwegian cargo ships were admirably timed. This one necessitated leaving school a whole day early, and provided us with an excuse that even a headmaster would accept. A day, moreover, was composed of twenty-four hours, or 1,440 minutes, which ever way you look at it.

At last it arrived. The end of term was always an occasion of wild excitement, just as the last day of the holidays was one of profound gloom, but never had I felt such mad joy as on the last morning of that particular summer term. Sitting in the train, I pointed out to Gustav the highest point of the Chiltern Hills, and we laughed heartily at the idea that these ridiculous little bumps should even be called hills. We could afford to laugh, for we were both experienced mountain travellers – he in the wild mountains of Norway, and I with my great experience in the Pyrenees.

We spent one night in London. I had a delicious feeling of superiority which always preceded and followed my early mountain adventures. I was genuinely sorry for all those silly people at the theatre that evening who were not sharing our enterprise, and I hoped that they would find something to compensate them for their sad misfortune. The next day we travelled to a place called Blyth in Northumberland. I was in a fever lest our ship had left without us. But after a long search among grimy docks we found her lying passively in a cloud of coal dust, and with no evident intention of moving. Indeed, we had to wait for twenty-four hours before we set sail, and I began to revise my opinion of the excellence of Norwegian time-tables. Also the appearance of the ship itself was a bit depressing. She was of the type that one imagines for ever fastened to the quayside, idly loading and unloading some mysterious cargo. But the warmth of our welcome by the captain and crew soon put us in better spirits.

We were given comfortable berths in the sick-bay. Most appropriately as it turned out. I am not as a rule worried by rough seas, but on this occasion I had been introduced to that brown Norwegian cheese known as Mesost. It is very sweet. I thought it was great stuff, and spent much of my twenty-four hours in Blyth eating it. The result of my gluttony was twofold: though the sea was not unduly rough I was very ill, and I have never been able to eat Mesost since. Gustav was ill too, which mitigated my sufferings a little. But some three mornings later we awoke to find ourselves moving smoothly up the Christiania Fjord (as it was called in those days) with the rocky pine-clad shores of the promised land close at hand. We left our ship at Fredrikstad and went by train to Christiania (Oslo), where we spent two days buying boots and eating enormous quantities of strawberries and cream. Strawberries in Christiania were remarkably cheap: I have never understood why.

On the night before we left the capital, Gustav gave me lessons in oiling boots and packing a rucksack. The latter task was a most serious affair, and appeared to require as expert a hand as packing valuable glass. I was made to do it over and over again before my efforts would pass muster. I am afraid that like so much of my education this lesson had no lasting effect, and in all the years that I have packed rucksacks since that early initiation, my only method has been to take the things as they came to hand and to ram them down with as much force as was necessary to get them all in; and when mere arm power failed to produce sufficient compression, feet generally did the trick.

The main trouble about those rucksacks was their weight. But this was only forced upon my notice later, and even then it did not occur to me that it was largely due to all the unnecessary things we carried. I simply accepted the idea that a spare pair of trousers, pyjamas, and a change of underclothing and shoes were necessities, and tried to forget my aching, untrained shoulders. We even took washing materials, which in view of my later ideas of 'travelling light' seems incredible. Soap was the first of the civilised amenities that I learnt to dispense with. Indeed, my sister still maintains that the only reason I climb is that it provides me with an opportunity to avoid washing.

Our journey to the Jotunheimen was first by train through endless rocky pine forests, and then by bus climbing up and up above the trees, through wide valleys of rough grass and boulders, to Bygdin at the end of the road. The next day the real adventure began. It was a sad anti-climax to those months of eager anticipation. After half an hour my shoulders began to ache from the drag of the rucksack straps. It rained in torrents, and I was soon wet through and very cold. I could only see a few hundred yards in any direction, and what I could see was bleak and dismal. My enthusiasm for mountains evaporated, and I could only think of the end of the day's march and wonder how much farther we had to go. I did not dare to complain, and plodded wearily behind my companion in morose silence. But soon I was to discover that the pain and weariness of physical effort are quickly forgotten in a glow of retrospective warmth, and even before we had entered the rest house at the end of our first day's march my spirits had revived. A fire and a huge meal restored to mountains their lost enchantment.

Our trip to the Jotunheimen was a simple walking tour, and we did not attempt any serious mountaineering. But I think on the whole it justified my high expectations. After a few days my stiffness and fatigue left me, and I was able to take an intelligent interest in the country and in the thrilling business of identifying it with our large-scale map. I even became resigned to the weight of my rucksack, though I never really liked carrying a load, and my shoulders still ached. The mountains were very different from those I had seen in the Pyrenees. They were smaller and rounder, and the peaks seemed to be less aloof and mysterious. There were none of those tremendous forest-filled gorges. But the country had a different kind of fascination; a grand desolation and an endless breadth. Walking on and on from place to place through an ever changing scene was a most satisfying experience. Sometimes we stopped for a day to climb an easy peak. These days were all the better because I could leave my hated load behind. One day Gustav was ill and stayed in bed, while I walked to the head of the valley we were in. Here I found a glacier which came down from a hidden world of ice peaks. In a state of glorious excitement I started to walk up by the side of the glacier, and before long I was forced to get on to the ice itself. But soon I was brought up short on the brink of a crevasse. I had read about these sinister monsters, and I was suitably scared, so I decided not to proceed any farther with my exploration of the glacier. It was very tantalising, but my disappointment and my fright only increased the delicious mystery of the region above. Later on we joined another party with a guide to cross a glacier pass. For this we had to be roped together.

We finished our holiday with two weeks at the Sommerfelt family hut in the forest of Hardanger, where we spent our days idly pulling pink-fleshed trout out of the lake, eating them and discussing our mountain journey. The weather in the Jotunheimen was almost always bad. We had cursed it heartily, but it had not upset our plans. Besides, bad weather in mountains, though it generally puts a stop to serious climbing, does not spoil the mountains themselves. In fact, I have come nearer to being bored with mountain scenery during a long spell of cloudless weather than I ever have in rain and mist.

That trip to Norway opened the door to all sorts of wonderful possibilities. One had only to look at the map of Europe to sow the seeds of some new project. In those days it was not mountaineering as such that attracted me. I did not think much about climbing except as a means of seeing mountains. No, it was all the strange and wonderful things about the mountains themselves, as described by Whymper and Tyndall and now seen by myself. But the most fascinating of all these phenomena was volcanoes. I bought all the books I could find on the subject. Some of these plunged me into a sea of geological and physical technicalities that I did not understand, but most of them were by nineteenth-century scientists who told a simple story of fantastic events, and provided nice easy explanations.

So, most of all, I wanted to go and look at volcanoes. For a long time I thought about Iceland, but unfortunately no Icelander turned up at school, and on the mountains. Wyn had been sent to an inaccessible spot near Lake Rudolf, and Gustav and I were now working on the same farm and could not get away together. But it was not difficult to find people with whom to climb. Nearly a year after that first expedition I went to Mount Kenya again with Pat Russell. I wanted to explore the north-west approaches to the peaks, but a week of our time was wasted by my being laid up with an attack of fever. When I had recovered we had time only to work round to the south-east and climb the peak by our old route, though we managed to climb Point John as well.

Early in 1930 I had a letter from H.W. Tilman, who had been given my address by Mefhuish. This turned out to be a most fortunate contact and we were destined to share many mountain ventures together. At that time Tilman had not done much climbing, having only started during his last home leave in the Lake District. But I have met few people so admirably adapted to it both physically and temperamentally. He was very strong and tough, he had a natural aptitude for moving about difficult country, I have never known him rattled, and he had a remarkable ability to put up with – even a liking for – unpleasant conditions. He said very little, too little I thought, but, like many quiet people, when he did speak he was generally worth listening to. As a companion the qualities I liked best were his tremendous sense of humour and his constant readiness to embark upon any project. When I first knew him he was a recluse, and, to my way of thinking, too anti-pathetic towards the softer forms of human pleasure, such as novel reading, cinemas or any form of social intercourse. Most of our occasional quarrels arose, I think, from our disagreement on these matters. Though still at school when the last war began he had served nearly four years of it in France as a gunner in a battery commanded by Major (now Lt-General) Norton of Everest fame, and had won the Military Cross and bar. He came out to settle in Kenya soon after the last war and had spent most of his spare time hunting elephants and other big game.

Our first trip together was to Kilimanjaro. It was a most interesting journey, through the great game reserve south of Nairobi and across the Tanganyika border to Moshi, near the southern foot of the mountain. Like Mount Kenya, Kilimanjaro is an old volcano. It has two main peaks, Kibo, the higher, and Mawenzi. Though Kibo (19,000 feet) is nearly 3,000 feet higher than Kenya, there are no real difficulties in the ascent. We must have gone there at the wrong season for we struck continuously bad weather and reached the top of Kibo only after a hard struggle through masses of soft snow. To see better in the bad visibility we removed our snow-glasses and suffered for it a few hours later with a mild dose of snow blindness. This is a most painful affliction; it feels rather as though the insides of one's eyelids have been lacerated and then filled with sand. When we had recovered we climbed Mawenzi, which, in those conditions, presented us with quite a tough proposition.

Some six months later Tilman and I joined forces again, this time with a more serious ambition of traversing the twin peaks of Mount Kenya by climbing Batian from the north-west and descending by our old route to the Lewis glacier. I was then living in Turbo near the borders of Kenya and Uganda, and Tilman lived in Sotik, south towards Victoria Nyanza. We met at Nukuru and the difficulties of getting to that country by myself seemed to be insuperable. The extinct volcanoes of central France presented me with a poor alternative. Here things were easier. The journey was easy; the exchange made it far cheaper to travel in France than to take any sort of a holiday in England, and my mother had an old friend called M. Chalus who lived in Clermont-Ferrand and who offered to provide a companion for me, thereby overcoming the quite unreasonable objection to my going alone. Moreover French, unlike Icelandic, was part of my school curriculum, and therefore provided a more effective weapon of persuasion. Once I had made up my mind to go, there was no 'poor alternative' about it, and the Auvergne appeared to be the most alluring place in Europe. In achieving this role it was greatly assisted by engravings in my Volcano books. My prospective companion somehow disgraced himself in the eyes of his family, and as a punishment was forbidden to take a summer holiday that year. I was sorry for my unknown colleague, but deep down I was truly thankful, for it seemed unlikely that a stray Frenchman would have shared my passion for gazing at extinct volcanoes. Besides, it was good to feel entirely free. It required little argument to overcome the objection to my going alone. I owe a great deal to my mother's broad-minded attitude towards my activities.

But these plans were for the following summer, and in the meantime I quite unexpectedly started climbing. My sister and I were taken to Adelboden in Switzerland for winter sports. Rising above the village was a mountain called the Gross Lohner, 10,000 feet high. I had spotted it on the map, and, before I left England, I was consumed with a longing to climb it. But I knew enough to realise that mid-winter was not the right time for climbing mountains. Fortunately that year there was no snow in the lower valleys for skiing, and I managed to persuade five other people in the hotel to share with me the expense of two guides and attempt to climb the Gross Lohner.

It was the most thrilling experience I had ever known. For once the event was even better than the anticipation of it. We spent the night in a snow-bound hut below the Wildstrubel and started several hours before dawn the next morning. The climb was not difficult, but in winter conditions difficult enough to impress me. We were roped together; there was some step cutting to be done by the guides, and we wore snow goggles just like the pictures in Whymper's book. I was tremendously impressed by the lovely easy movements of the guides on difficult ground, by their power and self-confidence, and I longed to emulate them. The day was fine and the view from the summit was magnificent. I do not think that wide views of mountains in winter can compare with those in summer; the mountains look untidy and crowded together, and the lovely contrast between green valleys and white peaks is lacking. But the view from the top of the Gross Lohner was good enough for me. The guides pointed out the Matterhorn and Weisshorn of the distant Pennines and the nearer giants of the Oberland. Then the descent: the slow cautious movements down the steep upper face; the sudden freedom when the difficulties were passed; the joyous plunge down long snow slopes to the trees; the tired, happy plod along the forest paths. I felt when I got back to the hotel that all my senses had been sharpened and my whole outlook changed by the crowded experiences of the last 24 hours. In the Gross Lohner I now had a priceless possession. I bought a big picture of the mountain, looking in its mantle of winter snow as fine as any Himalayan giant, and hung it in my room at home.

There were two more climbs that holiday; one, alone with a guide up a gaunt rock spine, where I discovered that looking down a vertical drop from an exposed rock ledge was not half as bad as I had feared; the other with two French experts who had climbed the Matterhorn.

The Easter holidays were spent in northern Italy, where I saw another aspect of the Alps and managed to get a little more climbing by making a hazardous expedition to Monte della Disgrazia. So by the time the next summer holidays came round my attitude towards mountains had undergone a considerable change. The desire to explore them had found a practical expression in the sport or art of mountaineering, and this new-found passion was soon to eclipse for many years the wider view. I had not, I am glad to say, lost interest in the Auvergne, but school summer holidays are long and there would be plenty of time to visit the Dauphiné Alps as well. Life was very full.

In Clermont, I was treated by the Chalus as a member of the family. Indeed, I found it hard to get away. When eventually I managed to persuade them to let me go, my kind host rushed off to the tourist bureau and booked me a seat in the Mont Dore bus. I had considerable difficulty in persuading him that I proposed to walk. At first he regarded it as a joke, but when he saw that I was serious he became very perturbed. After the generous treatment I had received I was most reluctant to upset these kind people, but what could I do? Many of the most interesting old volcanoes lay between Clermont and Mont Dore, and my plan had been to walk slowly over them and to linger in the places that took my fancy. I might, of course, have started in the Mont Dore bus and left it when I was well out of Clermont. But this would certainly have led to complications, and I thought it best to have the matter out there and then. I do not think I convinced them of my sanity, but at length they acquiesced with eloquent shrugs. However, I evidently repaid them for their anxiety by providing a story which was recounted and embroidered for many years.

There is a lot to be said for travelling alone. Contact with the country and the people is more intimate, and the traveller has only himself to consider in his day to day plans, and in the satisfaction of his whims. I was very young, and the whole thing seemed a tremendous adventure. At first I was rather lonely and felt very foolish tramping along a main road with an enormous pack on my back while cars flashed by, blinding me with their dust. But when I got into wilder country and learnt to seek my food and rest in peasant cottages, I began to feel more at home, and there was too much to occupy my attention and too much to do, to notice that I was alone. Anyone who has read Stevenson will understand the charm of that country, certainly a great deal better than I can ever describe it. I had not at the time read his famous 'Travels', or I might have been tempted to take a companion to carry my load. This was still ridiculously heavy, and caused me much pain and grief.

This journey took place a very long time ago, and as I did not keep a diary most of the details of times and place-names and the exact sequence of events are forgotten. I have sometimes tried to keep a diary, but writing down the events of the day has always seemed rather silly at the time, and it is not until long after that the little mundane entries can do their work of romantic reconstruction. Never having had much of an eye for the future, my occasional efforts at diary writing have rarely survived the first few days of an expedition. But though the details are gone the essence of the experience remains, and can be vividly reproduced in thought and feeling.

So far as I can remember I walked for about three weeks in the Auvergne and the Cevennes, generally along the smaller roads, sometimes across the mountains. There is no better way of getting to know country than by walking over it, and I had a delicious feeling almost of personal possession, such as I had already felt for my first Alpine peaks, and which comes from a true understanding of the country. It was not, in fact, the long unbroken sensation of glorious enjoyment that it seems now in memory. My load dragged as unpleasantly as ever; I was often hot and painfully thirsty; I developed enormous blisters on my feet; a strained Achilles tendon was rubbed mercilessly by my boot; once I was rather frighteningly lost in the mist amongst some wild mountains. But I became so absorbed in my adventure that I hardly thought about the more spectacular Dauphiné plans, and towards the end I was tempted to continue my wanderings in central France for the whole of the holidays. I found I could live quite comfortably on ten francs a day, which at the rate of exchange then prevailing, amounted to about 1s. 3d. At first I made few friends, being much too shy to display my school French more than was absolutely necessary. However, this mood soon passed, and presently I was conversing happily with anyone I met. Once I met a Greek at an inn and travelled with him in a punt through the wonderful gorges of the river Tam.

Eventually I returned to Clermont by a different route. M. Chalus was away in Paris and the only occupants of the house were his mother who was over eighty, and her nun companion. These two ladies were profoundly shocked by my disreputable appearance, grimy, sun-scorched and tattered. I had not realised my beggarly appearance, or I doubt if I should have had the courage to enter that select and spotless establishment. But I soon discovered that their concern was for my apparent discomfort and not for the impropriety of entertaining a tramp. I was plunged into a hot bath, provided with endless luxuries and petted and pampered in a most delicious manner. After basking in their heart-warming hospitality for a day or two I set out for the Dauphiné and the high mountains.

This then was my approach to the hills. It was a devious and round-about route that led by a series of accidents to a passion that has had a decisive influence upon my life. Some start climbing because their fathers before them have climbed, others because of tutors or friends. These ways of introduction have many advantages. I prefer my own line, as the next man will prefer his. But in any field of human activity it is not the road of approach that matters, but the attitude of mind; for whatever changes time and experience may bring, whatever conceits or failures, something of the early feeling will always remain. Best of all is the eager humility of a child.

2 The Alps

It is impossible of course to provide an entirely satisfactory explanation for any recreation. The predominant motive in any human activity varies according to the temperament of the individual. Mountaineering provides good exercise in pleasant surroundings, a sense of satisfaction in overcoming difficulties, the joy, akin to dancing, of controlled rhythmic movement, a stimulating contact with danger, a wealth of beautiful scenery and a release from the tiresome restrictions of modern life. The expert likes to practise or display his skill. Some confess to having been drawn to climbing by a physical inferiority complex engendered by their failure at school to hit a ball straight and far. These motives are probably sufficient in themselves, and they certainly form the basis of many other sports. But in the deep devotion to any form of active endeavour there is generally something else we seek. In the case of mountaineering it is a kind of personal identification with the hills themselves, which comes of intimate understanding and strenuous contest and which brings with it a wealth of philosophical content. Above all, in my view, the attraction lies in the memory of those rare moments of intellectual ecstasy which occur perhaps on a mountain summit, perhaps on a glacier at dawn or in a lovely moonlit bivouac, and which appear to be the result of a happy coincidence in the rhythm of mind and scene. These moments are not of course peculiar to mountaineering; they may be realised in deserts, on the sea and elsewhere. Such exaltation of feeling is achieved more often, I imagine, and in more normal circumstances by the mind of the creative artist, but for ordinary folk it would seem that it is more readily found in close contact with nature.

Mountaineering is an art in the same sense that sailing is an art, or horsemanship, or big-game hunting. The thorough mastery of each of these crafts requires a combination of technical skill, knowledge and experience. It is possible to become proficient at handling a boat on the Norfolk broads and yet to know nothing of sailing in its wider aspects of navigation and deep-sea travel, to ride well without becoming an expert horseman or to shoot a tiger and remain ignorant of jungle lore. Many people, owing to circumstance or inclination, are content with such superficial contact. In the same way the experience of climbing behind guides on well-known ground is very far from being the whole art of mountaineering.

The sport of climbing as we now know it began somewhere in the middle of the nineteenth century. Mountains were climbed long before that, but then motives appear to have resembled more closely those attributed by the general public to the would-be scientific purpose. It was not until about the 1850s that people started to go to the high Alps for sport and recreation. At first of course their objective was the climbing of the great peaks by the easiest way they could find and the crossing of high passes. Later, as the number of unclimbed peaks diminished and mountaineering technique developed, interest began to centre less on the summits themselves and more on the great faces and ridges of the mountains. To-day not only all the peaks of the Alps, but nearly all the faces and ridges, too, have been climbed, and the mountaineer in search of new conquests must look to the more distant ranges, in some of which the field is practically unlimited.

But for all that, the Alps still provide as good climbing as can be found in any other range in the world. Certainly there is nowhere that offers such a good training ground for mountaineers. The reason for this lies in the combination of three factors; variety, accessibility and expert tuition. Almost any kind of climbing can be found there, from the rock pinnacles of the Dolomites to the great ice precipices of Mont Blanc. The mountains themselves are so easily accessible and so well provided with hotels and huts that most of one's time there can be spent actually climbing. Moreover the size of the peaks is exactly right from the climber's point of view; anyone, with say, a fortnight's holiday can go to a hut and, if he is energetic enough, can do a dozen climbs in the time. It is obvious then that the opportunities for practice and training are far greater than those offered by the Himalayas, for example, where it may take weeks to get to the foot of a mountain, besides the laborious business of establishing high camps and the unpleasant effects of rarefied atmosphere. Finally, expert guides are to be found in almost every district of the Alps; this and the large number of people who climb there set a very high standard of performance.

There are only two satisfactory ways for the novice to start mountaineering. One is to be taught the rudiments by an expert amateur; the other is to engage a professional guide. In many ways the former is the more satisfactory method. A guide is too often interested only in the business of getting the climb done; it is difficult for an inexperienced amateur to assert himself and he is very liable to remain a mere passenger. Usually, too, the guide is climbing on ground with which he is thoroughly familiar, and for him the element of exploration, which is one of the most serious and the most attractive aspects of mountain craft, does not enter into the problem.

In the early days of mountaineering when the Alps were comparatively little known, these objections to guides did not exist to the same extent, and the relations between guide and employer were much less professional. This is probably one reason why the pioneers were content for so long to climb with guides; they themselves had an important function in the team, and were not treated as so much baggage to be got up the mountain and down again with the least possible delay. But it is not so easy to understand why the guide continued so long to be regarded as indispensable. For a time guideless climbers were regarded as reckless heretics who were bound sooner or later to come to a sticky end. There seemed to be something mystic about a guide's powers. Accidents, when they occurred to guideless parties were frowned upon as a result of folly, when they happened to guides they were attributed to events beyond human control. Certainly a guide's local knowledge is a considerable safeguard, but to insist upon local knowledge being present in all climbing parties would be to set such limits to the scope of mountaineering as to rob it of most of its charm. Of course this prejudice against guideless climbing was bound eventually to die. It was gradually recognised not only that an amateur could master the whole of his craft, but that he must strive to do so if he were to taste all its joys.

The average Alpine guide has his limitations. When a man has climbed all his life in the same district he will acquire sureness on his particular peaks, and will tend to rely upon his memory for the ground that he has covered so often. His instinct for finding his way in new country remains undeveloped. A peak that is climbed for the second time presents only a small proportion of the difficulties that were met on the first occasion; if one were to climb it fifty times the procedure would become almost automatic; many of one's mountaineering faculties would be lulled to sleep. Handicapped though he is by the lack of continuous lifelong training, the experienced amateur has this one great advantage over the average guide, by far the majority of his climbing is on ground that is new to him, so that his experience of dealing with new situations is constantly growing, and his capacity for mountain exploration is developed alongside his capacity for mountain climbing. Moreover, different types of mountains require various modifications in technique. For example, anyone who has spent all his time climbing on the sound granite of the Chamonix Aiguilles would probably be at a loss on the friable rock of the Dauphiné, and a climber in the Dauphiné has little opportunity to acquire the gymnastic skill required on the Aiguilles. Many good guides have disappointed their employers when taken out of their native districts.

But this criticism does not apply to the really great guides – and there are and have been many such – who will always be a step or two ahead of the best amateur in most branches of their craft. In mountaineering as in everything else it is the professional who reaches the highest peaks of perfection. For this reason, whether the beginnings are made with amateurs or professionals, the experience of climbing with a first-class guide is an important part of the education of a mountaineer.

Knowing no one who was interested in climbing I had no alternative but to start with guides. My early reading had been confined to the work of the pioneers, and in consequence it never occurred to me that big mountains could be climbed without guides. I imagined that my career as a mountaineer would be severely limited by the amount of cash I could scrape together for their hire. I had acquired a copy of Abraham's 'Swiss Mountain Climbs' which set out in depressing detail the official tariffs for the great peaks, the study of which acted as a constant check to my ambitions. I did not see how I could ever aspire to more than a few minor climbs. But the prospect of climbing any mountain made me wild with joy, and even to wander about the valleys and look at the peaks I had read about would be thrilling enough.

I was sorry to leave the Auvergne where I had enjoyed such delicious freedom and adventure. But when I found myself in the train bound for the Alps my regrets were swamped by a mounting excitement. My plans were vague and I had very little idea what I was going to do. The obvious thing seemed to be to make for La Bérarde, which lies in the heart of the highest mountains of the Dauphiné, and I had intended to walk there from Grenoble. I stopped in a pension in Grenoble to give my still painful Achilles tendon a few more days to recover. My time there was divided between watching the local lads trying to climb a pole at the Exposition, wishing I had the moral courage to try myself, and gazing at the windows of the tourist bureaux. Here I saw pictures of wonderful peaks with names straight out of Whymper's book. Mont Pelvoux, Les Écrins, La Meije. This was too much. Here I was wasting my time dallying on the threshold of Paradise. I packed my rucksack and boarded a bus for La Bérarde.

It was a dismal morning. Rain had been falling for days and leaden clouds covered all the peaks. My fellow passengers were making a day trip to La Bérarde. Their talk was gloomy. Never had there been such a summer. The sun had not appeared for weeks. The higher valleys were not really worth visiting for one could never see more than a few hundred yards; but one had to do something with a holiday. I was incautious enough to remark that I was going to stop in La Bérarde in the hope of climbing. The idea appealed to that lugubrious sense of humour peculiar to the French, and I became the butt of sarcastic witticisms.

But when we reached St Christoph the clouds were retreating up the mountain sides. Presently a window opened and framed a sharp white peak which seemed to be hanging almost directly overhead; it glistened like a great diamond. Then another appeared and another, and at last sunlight filled the valley. I could not have asked for a better introduction to the summer Alps.

We made a long halt at Les Etages, a tiny hamlet a few miles below La Bérarde, while our driver refreshed himself, and his passengers photographed one another. At the inn I enquired for a guide and was promptly introduced to a bandy-legged little man named Elie Richard. Yes, he would act as my guide. It had been a terrible summer, very little climbing had been possible in August and now the peaks were heavily laden with new snow. But we would climb, and from now on it would be fine. He seemed to be as keen as I was to get going and announced that on the very next day we would climb the Pic Coolidge, which despite its 12,000 feet was not difficult. After that the new snow would settle and we would go after bigger game. This all sounded too good to be true. I broached the question of finance by explaining that I had very little money to spend. But this obstacle was brushed aside as lightly as the weather and the new snow. He would charge me sixty francs (then about 7s.) a day, we would climb every day if I wished, we would live in huts which cost nothing and the cost of our bread would not amount to much. It was settled then; Richard would be at La Bérarde, with a spare ice-axe for me, at one o'clock the next morning. I climbed back into the bus with a joyous heart.

I found pleasant company at La Berarde. There were very few people staying in the small hotel, and they were all climbers. Everyone was friendly. We sat together at one table and the talk was all of mountains. The others seemed very expert and talked of their lofty ambitions which could not be attempted until many days of fine weather had settled the new snow. I felt very raw and shy, but I basked blissfully in the company of the gods. In the evening some of them invited me to go for a walk with them up the valley. All the clouds had gone, I learnt the names of the peaks in view and we watched the sunset glow touch the western face of the Ailefroide.

The ten days that followed were beyond my wildest expectations. Hitherto I had looked upon the climbing of mountains as isolated experiences, and I had not conceived the idea of linking them together into a continuous mountaineering journey by travelling from place to place over the ranges and even by crossing the peaks themselves. Elie was as good as his word, we used every day, and his optimism about the weather was amply justified. Every day we crossed a high pass or climbed a peak, and each night was spent in fresh surroundings. From each new summit we looked across the scene of our previous wanderings, and beyond over great ranges of unlimited promise. I found this new view of mountains profoundly impressive.

The climbs we did were not difficult, but I was not disappointed by that; indeed I was rather relieved, and anyway I found them fully satisfying. I was pleased to discover that the art of mountaineering consisted, not in getting into difficulties as I had once supposed, but rather in avoiding danger. There were all sorts of little things to learn which later became matters of commonplace routine in thought and action: the hot sun loosens rocks that have been split off but held in place by frost, so that a gully which is safe in the early morning may become a death trap later in the day; new snow lying on old is liable to avalanche; the rope which links the members of a climbing party, if

properly handled, is a very real safeguard, and is not merely intended to provide the comforting thought 'If I fall they all fall with me.' The height of the
peaks was sufficient proof that they were real mountains, and I was very grati-
fied by the memory of Whymper's dramatic descriptions of the first ascent of
Les Écrins. I had yet to learn that following a guide up a well-trodden peak was
a very different matter from discovering a route up an unclimbed mountain.

There were many things I did not like about climbing, and there were brief
periods of bitter disappointment: being woken at 1 a.m. from a deep sleep of
real physical fatigue, and having to turn out into a cold hard world of stale
bread and boots and cracking lips – it is not easy to break with sleep in one's
'teens, and it was many years before I became resigned to that grim business of
the midnight start; the endless trudge up a slope of soft snow with nothing to
divert the attention from aching thighs and a raging thirst; moments of clumsy
fear that made me feel supremely helpless and foolish. But all these things vanished in the ecstasy of gaining the summit, and in the retrospective view of the
day. Besides, even then I must have realised that contrast sharpened appreciation: the sudden rush of life that came with the dawn after the dead monotony
of the night approach; a cup of water collected from a rock outcrop at the top
of the snow slope; the gradual achievement of rhythmic mastery over steep
unstable rock.

The end of the ten days was also the end of my holiday, as well as the end of
my purse. But my mind was too full of the unexpected success of my first real
Alpine season and the glorious possibilities that it opened for the future, to
leave any room for regrets. Even my rucksack felt light as I swung down the
road towards Grenoble.

When still at school it is easy to achieve singleness of mind. The problems of
having to make a living are still remote, and in spite of the warning of elders,
life continues to revolve round a new-found passion. The shock of finding that
it cannot always remain the only important thing is severe, but the illusion is
good while it lasts, and perhaps it contributes a measure of peace in after life.
I had found in mountaineering a fulfilment of all my early longings; I had no
doubt about it. Looking at pictures of the Alps I experienced such a wild surge
of feeling and memory that I could not understand why everyone did not
want to climb. I supposed that it was either because they could not get to the
mountains or because they had not discovered them as I had; I longed to talk
about the Alps but I also wanted to keep it as a jealously guarded secret.

After that first season, time was divided into two categories: the summer
holidays and the ten months between them that unfortunately had to be lived
through as well. A stupid and ungrateful attitude, particularly as the winter
holidays between included, among other good things, a Christmas spent in
Gustav's hut in the Norwegian forests and an exploration of the volcanoes of
Tenerife, both of which were thrilling experiences.

My second Alpine season was again spent in the Dauphiné. The value of the franc had dropped to 240 to the pound. Elie was still willing to climb with me for sixty francs a day, and the use of the huts was free so long as one was a member of the French Alpine Club, which could be joined by anyone for the payment of a very small sum. We lived nearly all the time in huts.

The high Dauphiné is barren country, with narrow rocky valleys in which there are few trees and little pasture land. Scenically it cannot compare with most of the Swiss Alps, but its grim austerity has a great fascination. From the mountaineering point of view, too, it has many advantages, and it would be hard to find a place better adapted for learning the game. There is an extraordinary profusion of peaks, the large majority of which are rarely visited. We climbed twenty that season and on only two or three occasions did we meet another party on a mountain. In those days Elie was a 'Guide de Deuxième Classe', and was anxious to be promoted to the first rank. So with this in view he was very keen to get to know as many peaks as he could; and far from having to be urged to work for his sixty francs, it was often that he forced the pace. Much of the ground that we covered was new to him, and I soon found myself sharing in the problems of finding the way and of deciding which routes were safe and which were not. As before we traversed the peaks from one valley to another, and before long I began to have that exciting feel of connected knowledge of country.

A thing that surprised me about climbing in the Alps (and indeed which still rather surprises me on looking back) was the number of long days one did. Most of our climbs that year took anything from twelve to sixteen hours. We would do four such days consecutively, then a morning off with a three or four hour walk to a hut in the afternoon, followed by another four long days in succession. I remember feeling very tired at night, so that my whole body ached when I lay down, and the early morning starts were hateful; but the fatigue of one day never lasted long into the next, and my appetite for food was prodigious. Off days were occasionally forced on us by the weather, but very rarely. I hated them, and it was a long time before I acquired the philosophy that could find pleasure in a day of rest in the valley.

It would be a mistake, I think, to begin climbing in one of the famous centres like Zermatt or Chamonix. For one thing the peaks are so well known, and the various routes up them are tabulated in such detail that one might easily get the wrong impression of mountaineering. Each climb would seem like a set piece in which one was forced by convention to stick to a rigid series of steps, each with a name and a history. In a less frequented district there is a sense of freedom of choice, and it is easy to imagine that the route one takes has never been climbed before. This presents mountaineering in a totally different light, and as first impressions are important it is better that this exploratory aspect of the game should predominate at first. Also to begin by climbing famous peaks might lead to a scornful attitude towards lesser ranges, and to despise any mountain is a cardinal error both of philosophy and practice. It is wrong to suppose that because a mountain is in a well-known district and is itself famous, it necessarily provides good climbing. From the mountain point of view there is no finer mountain in the Alps than La Meije in the Dauphiné, and a traverse of, say, Les Bans is every bit as good a climb as, for example, a traverse of the much more famous Zinal Rothhorn.

Elie Richard was an excellent companion and his desire to climb little known peaks from unusual directions suited me admirably. I owe a great deal to his friendly interest and encouragement. He was not at the time a really first rate guide, having had no experience outside his native Dauphiné, but I should say that in temperament and ability he had the makings of one, though he was very shy and modest. The next summer I was fortunate enough to climb on some of the Zermatt peaks with Theophile Theytaz, who was a very much more forceful character.

It is impossible to climb for long without meeting other climbers, and when those contacts came I found a new source of joy in talking of mountains with understanding. This also suggested the exciting possibility of climbing without guides, which was strengthened by an Easter holiday of rock climbing in the English Lake District.

To those who wonder at the reason for mountaineering, this rock climbing on British mountains must seem quite incomprehensible. Its object is not to reach the top of mountains but to climb up some particular part of a precipice. A cliff three hundred yards long by a couple of hundred feet high may have as many as fifty routes up it each bearing a name, such as 'Eagle's Nest Ridge' or 'Great Gully', and each classified according to an accepted standard of difficulty. It is a fascinating sport; there are those who prefer it to Alpine climbing, and of course it provides excellent practice in rock climbing. But rock climbing is only a small part of a wider art. Climbing on British crags is to mountaineering as yachting on the Norfolk Broads is to sailing.

Just as the relative smallness of Alpine mountains enables one to tackle far harder climbs than would be possible on the great peaks of the Himalaya, so the standard of rock climbing difficulty on Welsh or Lake District crags is a good deal higher than is normally met with on Alpine climbs. It is a highly specialised and a restricted technique. When I started climbing in the Lakes I was extremely frightened and not a little humiliated. The climbs that were dismissed by the initiated as easy, struck me as formidable. Seeing a nice easy grass slope a few yards to the side while I was spread-eagled on a giddy precipice seemed to increase my discomfiture tenfold, and I began to wonder if I really liked mountaineering after all. Like most things it was simply a question of adjustment to environment. After a time I found the knack of easy poise and with it came a sense of security and a great exhilaration.

A day on the Lakeland fells is a joy second to none. In driving rain or in rare sunshine, it is the same clean, good country of soft, rich colour. The climbing gives a spice of adventure, and objective interest; like all good sport its real function is to provide a medium for experience, through changing moods, of the country itself. Not least of the day's delights is the evening spent in good company at a farm house, satisfying a mighty hunger with an endless Cumberland tea.

That Easter I climbed mostly with George Peaker (at least I thought his name was George and when our friendship had ripened I always called him that; he never bothered to correct me and it was not until ten years later that I discovered that it was not really his name). He was an experienced rock climber, though at the time he had not climbed much in the Alps. He nursed me through my initiation into Lakeland climbing. I had a great admiration for his imperturbable temperament. In moments of crisis he always spoke with absolute calm, using precise, well-chosen phrases as if he were engaged in an after-dinner discussion. I remember one occasion particularly, when he was leading up a steep wall, slashed by an icy wind-driven rain. He remained for some considerable time clinging to small slippery holds near the top of the wall apparently unable to get any further. Then he looked down at me over his shoulder and announced that he was going to fall off. This he proceeded to do, but it did not matter much as he had taken the precaution of tying himself to the top of the wall.

The following summer we went to the Alps together. George was a lecturer in mathematics, so that his long summer holiday coincided with my own. We had decided to start in the Graian Alps, and, by crossing peaks and passes, to wander from there in whatever direction seemed good at the time. Climbing without a guide seemed a great undertaking. I felt as though I were rediscovering all the delights I had found in previous years and many more besides. The new responsibility of decision and action, the feeling of self-reliance, the modest triumphs shared by a companion of equal standing and similar outlook sharpened the whole field of sensibility and deepened delight.

Our first experience was not a happy one. We arrived at Pralognan in the morning, after a sleepless night in the train, and set out heavily laden for a hut in the afternoon. Before long it started to rain in torrents, we missed the way and darkness found us lost on the hillside. Soaked through and tired we spent a long shivering night huddled together in a sheep pen and retreated to Pralognan the next day crushed and dejected. But after that the weather was gloriously fine – day after day, week after week hardly a cloud appeared in the sky and we never halted for a rest.

It is a further advantage of the lesser ranges of the Alps that they enjoy far better weather than their more lofty neighbours. All this time a continuous series of storms was raging over the peaks of the Mont Blanc group only a short way to the north. When we went there later we met friends who had spent their entire holidays waiting in the valleys for an improvement in the weather.

When we had climbed or traversed the more attractive peaks of the Graian Alps we crossed the frontier into Italy and climbed in the Gran Paradiso group. We got into a lot of unnecessary difficulties, due to bad judgement, and we often paid the penalty of being caught by night high up on the mountain side, though somehow we always succeeded in worrying through, and never, after that first occasion, had to spend the entire night out. We learnt slowly by our mistakes.

From the Paradiso we worked our way to the north and crossed the Mont Blanc range to Chamonix. We had intended to stay there, but the stormy weather seemed as if it were set for the whole season; so after some minor climbs we took a bus to the Dauphiné, where we continued our interrupted adventures.

Mountaineering used to be regarded as a rich man's game. If you stay at big hotels in the famous Swiss resorts, and climb with first class guides it certainly is. But there are ways of doing a mountaineering holiday which make climbing as inexpensive as any sport. From England the chief cost is getting to the Alps, but the third class fare does not amount to very much. Once there it is possible to live entirely in huts, which in many parts of the French Alps costs nothing. In my experience one gets so hungry that the simplest food is completely satisfying. I think I sometimes overdid the economising in food. In those days I knew nothing of balanced diets, and once or twice at the end of the season I suffered from boils, which were no doubt due to some diet deficiency. But a well-balanced diet costs little more than an ill-balanced diet, and it is only a question of care.

Many young continental climbers who could not afford the railway fare used to bicycle to the Alps. They had their counterparts in the north of England and in Scotland. A friend of mine met a young but experienced American climber at the Hörnli hut below the Matterhorn, who had brought himself a return steerage passage from New York to Antwerp. There he purchased a second-hand push-bike and rode it to the Alps. He could not afford even the price of the Swiss huts and was content to sleep outside. He ate nothing but bread. Sometimes he found a companion to climb with, when he did not he climbed alone. My friend who was also in need of a companion joined forces with him. When they parted the American cheerfully mounted his bicycle with only 6 Swiss francs in his pocket besides the return half of his steamer ticket.

But apart from these extreme cases, forced by necessity, there is much to be gained by this frugality. To my mind a large measure of the charm of mountaineering lies in its simplicity; a rope, an ice-axe, dark glasses and nailed boots are all the special equipment that is needed; the object is uncomplicated; the rest lies in the physical, mental and aesthetic contact of the climber with his mountains. The simpler the approach the easier it is to achieve a synthesis. At least that is the only way in which I can explain the feeling I have so often experienced on large and luxuriously equipped Himalayan expeditions, and on rare occasions when I have climbed from a big hotel, a feeling of having lost touch with the essence of the life I was subconsciously seeking.

My last season in the Alps was the best of all. Again I had Peaker as a companion and this time we were joined by H.M. Kelly, who was famous for his remarkable achievements on English rocks. We started with three weeks in the Zermatt valley. It was one of those seasons that one dreams about, and during the whole of our time there we were never troubled even by the threat of bad weather. It seemed to me almost a crime to waste any of it, though sometimes we were forced by exhaustion (or, more likely, laziness) to take a day off. But in the three weeks we managed to do eight of the classic climbs. The two I enjoyed most of these were the West ridge of the Dent Blanche, and the Zmutt ridge of the Matterhorn which is the finest approach to that lovely mountain. I had climbed it before with two guides and two other amateurs, but in spite of this I missed the way on the upper part and forced our party to climb a new and a somewhat spectacular chimney. I had some excuse for this mistake, for on the previous occasion the mountain had been sheathed in ice and it had taken us exactly twenty-four hours of continuous going to climb up the Zmutt ridge and down the north-east or Swiss ridge. This year we descended by the Italian ridge which is chiefly a matter of sliding down fixed ropes. When we reached the hut at the foot of the ridge, George and I wanted to go on down to the valley, as we had very little food with us. But Kelly refused, saying that he would rather go hungry than be arrested by the Italian police on a charge of espionage, which had recently been the fate of several unfortunate climbers who had strayed across the frontier.

Although our programme that year was a good deal more ambitious than it had been before, we never encountered serious difficulties. Increased experience, of course, had something to do with this, but I am certain that it was partly due to the fact that it is so much easier to find the way about well-known mountains, though with the exception of the Zmutt ridge all climbs we did were new to us. I regard this as evidence of my contention that in some respects the smaller ranges of the Alps provide a more complete training in mountaineering.

From the Zermatt mountains we made our way slowly along what is known as the High level Route to Chamonix stopping to climb on the way. We had hoped that Kelly would come with us to Chamonix, and we were looking forward to watching him display his rock-climbing genius by leading us up some of the more spectacular granite faces. But unfortunately he had to return to England at the end of our three weeks in Zermatt.

It is doubtful if there is any place in the world that can rival Chamonix as a climbing centre. The flawless granite of the Aiguilles offers almost unlimited scope for the rock climber, the bigger peaks provide ice as well as rock climbing of a high order, while the great southern faces and ridges of Mont Blanc, their scale unique in the Alps, are not far away. But Chamonix itself is a horrible place. It combines everything ugly and vulgar in modern 'tourism'; vast hotels sprout in unsightly clusters, charabancs roar through the streets, every kind of cheapjack is there to exploit the mountains. Unfortunately these horrors of mass touristdom are not confined to the main valley. In the height of the season the mountain huts overflow with trippers, many of whom having no intention of climbing, create an intolerable hubbub which continues far into the night, and they generally leave the huts in a state of filth and disorder. Even among the climbers there is an atmosphere of fevered competition. It is fairly easy to forget these things when one has some great adventure in prospect, but even in my brief acquaintance with the district I found myself longing for the peace of the Dauphiné or the quiet dignity of Zermatt, and I made a resolution never to return there after I had tasted some of the superb fare that its mountains offer.

Our first climb that year on the peaks of the Mont Blanc range was the traverse of the Grépon. By then we had reached a high pitch of fitness, and the feel of rough clean granite under toe and finger and the swift glides down the long rappel line were tremendously exhilarating. It is a remarkable climb, for although one is constantly poised over a sheer drop of thousands of feet, one has a feeling of perfect, almost careless security that I have never felt on any other mountain of similar difficulty. It was a day of supreme physical enjoyment. Then came the traverse of the two Drus, climbing up the Petit Dru and crossing from there over the summit of its taller brother. This was a much more serious proposition and its enjoyment of a more sombre kind.

Later we joined forces with Jack Longland and George Trevelyan, and climbed with them on the Rochefort Ridge and on Mont Blanc, where the weather spoilt our plan to climb one of the great southern ridges. Then the others went home. Having now no studies to return to, I snatched another week of this, my last Alpine season, and spent it on and around the Aiguille Verte, in company with Graham Macphee.

I left the Alps with a heavy sense that I was breaking with an episode in my life that would not be repeated. If I had been able to foresee something of what the next twelve years would bring I should not have been depressed. But in a way I was right. The Alps for all their limitations, their sophistication, their spoiling, have some qualities that I have not found in other ranges. It is difficult to describe these qualities exactly, but they are due I fancy to tradition, to the higher culture of the native inhabitants, to the easy friendships made and to the wonderful variety of scene small enough in scale to be easily appreciated and large enough to be wholly satisfying.

But the memory of my Alpine seasons has another importance to me, for they represent my first real contact with great mountains. Though experience has its own rewards – a wider view, a fuller understanding, a more sober and perhaps a deeper passion – inevitably something is left behind. We can never quite recapture the feelings of early youth; the mystery that lay behind each peak, and in the deep cloud-filled valleys at dawn; the wild joy that made one want to claw the ground that was part of this miracle. Oh yes, I continued to grow just as excited as each new vista appeared on my mountaineering horizon, but I suppose the other feeling was akin to those childish fancies that sometimes reappear in after life as a fleeting moment of absolute happiness.

3   First Climbs on Mount Kenya

In my experience the problem of what to do in life was not made any easier by those who were entrusted with my education. Looking back, it seems most odd that never once in all the years that I was at school was there any general discussion about careers. As presumably the main object of going to school is to prepare for after life, it surely would have been very easy and relevant to organise lectures or discussions designed to give boys a broad view of the enormous variety of occupations open to men of average intelligence? Of course many boys were destined from birth to follow their fathers' careers, but even these would have benefited by glimpses of a wider horizon. Often and often in after life I have come across people doing jobs that I had never dreamed of before, and which would have thrilled me had I been told about them at school. I suppose the reason for this extraordinary omission is that so many school masters had themselves such a restricted view. Spending all their time working to a rigid curriculum, the passing of examinations by their pupils gradually became the whole object of their working life. I recognise the importance of being made to learn things that one does not like, but surely it was not good to give the young mind the impression that all education was a form of mental gymnastics. For example, I used to find geometry rather fun, and, when I still had the naive idea that what I was being taught might have some practical value, I asked what geometry was for. The only answer I ever got was that it taught one how to think and to solve problems. If, instead, I had been told the simple fact that the word was derived from the Greek *ge*, the earth, and *metron*, a measure, and that the meaningless triangles that I was asked to juggle with formed the basis of geographical exploration, astronomy and navigation, the subject would immediately have assumed a thrilling romance, and, what is more, it would have been directly connected in my mind with the things that most appealed to me.

My experience in this connection may have been unfortunate, but it was by no means unique; many of my friends who went to different schools confess to a similar experience, and complain that when they had completed their school education they had not the remotest idea of what they wanted to do. Moreover I do not think that this curiously detached attitude towards education was confined to schools. It had been intended that I should go to one of the great universities. I was tepid about the idea myself, for I had developed a dislike for the very thought of educational establishments. However, the prospect of three extra seasons in the Alps was a considerable incentive, and by dint of an enormous mental effort, I succeeded in cramming sufficient Latin into my head to pass (at my second attempt) the necessary entrance examination. In due course I went to be interviewed by the Master of my prospective college. When I was asked what subject I proposed to take when I came up to the university, I replied, somewhat diffidently, that I wanted to take geology – diffidently, because I still regarded such things as having no reality in the hard world of work. The answer to my suggestion confirmed my fears. 'What on Earth do you want to do with geology. There is no opening there unless you eventually get a first and become a lecturer in the subject.' *A first, a lecturer-I*, who could not even learn a couple of books of Horace by heart! I felt that I was being laughed at. In fact I am sure I was not, and that my adviser was quite sincere and only trying to be helpful, but I certainly did not feel like arguing the matter. I listened meekly to suggestions that I should take Classics or Law, and left the room in a state of profound depression. 'O Lord,' I thought, 'even here I won't be able to escape from Kennedy's Latin Primer,' with which I had been struggling for ten years.

That interview was largely responsible for my decision not to go to University after all. Now it seems a spineless decision, and that I was remarkably lacking in determination. But at that age one is not always wise. In actual fact of course there were enormous opportunities open to a man who had specialised in any one of the natural sciences, but in those days I had never heard of the Geological Survey of India, oil prospecting, marine biological stations, the exploration ship *Discovery II* which has been working almost continuously in the Antarctic during the last two decades, manned by young specialists in almost every branch of natural science.

Farming in East Africa sounded a good sort of life, one which offered reasonable freedom of scope, not only for making a living but for wider interests as well. Moreover the map showed me that there were some high mountains at hand. I did not suppose that these would offer much in the way of climbing, and I pictured the ascent as being a matter of hacking a way through jungle to a gently sloping ice-cap on top. Somehow I had acquired the extraordinary notion that the Alps were the only mountains in the world that could offer real mountaineering, but I still felt that all mountains were good mountains, and I hoped that the interest that East African peaks lacked in technical difficulty they would provide in unexplored ground. I had read something about the Ruwenzori range, which lies between Uganda and the Belgian Congo, and I knew that this at any rate was one of the most fascinating parts of the world. Accordingly I set out for Uganda with the intention of settling there for the rest of my life.

As luck would have it the place I went to first with the object of learning my job was only about twenty miles from the foot of Mount Kenya. The evening on which I arrived at my first Kenya home was cloudy. But when I came out of my bungalow early the next morning I was met by a sight that made by heart leap. I stood on a ridge and looked through a break in the trees over wide plains, still dim in the early light. The whole northern horizon was filled with a gigantic cone of purple mist. The cone was capped by a band of cloud. Above this band, utterly detached from the Earth, appeared a pyramid of rock and ice, beautifully proportioned, hard and clear against the sky. The sun, not yet risen to my view, had already touched the peak, throwing ridge and corrie into sharp relief, lighting here and there a sparkling gem of ice.

On my way through Nairobi from the coast I had called upon Dr J.D. Melhuish who had made several attempts to climb Mount Kenya. He had shown me his magnificent collection of photographs and had told me much about the mountain, altering all my preconceived ideas. It was obviously a mountain that would stand comparison with any I had seen in the Alps. I was expecting something good, but the exquisite loveliness of that sunlit peak, floating high above a still sleeping world of tropical colour was far beyond anything I could have imagined.

Mount Kenya is an ancient volcano. It rises from a relatively flat tableland, the general level of which is about 4,500 feet above the sea. The base of the mountain is about seventy miles in circumference. From this it rises at a gentle slope to a wide ring of peaks which are the shattered remnants of the crater. In the centre of these, at the apex of the great cone, rises the main peak crowned by twin summits, and draped with fifteen glaciers. This central peak is composed of a kind of granite, a non-volcanic rock, which, when the volcano was active, had been forced up from below and choked the main pipe. The softer volcanic rocks of the crater gradually weathered away and left this hard plug or core standing thousands of feet above the present level of the ancient crater. The summit of the peak is 17,040 feet above sea level and is the second highest in Africa.

The mountain was first seen by a European, Ludwig Kraph, in 1849. Towards the close of the century the explorers Count Teleki (1889), Professor Gregory (1893) and Georg Kolb (1896) made their way through the forests that cover the lower slopes of the mountain, and reached the glaciers at the foot of the main peak. In 1899 Sir Halford Mackinder climbed the peak with two Alpine guides, the brothers Cesar and Joseph Brocherel. The story of his expedition (recorded in the Geographical Journal of May, 1900) is a great one. In those days the country was very wild and little known. The party had frequent encounters with unfriendly tribes and the piercing of the great forests was a long and laborious task. More than once they were forced to retreat for fresh supplies and their journey to the glaciers took several months. After some reverses, Mackinder and his guides reached a small and very steep glacier coming down from the gap between the twin peaks. The ice was so hard that they named it the Diamond Glacier. After what appears to have been a some-what desperate struggle they reached the gap, which they named the Gate of the Mist, and from here they climbed to the summit of the higher peak. Mackinder named the two peaks Batian and Nelion, after two famous Masai chiefs. Batian is slightly the higher.

For nearly thirty years after this, the highest peak had remained unclimbed, though repeated attempts were made, notably by Dr Arthur Melhuish, and Major E.A.T. Dutton, the author of the very charming book 'Kenya Mountain'. The summit of Nelion remained untrodden.

It was indeed a splendid prospect, and I could hardly bear to contemplate the months that must elapse before I could move towards this glistening prize. But it was wonderful to be able to look at it each day. It was generally clear in the morning, until about nine o'clock when the swiftly forming clouds clus-tered round the peaks and extended far down the great volcanic cone. In the evening the clouds would dissolve and the peaks would unveil. I looked for-ward each day to that time, and wondered just how the daily miracle would be revealed. Sometimes the two tips of the twin peaks would appear above the cloud mass – incredibly high they seemed; sometimes the lower glacier skirts would come first into view, grey and cold under the dark pall; sometimes a window would open and show a section of flying buttress and deep ice-filled couloir, steep and forbidding; sometimes the western clouds would break before the southern, and the peaks would emerge already bathed in the sunset glow, shreds of rose coloured mist clinging to their sides. Each evening, week after week, it was different, though I had learnt to know every detail of ridge and corrie. After a while the rains broke and the peaks remained hidden for weeks at a time. Those were dull days.

Arriving on an East African farm with an ice-axe, climbing boots and sev-eral hundred feet of rope seemed for some reason rather ridiculous. At first I managed to conceal these clumsy implements in my baggage, but soon the house servants discovered them and my secret leaked out. My enthusiasm for the mountain became a standing joke and I found few sympathisers among my neighbours. But there was quite a number of kindred spirits in the Colony. Among these was P. Wyn Harris, of the Kenya Civil Service. I knew him well by repute as he had been a prominent member of the Cambridge University Mountaineering Club, and I had been told by several of his friends to look him up. He had already made one attempt to climb Kenya the previous year. Most luckily he was due for home leave at just about the time that I could decently apply for a short holiday. We arranged to join forces for three weeks before his ship sailed.

Besides Harris there was my old friend Gustav Sommerfelt, the Norwegian, who had also come to settle in Kenya. Though he had not done any moun-taineering in the full sense, he was very tough and athletic and a splendid companion for such a project. He jumped at my suggestion that he should join us.

After months of gazing at the peak I had almost come to regard it as something unreal, and I found it hard to believe in our plans. I was haunted by the old feeling that something must go wrong to upset anything so perfect. Sure enough it did. One day in the jungle I fell from a cliff into the fork of a tree and broke my ankle. This seemed a bit unanswerable at first, but the ankle mended after a fashion. Then a telegram came from Wyn to say that he could not get away after all, owing to some tribal disturbance in his district. However at the last moment another telegram arrived to say that all was well.

The three of us met in Nairobi. We had about three weeks before us, the limit being set partly by the length of Gustav's and my holidays, but mainly by the date on which Wyn had to reach Mombasa to catch his ship. Three weeks was enough time in which to make a strong attempt on the peak and get back, providing everything worked smoothly. But it allowed very little time for reconnoitring routes, for bad weather and for failures. So, to give ourselves a chance of success, we could not afford to waste time on our journey to the mountain, and up to the foot of the peak. We hired a lorry with a native driver to take us to Chugoria, a little village in the forests at the foot of the mountain. Innumerable delays occurred, due chiefly to Wyn having to report at the secretariat and the congenital inability of our driver to realise the need for haste. Following the practice of his kind he waited the entire morning while we were busy with our several chores, then when at last the lorry was loaded and all appeared ready he decided to fill up with petrol, an operation which required the partial unloading of our carefully packed goods. This done he disappeared for what, judging by the time it took, must have been a veritable banquet. However by two o'clock in the afternoon we were clattering out of Nairobi along one of its typical corrugated roads.

It is only 150 miles from Nairobi to Chugoria along one of the main roads leading to the Northern Frontier Province. But in those days even the main roads of Kenya were not always easy to negotiate, particularly in a lorry hired for its cheapness rather than its mobility. But we made fair speed, and we only had one tyre burst and one ordinary puncture – remarkable luck considering that on each of the wheels patches of inner tube were visible. By nightfall we were well into the forests that skirt the southern base of the mountain. Our driver stopped with the intention of spending the night by the side of the road. A pal of his, he said, had been attacked by elephants while travelling along this road at night not so long ago, the lorry had been wrecked and the driver killed, and it was not his intention to share the same fate. He could not be made to see that we would be much more vulnerable to attack by the side of the road than moving along it, and for some time he refused to budge. For our part, elephants or no elephants, we were determined to get to Chugoria before morning. We were three to one, and supported by the omnipotent ten shilling note we eventually succeeded in winning the argument.

Chugoria lies about four miles up a side track to the north of the main road. We had some trouble in finding this track in the dark and it was past midnight when we reached our destination, where we found a comfortable billet in a mud hut. Our arrival was adequately announced by the noise of the lorry and at dawn a large number of Masai villagers collected to welcome and inspect us. This suited us admirably as our next concern was the recruiting of porters for our *Safari* up the mountain. Our offer of a shilling a day was greeted with such enthusiasm that we were able to select fifteen of the most likely looking warriors from scores of eager volunteers. I fancy that the gorgeous blankets we had brought for distribution among those who came with us were the real attraction. This state of affairs had the additional advantage that we appeared to be conferring a great favour upon the chosen few – an illusion which held for a day or two at least.

We had not expected to get far that day, but the recruiting was completed with such despatch, and so eager was the rush to secure the lightest load, that our caravan was disappearing into the forest even before the sun had reached the clearing. We counted it as almost a whole day gained. The lorry driver was paid off and went back to Nairobi. We had made no arrangement for our return journey. With remarkable optimism we proposed to 'hitch hike' back when the expedition was over. The truth was, I think, that none of us, not even Wyn who stood to lose his ship and with it a month of his home leave, cared very much what happened so long as we climbed the peak.

There was much to fill the heart in the days that followed. The wonderful knowledge that we had really started, that nothing lay between our own endeavour, our mountain craft, and the great peak ahead; the sight of the naked Masai porters, erect and lithe, swinging along in front of us, their loads balanced gracefully on their heads; the eager talk of hopes equally shared. I kept trying to imagine how my present prospect would have appeared a short year before, and I had a struggle to convince myself that it was real. Not least of the joys was the passionate outflow of mountaineering talk; how good it was after so long, to discuss Great Gable, the Matterhorn, mutual friends, to hear a first-hand account of the ascent of the Brouillard Ridge of Mont Blanc.

The first part of the journey was through forest. The track was good, though slippery here and there where elephants had used it as a kind of toboggan run. It was cool all day in the shade of the giant trees. The gradient was steady and gentle. At 8,000 feet we left the forest and entered abruptly the zone of bamboo. In the forest we had seen little of our more distant surroundings, but among the bamboos our view was even more restricted. We might have been walking between walls of matting. But for the track it would have been an incredibly laborious job to hack a way through. At 10,000 feet the bamboo gave place to giant heath and presently we emerged into spacious park land. It would be difficult to imagine a more lovely spot. Many great trees, exiles from the forest, stood in grand solitude or in shady woods. Here, in place of the wild tangle of monkey rope and tropical creeper, they were draped with wisps of moss and lichen. There were clumps of tall bamboo, of giant heath, no longer engaged in their mad struggle for the predominance of their species, but content in the more temperate climate to live as friendly neighbours. The grass was tall and green.

In this idyllic place a Nairobi business man, Mr Ernest Carr, had built a comfortable wooden hut for the use of all who came. At this time the hut was occupied by Miss Vivienne de Watteville, who is well known for her adventurous African journeys made in the company of her father. She was stopping here for several months engaged in writing a book about her travels. It seemed unkind to disturb her peace, but she welcomed us with charming hospitality, and gave us a dinner that would have done justice to any English home. We would certainly have been tempted to prolong our stay, had we been less impatient to reach the glaciers. Our hostess promised to pay us a visit while we were there.

Above the hut the country was open downland, covered with thick tufted grass. Our way led up a wide ridge. It was a relief to be free from the confinement of the forest. The view in every direction was magnificent and ever wider as we mounted the flank of the vast cone. To our left was the deep ravine of the Gorges valley, holding the dark waters of a lake and dominated by a tremendous precipice and huge, fantastic spires. Below us was the wide belt of forest beyond which the plains stretched away towards the horizon, lost in the distance of infinite space.

Though Mount Kenya lies astride the equator we were already in the region of night frosts. Our porters thought they had gone quite far enough, and we had considerable difficulty in inducing them to face the morning stars. But they were cheerful people and easy to handle, and once they were warmed with exercise they went very well. They had long hair done up in a bun and dyed red. It never seemed to require attention and remained as neatly dressed at the end as at the start. Their great delight was to set a giant groundsel tree alight and to cluster round the warm glow. These curious plants, and the giant lobelias, are peculiar to the mountains of equatorial Africa. They grow in profusion at altitudes of eleven to fourteen thousand feet. They stand about twelve feet high on stems so soft and pulpy that it is quite easy to push the whole tree over. They look quite dead and rotten except for a cabbage-like growth at the very top. As this dies it is replaced by another and the dead leaves form a thatch below. The lobelia grows as a single feathery cone about six feet high.

Once we were above the forest and bamboo, the north-east faces of the twin peaks were in view, and so long as they remained clear of cloud most of our attention was concentrated upon them. Mackinder's ascent had been made from the south-east, and all subsequent attempts had been made from that direction. But after a careful study with the aid of field glasses it seemed to us that a route up the north-east face of Batian might be practicable. The lower part was screened by the surrounding mountains but we decided to gamble some of our precious days on an attempt from this side. As we drew nearer our optimism grew, and with it our impatience to get to grips with the peak. At last we reached a high saddle on the main axis of the mountain. From here, across the head of the Mackinder valley, we could see the whole wall from top to bottom. The face of Nelion appeared smooth, vertical and utterly unclimbable, but the face of Batian, though very steep, was broken by a network of ledges and gullies. The lower part, which before had been hidden from us, was certainly easier than the upper half, that our previous study had pronounced practicable. The faces of the two peaks were divided by a dark gully that plunged in one frightful sweep from the Gate of the Mist. No, there was no alternative, but we did not want one. Our mood of optimism had changed to one of complete certainty. Nothing but a heavy snowstorm, we felt, could now defeat us; and surely the weather which had held for so long, would not change before tomorrow.

It was still before noon when we reached the ridge. Wyn and I left Gustav to pitch our tent, pay off half the porters and send the other half back to the upper limit of giant groundsel, while we rushed off to reconnoitre the route. Plunging down a thousand feet of scree slopes, and skirting under two small glaciers, we reached the foot of the face. We were thrilled to find that the rock was as firm and clean cut as Chamonix granite. It was difficult, but though we climbed a long way up we found nothing to damp our confidence. We returned to camp just before dark with bursting lungs and high spirits. By the next evening, after a glorious climb, the summit of Batian would have been reached for the second time in history, and after a lapse of thirty years.

It was a cold, uncomfortable night and I slept badly, though this was due largely to sheer excitement. But at last it was time to start cooking our breakfast of porridge and bacon, and as soon as it was light the three of us were running down the scree towards the foot of the peak. As we had to move one at a time, with three on the rope, our progress was slower than it had been the day before, but it was steady enough and it seemed that we had plenty of time. Above the point that we had reached before, matters continued to be satisfactory for a while. But gradually the climbing became more difficult. Each new step demanded a more determined effort. Gully, ice slope and ridge were mastered ever more slowly and we began to get worried about the time. At last we reached a great slab, about 200 feet below the summit ridge.

The slab was smooth and offered only tiny finger and toe holds. It was not excessively steep, but above it was a great bulge which ran the whole width of the face and ended in the gloomy overhanging gully under the Gate of the Mist. We had seen this bulge through field glasses from our camp, but we had greatly underestimated its size. Moreover it had appeared to be split by a vertical crack, but this turned out to be no more than a shallow groove as smooth as the rest and overhanging in its lower portion. It did not take us long to recognise that we had arrived at a hopeless impasse; but we continued to gaze at it in silence, each hoping that the other would find some miraculous solution, each waiting for the other to pronounce the verdict he knew only too well.

I do not remember who had the courage to sound the retreat, but whoever it was it was none too soon. During the next few hours the surge of my disappointment was checked by the urgent necessity of getting off the face before nightfall. But it welled up again with yet greater bitterness as we stumbled and toiled up the long scree slopes in the dark. We were all very tired when we reached camp and several mugs of tea brewed on the Primus from melted snow was all we could face for supper.

We felt better in the morning. Our defeat on the north-east face had been complete and decisive. We were not tempted to try again, and so had no awkward decision to make. We still had five clear days before we need move down. Conditions were still perfect, all snow was hard, safe snow, all rock faces were clean. For failure we could blame nothing but our lack of skill and the intrinsic difficulties of the peak. If our confidence was shaken our enthusiasm was, if possible, keener and our goal more desirable than before.

The eastern side of Nelion is nearly vertical, but about half way down a sharp ridge abuts against the face, and leads down to a high saddle dividing a sharp little peak, known as Point Thompson, from Nelion. Through this peak the ridge continues in an easterly direction and climbs to the glacier-capped Point Lenana. At Point Lenana the ridge divides, one branch running north, to form the watershed on which we were camped, others, less well defined, fall away to the south and east. The north side of the ridge between Nelion and Lenana forms the head of the great Mackinder valley, while on its southern side lies the Lewis glacier, the largest ice-stream on Mount Kenya.

Early that morning the remaining porters arrived from below as they had been instructed. Our next task was to move our camp round Point Lenana to the side of the Lewis glacier. It was a tiresome journey. We had to carry loads ourselves, and the way was across steep slopes of shifting boulders. From the start we were enveloped in thick cloud, so that our view was restricted to a few hundred yards. But it was not difficult to find the way as all we had to do was to maintain the same altitude at which we started and keep on traversing. Also Wyn had been to the Lewis glacier a year before, and when we got close to our objective he was able to recognise the ground. His previous attempt to climb the peak had been frustrated by a heavy snowfall, and by his companion collapsing with paratyphoid while they were at their high camp.

We arrived at the side of the Lewis glacier at about midday, and pitched our tent by a small frozen lake. It had often been visited before, and was known as the Curling Pond or Skating Lake, the indefatigable Melhuish having practised both these sports on it. Mr Carr had also built a small hut there, but it had been wrecked by storms and only scattered debris remained.

The weather was still thick when we arrived, but I knew the south-east aspect of the peaks well from photographs. From this side Nelion dominates the picture. It has the appearance of a blunt obelisk supported by two sharp buttresses. One of these forms the upper part of the east ridge, already mentioned, and the other runs up from the south and joins Nelion to a sharp rock spire known as Point John. The south ridge meets the face of Nelion about half way up from the glacier. From the Curling Pond only the very top of Batian can be seen appearing over the south ridge.

By the time we had pitched our tent and sent the porters back to their lower camp and had eaten some lunch, the clouds began to lift and we could see across the glacier to the lower part of the peak. Wyn and I set off across the glacier to reconnoitre. The alternatives were few. The east ridge looked exceedingly difficult in its lower portion; half way up it was broken by a sharp cleft from which descended an ugly-looking couloir, and the rock face above its junction appeared sheer and smooth. The narrow part of the face of Nelion lying between the two ridges was very steep, and did not seem to offer much chance of success. This left only the southern ridge, which was easy to reach and appeared to be quite straightforward as far as it went, except for a small notch about half way up. It would at least give access to the upper part of the peak and we believed that, from its junction with the face of Nelion, Mackinder and his guides had reached the Diamond glacier. So it was on the southern ridge that we pinned our hopes.

The surface of the Lewis glacier was composed of bare ice, in which hundreds of locusts were imbedded. There had been a plague of locusts in Kenya during the previous year, and these must have been carried up by the wind. Crevasses were few and small, and we did not bother to put on the rope until we reached the other side. We found the rock here was as sound and clean as it had been on the north-east face, and we climbed quickly to the ridge.

Just before we reached it we came across a ladder. This was a surprising discovery, and it brought back a pleasant recollection of those early Alpine prints which depict fantastic glaciers on which dozens of little men are seen carrying ladders with which to surmount the crevasses and ice cliffs. We learnt later that this ladder had been left there by Dutton and Melhuish. We were by no means disposed to laugh at their idea.

From the crest of the south ridge we looked down upon the Darwin glacier lying below the south face of the twin peaks. The clouds were steadily lifting. The ridge was easy at first, but soon it became sharp and serrated like the edge of a huge saw. We soon reached the notch that we had seen from below. One glance across it through the thinning mist was enough to shatter our hopes again. It was easy enough to get down from our side on to the narrow level terrace that formed the floor of the notch, but we could see no way of getting up or round the opposite side. This was a thin vertical buttress, smooth like the prow of a ship; at both sides of its base it overhung. Again the verdict was distressingly simple.

Until then I do not think that I had seriously entertained the idea that we should not reach the summit. Before the expedition had started all the gloomy forebodings of my friends, all their statements that the peaks were unclimbable (many of them did not believe that Batian had ever been climbed, though of course they had no justification for their disbelief) had fallen on deaf ears, and had only increased my determination to prove them wrong. Some of the people I had met had themselves been up to the glaciers and had seen the peaks at close quarters so that they knew much more about it than I did. Melhuish was the only man I had met who had actually attempted the peaks. He, of course, knew that Batian had been climbed and rightly assumed that it could be climbed again.

Wyn had encountered the same cynical attitude, and had felt as I did. Our reverse on the north-east face had been a salutary check to our over-confidence, but our failure to reach even the upper end of the south ridge, where the real difficulties, it seemed, would only begin, was a much more severe blow and it left us feeling rather hopeless.

It was now about six o'clock. The mists were clearing rapidly, as I had so often seen them from the farm more than forty miles away. I wondered if anyone were watching from there now. For us, in the midst of the scene, a part of it, it was profoundly impressive. First Point John appeared as we were nearly level with its summit, an island in a restless sea of soft pink and grey. Then, all about us were spires and wild buttresses, floating, moving; and above, infinitely high, the rocky dome of Batian. The level rays of the sun had broken through. We looked towards the east and saw there a great circle of rainbow colours, sharp and clear, framing our own dark silhouettes. It was the Spectre of the Brocken – the only one I have ever seen. Mountains have many ways of rewarding us for our pilgrimage, and often bestow their richest treasures when least expected. For my part, all disappointment, all care for the future were drowned in the great joy of living that moment. We climbed slowly down the ridge and crossed the glacier back to camp.

In my experience, the lofty thoughts, the enthusiasms and good intentions of the night before seldom survive the early interruption of sleep, the hateful business of making and eating an early breakfast, the sullen struggle with frozen boots. The next morning was no exception. I could think of nothing but the futility of renewing our efforts to climb this confounded peak. But yet it had to be done, there was no way out. Anyway in a few hours I would be back again to resume my blessed slumbers.

Gustav had slept badly, and had a headache, so he stopped in bed. Wyn and I slouched across the glacier and sorted ourselves out on the other side. It was still very early and very cold. The peak was black and hard against a clear sky. Our only hope now was straight up the face of Nelion between the junction of the south and east ridges. I gazed up at it in dreamy bewilderment, without the faintest idea of how to start. But a fiery spark seemed to have kindled in Wyn during our short halt, and as soon as we had roped together he led off up the rocks with such energy and decision that he might have been an Alpine guide climbing a familiar peak. First up a gully to the left, then to the right along a broken terrace under a smooth wall – this was fine, I began to come to life. But it was too good to last. Our terrace ended abruptly against a vertical rib, and there was still no sign of a breach in the wall above us. Descending a little, Wyn disappeared round and below the obstructing rib, while I belayed the rope and prepared for the worst. The rope went out slowly, and I waited. Then came a wild cry from round the corner. I thought Wyn had fallen off, and braced myself to receive the jerk. But instead came an excited 'All right, come on!' When I joined him on a square platform I saw the cause of the excitement. A steep and narrow gully led up from the platform, and down it dangled a rope, white with age. It could only have been put there by Mackinder's party; no one since had succeeded in getting so far up the face. Though the rope was too frail to use, the discovery was a tremendous encouragement.

Wyn had found the way, and it was now my turn to take a hand. I led off up the gully and, after struggling for some time below the overhang, at last succeeded in reaching a firm hand-hold away to the right and swung myself, breathless, above the obstacle, where I pulled in the rope for Wyn to follow. The gully was certainly the key to the lower part of the face, and after some straightforward climbing we reached the place where the south ridge abuts against the upper wall of Nelion.

Flushed with our success we sat down to reflect. It seemed amazing to find ourselves here after the hopelessness of the early morning. The day was still young and fortune appeared to be on our side. The sky was clear and the rocks were warming in the sun. We looked out over a vast sea of billowy white clouds, gently rising. They would envelop us before long. To the south, above the clouds, stood a great dome of shining ice. That was strange. We knew there was no peak of that shape and size in the Kenya massif. Yet there it was clear against the blue sky, and it seemed quite close to us. Then suddenly we realised it was Kilimanjaro, the highest mountain in Africa, 250 miles away. The atmosphere over East Africa is remarkably clear. I do not think I have seen mountains at that distance anywhere else.

But we could not spend long enjoying the view, and we had almost at once to turn our attention to the immediate prospect. This was far from encouraging, and our spirits soon clouded. It must have been from here that Mackinder's party had reached the Diamond glacier, and here too that they had been forced to bivouac after their successful but prolonged struggle with it. Above and to the left the great cliffs of Nelion bulged over steep white slabs that fell away to the Darwin glacier. Along the top of these slabs there was a possible line of traverse. But it was an ugly-looking place, and the rocks were plastered with ice. Even if it were possible to climb along the slabs in these conditions, which was very doubtful, we would then be faced with the Diamond glacier. We decided to try to climb the face of Nelion direct. It did not look very promising, but it was the only alternative to those ice-covered slabs.

We climbed to a little recess at the end of the ridge. Behind this was a smooth wall some sixty feet high. But in its lower part there were some tiny holds, and balancing on these I started climbing, hoping to find more holds higher up. But before I had got 15 feet up they petered out. I managed to make a little progress to the left, but without gaining height, and there I clung until my fingers and feet were aching painfully. Working my way back above the recess I tried to the right and here found a narrow sloping hedge that led round a corner out of sight. It was an airy place above a sheer drop whose depth I did not bother to estimate. But before I had got far round the corner I found a shallow crack which split the surface of the wall above me. It was obviously the only line of possibility and I took it, though I was not at all happy. The crack was not wide enough to wedge my foot in it, and the only holds were smooth and sloping outwards. My progress was painfully slow, but soon the prospect of beating a retreat was even more repugnant than climbing on up. At length I reached the top of the crack and found myself on a fairly wide platform above the wall. I felt rather ashamed of myself for wasting so much time on a fool's errand.

But Wyn, when he joined me on the platform, was jubilant, though what there was in our situation to be pleased about I could not see. For the next hundred feet or so the ground was certainly easier, but above that the upper cliffs of Nelion frowned over us in a fearsome overhang, which, even in my somewhat desperate frame of mind, I could not imagine myself attempting.

We climbed on until we were directly under the overhang. From here a wide gully ran steeply down to the right and plunged out of sight. By climbing a little way down this it seemed that we could cross to the buttress on the other side, which formed our skyline in that direction. But if we could get round this it would only bring us out on to the terrific precipice of the eastern face of Nelion. However it was the only way, and Wyn led off down and across the gully. The full length of the rope was stretched taut across the gully before he found a suitable stand and I could join him. Then we climbed diagonally up the buttress. Before it disappeared round the corner, I looked back and saw that we were already above the overhanging part of the southern face of Nelion. We crossed the crest of the buttress, expecting to be faced with a smooth perpendicular cliff. Instead, to our incredulous delight we found that easy broken rocks led on upwards. We could not see the summit, but it was clear that we were above the great wall of the east face and that there was nothing now to stop us. This sudden change from hopelessness to the certainty of success was among the most thrilling experiences I have known. There followed only a swift joyous scramble and we were there, on the hitherto untrodden summit of Nelion.

By now the cloud was all about us, though we could still see the Lewis glacier below. Gustav had been watching the summit through field glasses. He saw us now and let out a tremendous shout which came faintly to our ears. Across the gap, filled with swirling mist, we could see dimly the rocky dome of Batian.

After a short rest we started down the ridge towards the Gate of the Mist. Our first attempt to reach it failed, but by cutting steps down a hard snow slope on the northern side of the ridge we turned an overhanging pinnacle and got down to the floor of the gap. Thence we reached the summit of Batian.

In climbing a peak, or a ridge, or a mountain face for the first time, the anxiety of finding the way, not knowing where each step is going to lead or how far to press home the attempt upon each difficult section, the ever-present fear of being placed in a false position from which there is no retreat, the nagging time factor, all these things enormously exaggerate the actual difficulties of the climb. Wyn and I were so impressed by our ascent of Nelion that we were seriously worried about our ability to get down by the way we had come. We actually contemplated cutting our way down the Diamond glacier and crossing the ice-covered slabs which, only that morning, we had dismissed as impracticable.

I have since repeated the climb several times, and each time I was more amazed, not only that we should have thought of such a desperate alternative, but that we should have regarded the ascent of Nelion as so very difficult. Each step became so engraved on my memory that it seemed commonplace and perfectly straightforward. Even the crack in the sixty-foot wall, that had turned out to be the key to the upper part of the mountain, was no longer formidable. This experience of repeating a climb, the first ascent of which I had made myself showed me very clearly how it was that mountains in the Alps, which had resisted the attacks of the pioneers for so long and had appeared to them such desperate ventures, should come to be regarded as quite easy. To a lesser extent, too, this illustrates the main difference between 'guided' and 'guideless' climbing in the Alps.

Most fortunately for us, Wyn and I resisted the 'temptation' of going down the Diamond glacier, and, with a good deal of anxiety about the time, we climbed down into the Gate of the Mist again and recrossed the summit of Nelion. Most of the way down from there Wyn occupied the more responsible position of rearguard. My job of finding the way was easy. We avoided the crack by roping down the sixty-foot wall. I felt better when the upper half of the mountain was behind us, and I let my mind dwell upon the glorious knowledge that the peaks had been climbed.

For all our misgivings the climb was perfectly timed, and we reached the foot of the peak as the clouds were breaking in the evening light. We made our way across the glacier in the soft glow of the setting sun. I was tired and utterly happy.

Two days later we repeated the ascent of the twin peaks, this time with Gustav. I must confess that neither Wyn nor I were very keen on the idea, but we were well rewarded by enjoying much that in the excitement of the first ascent we had failed to appreciate. When we returned that evening we found that Miss de Watteville had come up with three of her porters to the Skating Lake, as she had promised. We had intended to go down the next day, but her visit provided us with a welcome excuse to allow ourselves just one more day, and the next morning the four of us set off down the Lewis glacier. The sky and the peak remained free from cloud all day, a rare occurrence on Mount Kenya, and one which, in my experience, usually heralded a storm.

We walked round the foot of Point John, and from there climbed to a rocky gap that gave us a splendid view across the Darwin glacier to the southern face of the peaks, crowned by the Diamond glacier. It is pleasant after a climb to have leisure to trace from afar the scenes of recent adventures. Above our gap to the west stood a rock peak, as slender and graceful as the spire of Salisbury Cathedral. Later this came to be known as Midget Peak, and was to be the scene of an unpleasantly exciting adventure.

We went on down to the Lewis glacier and crossed the valley of the Tyndall glacier to Two Tarn Col. Here we spent a blissful hour basking in the sun and gazing up at the great western face of Batian. The principal features of this face are two hanging glaciers. These treated us to a wonderful display of ice avalanches.

That night there was a heavy snowstorm. It is remarkable how satisfactory bad weather can be when it comes at the end of a successful climbing season. The otherwise dismal scene outside our .tent next morning seemed to provide a perfect climax. We had intended to carry our things down, but before we had struck camp our porters appeared through the mist and falling snow. It was a gallant gesture, for they were not equipped for such conditions. Miss de Watteville's men had stayed up at the Skating Lake.

Walking down hill was delightfully easy, and we reached the hut above the forest by evening. A huge meal was followed by a most remarkable rum punch for which our resourceful hostess had all the necessary ingredients. The next morning we said good-bye to her, and plunged down into the forest. After even so short a time in the sterile world of ice, it was a glorious feeling to be amongst trees again. When we reached Chugoria we waited for two days camped by the side of the road. Poor Wyn began to despair of reaching the coast in time to catch his ship. But on the third day a lorry belonging to a Dutch *padre* came along and gave us a lift into Nairobi, where we arrived in time but with none to spare.

4 Mount Kenya – the West Ridge of Batian

Kenya Colony was a land of wonderful variety and great promise. But so far the promise has not been fulfilled. Of the large number of people – Britons, Danes, Russians, Dutch, Swedes, Norwegians, Germans – that went there after the last war to make their homes, probably the majority found only disillusionment. It was not that these people were not prepared to work or that their one idea was to 'get rich quick'; this was a belief that originated in the malicious and quite misleading publicity to which the colony was subjected in the 1920s. Most of the settlers were honest, hard-working folk whose object it was to build this new and beautiful land into a prosperous and developed country.

Undoubtedly the colony was over-capitalised; banks tumbled over each other in their rush to open branches in all the small towns and to advance huge sums to the farmers, large grocery and drapery stores were opened, grand hotels sprouted amongst the low corrugated iron roofs of Nairobi. These parasites lived on the capital rather than the income of the farmers, and when this was exhausted, or the farmers became too wise to fall for their blandishments, they had to close down. Though this did a good deal of harm, the real trouble was that no one knew what to grow or how best to grow it. This is no new problem in a young country, but it was aggravated by a great wave of optimism, for which the government publicity department was largely responsible, and which induced otherwise level-headed people to sink all they possessed in what were at best very doubtful projects. For example, it was found that flax grew well in some districts. The price of flax at the time was £300 per ton which would certainly show a very handsome profit. Farmers put all their land under flax and raised enormous overdrafts at the bank to install the machinery necessary for dealing with the raw product. Then without warning, and almost overnight, the price of flax dropped to £20 or £30 per ton. The crops were not worth reaping at that price, the land became valueless and the farmer was faced with a debt that he could not hope to settle. Again, coffee had been grown with some success in Kiambu and Nyeri; therefore it was assumed that coffee could be grown in other parts of the colony and farmers with good land on the slopes of Mount Elgon and in the Ushin Gishu planted it. Coffee was then fetching £100 or £130 per ton. When the coffee trees were young they appeared to flourish and everyone became excited and planted coffee. But when after five years the trees reached maturity and should have begun to produce their beans, they assumed a woe-begone appearance and produced nothing, no matter with what manurial delicacies they were fed, how much they were petted and pampered, shaded and irrigated. But you do not abandon five or six years' work without a struggle and it was twice that time before people could be induced to realise that they had failed. A few were more lucky and actually succeeded in producing regular annual crops, only to find that the bottom had dropped out of the market. Although there were millions of people in Europe who had to use maize and other things with which to make synthetic coffee, the genuine article could not be sold. Thousands of tons of Brazilian coffee were dumped every year into the sea in an endeavour to induce the middle-men to raise their offers. It may be noted too that although the producer was getting a fifth of his former price, if he were lucky enough to sell at all, the well-do-do English housewife who could afford to buy coffee paid exactly the same price for this expensive luxury as she had paid before.

Flax, coffee, maize, dairy farming, sheep, pyrethrum, fruit, sisal – they were all tried, occasionally with success, usually without. Strange diseases attacked crops and livestock, plagues of locusts, never seen before within living memory, laid waste the land, the rains failed. No, it was not easy to make a living against these odds; everything was too experimental, too little was known.

But for all that it was a good life, full of interest and variety, and there was a great sense of freedom. Each day's work showed a concrete result in so much land cleared or ploughed, a drain dug, trees planted, a wall built – too few occupations in our modern world yield this satisfaction. One was always engaged in some experiment, thinking out new schemes, discussing them with neighbours, visiting other districts at week-ends where friends were engaged in some totally different undertaking – breeding polo ponies for the Indian market, or forestry. Some people spent months exploring the deserts of Turkana and the shores of Lake Rudolf in search of gold, while their partners ran the farms; others secured government contracts to build roads or bridges near their land; others again set up as 'white hunters' and made a good living by conducting wealthy tourists who had come out to shoot big game.

Although there was always plenty of work to do, some seasons were not so busy as others. One could generally manage to get away for a short holiday once or even twice a year. There was an infinite number of things to do, and if one kept away from the big towns these holidays cost very little. I spent all mine on the mountains. Wyn had been sent to an inaccessible spot near Lake Rudolf, and Gustav and I were now working on the same farm and could not get away together. But it was not difficult to find people with whom to climb. Nearly a year after that first expedition I went to Mount Kenya again with Pat Russell. I wanted to explore the north-west approaches to the peaks, but a week of our time was wasted by my being laid up with an attack of fever. When

I had recovered we had time only to work round to the south-east and climb the peak by our old route, though we managed to climb Point John as well.

Early in 1930 I had a letter from H.W. Tilman, who had been given my address by Mefhuish. This turned out to be a most fortunate contact and we were destined to share many mountain ventures together. At that time Tilman had not done much climbing, having only started during his last home leave in the Lake District. But I have met few people so admirably adapted to it both physically and temperamentally. He was very strong and tough, he had a natural aptitude for moving about difficult country, I have never known him rattled, and he had a remarkable ability to put up with – even a liking for – unpleasant conditions. He said very little, too little I thought, but, like many quiet people, when he did speak he was generally worth listening to. As a companion the qualities I liked best were his tremendous sense of humour and his constant readiness to embark upon any project. When I first knew him he was a recluse, and, to my way of thinking, too anti-pathetic towards the softer forms of human pleasure, such as novel reading, cinemas or any form of social intercourse. Most of our occasional quarrels arose, I think, from our disagreement on these matters. Though still at school when the last war began he had served nearly four years of it in France as a gunner in a battery commanded by Major (now Lt.-General) Norton of Everest fame, and had won the Military Cross and bar. He came out to settle in Kenya soon after the last war and had spent most of his spare time hunting elephants and other big game.

Our first trip together was to Kilimanjaro. It was a most interesting journey, through the great game reserve south of Nairobi and across the Tanganyika border to Moshi, near the southern foot of the mountain. Like Mount Kenya, Kilimanjaro is an old volcano. It has two main peaks, Kibo, the higher, and Mawenzi. Though Kibo (19,000 feet) is nearly 3,000 feet higher than Kenya, there are no real difficulties in the ascent. We must have gone there at the wrong season for we struck continuously bad weather and reached the top of Kibo only after a hard struggle through masses of soft snow. To see better in the bad visibility we removed our snow-glasses and suffered for it a few hours later with a mild dose of snow blindness. This is a most painful affliction; it feels rather as though the insides of one's eyelids have been lacerated and then filled with sand. When we had recovered we climbed Mawenzi, which, in those conditions, presented us with quite a tough proposition.

Some six months later Tilman and I joined forces again, this time with a more serious ambition of traversing the twin peaks of Mount Kenya by climbing Batian from the north-west and descending by our old route to the Lewis glacier. I was then living in Turbo near the borders of Kenya and Uganda, and Tilman lived in Sotik, south towards Victoria Nyanza. We met at Nukuru and motored in Tilman's car via Nairobi to Nanyuki near the western foot of the mountain. Motoring in Kenya in those days was an uncertain business, and one generally set out in the expectation of spending a considerable portion of the day digging the car out of a morass, for which the equipment of shovels and crow-bars was as necessary as the supply of petrol and oil. In some places, even on the main roads it was fatal to go where other cars had been and so slip into their deep rutted tracks. Each car had to plough a furrow of its own if it were to stand a chance of getting through. Things, I believe, have changed since then, and now metalled causeways span those uncharted seas of black cotton soil.

Unlike Chugoria which was in a native reserve, Nanyuki was in a European settled district. The surrounding country was a wide open prairie lying between Mount Kenya and the Aberdare Mountains. The farmers of the district went in mostly for cattle. Nanyuki itself was a typical Kenya township of tin roofs, shapeless and unlovely. It had the usual small and sprawling hotel, the Silverbeck, run by a retired naval officer, Commander Hook. These small hotels were a very pleasant feature of Kenya, and were to be found at remarkably frequent intervals along the roads through the settled districts. They were generally spotlessly clean, most efficiently run and the food was excellent. They combined the friendly unpretentiousness of an English inn with a service that left little to be desired. They were miles ahead of anything I have ever met with in India.

It was said that the bar at the Silverbeck had been built across the Equator, though geodesists would no doubt deny that such an exact determination of latitude was possible. However, it appears that the legend was popularly believed, for a famous chess match had been played on it between representatives of the Northern and Southern Hemispheres, each sitting on his respective side of the Equator.

Raymond Hook, the brother of the Commander, combined farming with professional big-game hunting – a remarkably pleasant way of life. He had kindly undertaken to arrange for out modest requirements of pack ponies and drivers for the journey to our base near the head of the Mackinder valley.

Having completed the 250 miles from Nuruku to Nanyuki in a single day without a hitch, we proceeded to get firmly stuck in the mud between the Silberbeck and Raymond Hook's farm, about four miles to the east. As it was getting dark we abandoned the car and walked the rest of the way. We returned the next morning to salvage the vehicle and its most precious load, with the result that we did not start with our small caravan until two o'clock in the afternoon.

I do not think that the route up the mountain from Nanyuki is as attractive as that from Chugoria. That may be partly because I saw the eastern route first, but the forest on the western side is not so magnificent, and there is nothing to compare with that wonderful belt of parkland which on the other side divides the zone of giant heath from the open downs above. But the Nanyuki route is nevertheless very lovely.

We camped the first night in a grassy glade on the outskirts of the forest. I always enjoyed the first camp. One felt so deliciously free, stretched luxuriously on the soft grass in front of a blazing fire that flickered on the dark clumps of jungle, listening to the strange night noises. All the senses seemed to be sharpened by the contrast with one's normal surroundings, just as they were on returning to the forest from the glaciers. Early the next morning as we were eating our breakfast we were startled by a fearful trumpeting close behind us. Perhaps I should say I was startled, for Tilman exhibited no more than a mild interest. Looking round I saw an elephant. We had no means of defending ourselves, but the beast appeared to share Tilman's nonchalance, and to my relief he turned and trundled off into the forest. An African elephant is an impressive sight in its natural surroundings. Later in the day we were fortunate enough to see some rhinoceroses, prehistoric-looking creatures, again to my relief going in the opposite direction.

The forests were full of strange creatures. One of the most interesting, I thought, was the honey-bird. He would follow you about all day flitting from branch to branch above your head, singing all the time. In this way he would try to induce you to follow him, for then he would lead you to a bee-hive. You were then under a gentleman's agreement to smoke out the bees, take your share of the honey and leave him the rest. I never had time to try the experiment but I have it on good authority that it is perfectly true. The Wanderobo carry the tale further. They say that if you do not leave the honey-bird a sufficient share of the loot, when next you meet he will lead you to a snake.

The Wanderobo are a tribe of forest dwellers in Kenya. They are a somewhat mysterious people, very shy, and rarely show themselves unless they have reason to know that you are friendly and have a supply of tobacco to trade for money. They are nomads, living entirely by hunting, of which they are probably among the greatest human exponents, and, presumably, by following honey-birds.

Our way led diagonally up the northern side of the mountain, and so into the Mackinder valley. When we reached the upper part of the valley we found a cave, a mile or so from the northern foot of Batian and about 14,000 feet above sea level. It offered us a most excellent base camp. Being just about at the upper level of giant groundsel it was amply supplied with fuel and a great improvement upon our bleak, comfortless camp by the Skating Lake. The floor of the cave was swampy, but by draining it, drying it with a huge bonfire built at the mouth of the cave, and laying down a carpet of grass and groundsel leaves, we made a very pleasant home for ourselves. We sent the ponies and their drivers down with instructions to return after ten days. I had brought a Wagishu tractor driver, named Masede, from the farm in Turbo. He stayed at the cave with us, where we spent a happy time sleeping and eating until our food ran out.

We spent the first day climbing two sharp granite pinnacles on the ridge forming the western side of the valley. Besides a lot of fun, these peaks provided us with a most comprehensive view of the northern aspect of Batian. I know no mountain in the Alps, with the possible exception of Mont Blanc, that presents such a superb complexity of ridges and faces as the twin peaks of Mount Kenya – a complexity that would delight the heart of any mountaineer. Each feature is clear-cut and definite, none is superfluous to the whole lovely structure. It would take many years of climbing holidays to explore them all, and each would involve a high standard of mountaineering.

From the summit of Batian a sharp, serrated ridge runs north. After some distance it divides and plunges down in two main buttresses, one towards the north-east, the other to the west. The north-east ridge forms the northern boundary of the wall up which we had made our first attempt to climb the peaks, nearly two years before. The west ridge is, to my mind, the finest feature on the whole mountain, though perhaps I am prejudiced. From its junction with the north-east ridge it descends in a series of sweeping steps, each larger than the one above, until the ridge takes its greatest plunge in what I unimaginatively named the Grand Gendarme. From the foot of this the ridge rises to a pinnacle – the Petit Gendarme – and then drops to its lowest point, a snowy saddle dividing Batian from a massive peak known as Point Piggot. Point Piggot is really a continuation of the west ridge which gradually curls south to enclose the basin of the Tyndall glacier, and sinks finally to the grassy slopes of Two Tarn Col.

Planning a climb is a fascinating occupation. In some respects it is even more fun than the climb itself, though of course it would lose most of its charm without the knowledge that the plan would be put into operation. The imagination is free to wander over the entire gigantic scene, to dance on the toes of fancy up sunlit rock and shining silver crest, to shudder in warm security at precipitous ice gullies and airy crags, to trace link by link the slender chain of possibility.

The triangular face between the two main ridges was guarded by a hanging glacier terrace, from which the risk of ice avalanches precluded any prolonged operations on the steep polished slopes below. The north-east ridge was supported by two massive buttresses, smooth and steep, and divided by a straight, deep cleft. For all its forbidding grandeur the west ridge seemed to offer the best hope of success. It was very long and complicated and there was much that we could not judge from a distance, many links that had to be taken for granted.

The first thing to do was to get a closer view of the lower part, which might give us an insight into the all-important time factor and the nature of the ice and snow and rock of which the ridge was built. So the next day we set out for the high saddle between the Petit Gendarme and Point Piggot.

It took us most of the morning and a lot of hard work to reach it. Crossing a low gap in the western wall of the Mackinder valley we climbed down to the lower edge of a great circular sheet of ice that sloped steeply down from the foot of the main peaks. This phenomenon goes by the name of Joseph glacier, after one of Mackinder's Alpine guides. Brother Cesar has been immortalised by a similar slab of ice farther to the east. Immortalised is perhaps hardly the right word, for I fancy all the glaciers of Mount Kenya are dying. Indeed it is a mystery how they contrive to maintain themselves on their present meagre diet of snow. Situated directly on the Equator they have no winter in which to recuperate their strength. In the Himalayas, which at their nearest point are a very long way from the tropics, isolated peaks of 17,000 feet are not usually festooned with hanging glaciers. The daily cloud cap over Kenya no doubt affords some protection to the ice. Admittedly I have taken pains to visit the mountain when I was most likely to meet with fine weather, but I have been there at several different seasons and have observed it during the whole of one 'rains', and I confess that I am puzzled to reconcile the appearance and disposition of the glaciers with the small quantity of snow that appears to fall on the mountain. But then I have never quite satisfied with the accepted explanations of glacial phenomena, and still cling to a sneaking belief that they are just put there by some beneficent power for the delectation (or grief) of mountaineers.

We spent a long time cutting steps up the Joseph glacier to a steep snow and ice gully that led to the saddle. Here we had to negotiate a bergschrund (a kind of crevasse that divides the main body of the glacier from the steeper ice or rock above). Above this a lot more step cutting was required, and by the time we reached the saddle we were dismally conscious that we had undertaken a very tough proposition. Nor was the immediate prospect above us in any way reassuring. By now the upper part of the peak was hidden by cloud. The Petit Gendarme frowned down upon us like an ogre that resented our intrusion. If it had been his scalp that we were after we might still have been over-awed, but he was only an incident on the great ridge, the first of a long series of obstacles. A direct assault seemed to be out of the question and we must outflank him. This we could only do by climbing diagonally up a very steep slope to the right. Whether this slope was composed of ice or snow we could not tell from where we stood. It was a matter of considerable importance, for if it were ice, cutting steps up it would involve a good day's work to reach the ridge behind the Petit Gendarme. Above and beyond we could see the vertical flanks of the Grand Gendarme thrusting up into the clouds.

We sat down on a rock shelf to reflect, our legs dangling over the Tyndall glacier several hundred feet below. It was a grand view. Across the way was the great west face of Batian, so close that we might have been hanging from a balloon before its ice-scarred ramparts. We were about level with the lower of the two hanging glacier terraces; the lace fringe of the upper terrace was just visible through the cloud. These monsters were silent now, which was a pity, for here we had front seats in the dress-circle from which such an avalanche display as we had seen from Two Tarn Col would have been a fine spectacle. To our right the ridge mounted in a series of jagged spires towards Point Piggot, to our left-, we averted our eyes; we had learnt as much of the west ridge as we could digest in one lesson. The stage was set and tomorrow the chosen day.

How I hated Tilman in the early morning. Not only on that expedition, but through all the years we have been together. He never slept like an ordinary person. Whatever time we agreed to awake, long before that time (how long I never knew) he would slide from his sleeping bag and start stirring his silly porridge over the Primus stove. I used gradually to become aware of this irritating noise and would bury my head in silent rage against the preposterous injustice of being woken half an hour too soon. When his filthy brew was ready he would say 'Show a leg', or some such imbecile remark. In moments of triumph on the top of a peak I have gone so far as to admit that our presence there was due in large measure to this quality of Tilman's, but in the dark hours before dawn such an admission of virtue in my companion has never touched the fringe of my consciousness.

The next morning was no exception. I remembered that it was my birthday, which seemed to make matters worse. We issued from our lovely warm cave soon after three o'clock, leaving Masede in full possession, and plodded slowly up the side of the valley in the bright moonlight.

I began to feel more human when we reached the Joseph glacier. We supplemented the light of the moon with that of a candle lantern and climbed rapidly. Our steps of the previous day, large and comfortable, were still intact. Hours of toil now sped beneath us with an effortless rhythm of hip and ankle joints, as we climbed towards the dawn. Daylight was flooding in upon us as we crossed the bergschrund. Half way up the gully above, we branched to the left so as to reach the ridge beyond a small but difficult section east of the saddle. In this manoeuvre we were delayed by some difficult climbing on ice-covered rocks, but even so we reached the crest below the Petit Gendarme with the whole day before us. And what a day! Crisp, sparkling, intoxicating. I have never known more complete physical well-being. The western face of Batian caught the full light of the newly risen sun, and every lovely detail of ice fretwork and powerful granite column was hard and clear.

Though what we could see of the west ridge towering above us looked no less formidable than before, we were now in a very different frame of mind, and we paused barely a minute. But the slope under the Petit Gendarme soon began to exercise a sobering effect. It turned out to be composed of hard ice covered by a layer, not more than an inch or two thick, of frozen crystalline snow. It was exceedingly steep and ended below in a sheer drop to the Tyndall glacier. While we were both on the slope together a slip on the part of either of us would have been almost impossible to hold, since we were traversing diagonally across it. It was possible, by kicking small toeholds into the hard layer of snow and by sticking the blade of the axe in for a hand rail, to climb up and along the slope with reasonable security. But this security would only remain so long as the snow held firm. The slope was still in shadow, but an hour or so after the sun had climbed above Point Piggot the snow would begin to melt and would no longer offer any hold. The proper procedure would have been to cut steps through the snow into the ice below, but this would have taken nearly all day, and we were still at the very beginning of the climb. This is a common problem in mountaineering, and each case must be judged by the circumstances. We must have a line of retreat in the event of failure higher up, particularly as that event was very probable. Cutting steps downhill, besides being very slow and exhausting, is apt to be a hazardous business when prolonged for many hours on so exposed a slope without any sort of anchorage. In this case I was fairly confident that we could climb over the top of the Petit Gendarme from behind and rope down its western side. Even if this line of retreat failed, we could always wait until the following morning and come down the slope when it was again frozen. So we decided to risk it and to use the snow layer covering the ice.

Even so it was a long job. In some places, near rock outcrops, the snow was too thin to provide any foothold, and steps had to be cut in the hard blue ice. It took us several hours to regain the crest of the ridge behind the Petit Gendarme. We halted for five minutes to eat some chocolate and look about us. The peak was already covered in cloud. It was obvious that we could not get very far unless things improved, and at first sight there did not seem to be very much chance of that. For a short distance the ridge was fairly easy, but then it rose up like a mighty wave, several hundred feet of vertical and unbroken rock. It was hopeless to think of climbing this direct, and the only chance was to look for a way of turning it on the left. We traversed out on to the north face and reached a gully that led directly upwards. Here the climbing was more straightforward, and except in a few places we could both move up together. We could never see very far ahead, and had little idea where we were getting to. Suddenly after about an hour and a half we reached the crest of the main ridge again, and were delighted to find that we were standing on top of the Grand Gendarme. This was a very welcome surprise, and our hopes began to revive, until we came to examine the next obstacle.

This appeared to us as a red pinnacle, but it was, in fact, a step in the ridge similar to the Grand Gendarme on a much smaller scale. It was extremely steep and was undercut at its base. This time there was no chance of getting round the obstacle. To the right there was a giddy drop to the hanging glaciers of the west face; to the left the scoop at the base of the pinnacle ran downwards in a groove towards the centre of the narrowing north face, over-hung by a continuous line of ice-polished slabs.

There was a good ledge below the pinnacle, and by standing on Tilman's shoulders I could just reach two finger holds. Hanging on these, and with a final kick off from Tilman's head, I managed to swing myself up to grasp a hold higher up and also to find some purchase for my feet to relieve the strain on my arms. After an exhausting struggle I established myself above the over-hang. Then followed some very delicate work. The wall of the pinnacle was nearly vertical, and the holds were only just large enough to accommodate a boot nail. But the rock was perfect, and at first the holds, though few, were well spaced. Half-way up, however, there was an extremely nasty bit. It involved a long stride from one nail to another with nothing but a few rough excres-cences for the hands with which to maintain my changing centre of balance. I contemplated this stride for a long time, before cautiously swinging my right foot to the upper hold. It felt so unpleasant that I hastily brought my foot back again for further contemplation. After repeating this faint-hearted operation about half a dozen times, and prompted largely by my increasing distaste for the present position of my left foot which was beginning to hurt, I gradually transferred my weight to the right foot, which to my intense relief did not slip, and by clawing at the face of the rock managed to hoist myself into an upright position.

Fortunately, after this the holds, although still small, became more profuse. But by now there was a new source of anxiety. The rope between us was clearly not going to be long enough to enable me to reach the top of the pinnacle. It was no use Tilman unroping, for he could not possibly get up the lower over-hanging bit without a pull from above. There was a little recess below the top, and I just reached it as the rope came taut between us. In this I wedged myself sufficiently tightly to support his full weight. I hauled up the ice-axes and the rucksacks and sent the end of the rope down again. In spite of my pulling, Tilman had a much more severe struggle than I had experienced. When he had succeeded I climbed quickly to the top of the pinnacle where I got into a really strong position. The rest was easy.

Nothing provides such a strong incentive to struggle on up at all costs as the memory of a really severe pitch below, and from now on we were infused with a pleasant sense of abandon. Time was our chief anxiety, and we hurried upwards as fast as we could. The steps that followed were difficult, but not nearly so bad as the red pinnacle which we had just surmounted. They grew smaller and smaller until at last we reached the junction of the north-east and the west ridges.

It was an exciting moment as we turned south to look along the final ridge leading to the summit. It is impossible to tell from below how difficult such a ridge is likely to prove. We had seen that it was long and serrated, and that the steepness of the west and north-east faces on either side of it would oblige us to stick to the crest. Much depended upon the width of this crest. We could not see far along it through the mist, and so the issue remained in doubt. At any rate, the short length of ridge that we could see, though very narrow and broken, was not hopeless. We started clambering along it, sometimes balancing along the top, sometimes sitting astride and sometimes swinging along the crest with our hands while our feet sought purchase on the wall below.

It was a splendid situation, thrust up infinitely high, isolated by the mist from all save this slender crest of granite along which we must find a way, the thrilling knowledge that the mighty west ridge was below us, mind and muscle set to a high pitch of rhythmic co-ordination. I have rarely enjoyed anything more. Somewhere down in the grey depths to the left was the great bulge of rock that had defeated us nearly two years before. To the right, below our feet, was a white glow, the upper hanging-glacier terrace of the west face. The rock was superb, as hard and strong as the granite of the Chamonix Aiguilles.

We reached a gap about thirty feet deep, and roped down into it. Our boats had already been effectively burnt, and there was no time to bother about cutting off our retreat still further. One after another pinnacles loomed into view, greatly magnified by the mist. One after another we set about the new problem that each presented, always expecting it to be the last. I soon lost count; the ridge seemed to go on for ever; but we were going with it, and that was the main thing. Surely nothing could stop us now.

At last, in place of the sharp pinnacle we had come to expect, a huge, dark grey mass loomed ahead of us. A few steps cut in the icy floor of a gully, a breathless scramble up easy rocks, and we were there beside our little cairn on the summit of Batian.

It was half-past four. There was no chance of getting down before nightfall, but no consideration of that sort could stem the flood of my joy and, let it be admitted, relief. I do not know what Tilman thought about it. He did not know the way down the south-east face. If he imagined it to involve climbing of a standard similar to that which we had just done he must have had some misgivings, though characteristically he expressed none.

There was no view to look at, and so, after swallowing a tin each of some meat essence, we began the descent. The rocks on the south side of Batian were plastered with snow, which delayed us. But we made up time between the Gate of the Mist and the top of Nelion which we crossed without a pause, and plunged down into the gully beyond. In our haste Tilman slipped and lost his ice-axe which vanished out of sight in a single bound. After that we were more careful. It was getting dark as we reached the top of the sixty-foot wall above the head of the south ridge, and night had fallen by the time we had pulled the rope after us at the foot of the wall.

It was here that I began to feel very sick. I imagine that the tin of meat essence I had eaten on the summit was bad. But an hour or so later I was sick, and after that I felt more philosophical about it.

The clouds had not cleared at dusk in their customary manner, and it looked as though we should have to stop where we were until the morning. It was already very cold, and the prospect was not welcome. But later, breaks began to appear in the mist, the moon came out and there was enough light to enable us to climb on down slowly. I felt very tired and the phantom moonlight, the shadowy forms of ridge and pinnacle, the wisps of silvered mist, the radiant expanse of the Lewis glacier plunging into soundless depths below induced a sense of exquisite fantasy. I experienced that curious feeling, not uncommon in such circumstances, that there was an additional member of the party – three of us instead of two.

It was not very difficult nor even laborious, dropping from ledge to ledge. I remembered every step of the way, and had no difficulty in finding it. We had some trouble in negotiating the chimney where we had found Mackinder's rope, but once below that the rest was easy. When we reached the Lewis glacier we started plodding up towards the saddle between Point Lenana and Point Thompson. But this demanded more physical effort than we had bargained for, so we altered course and made for the hut by the side of the Skating Lake. Here we huddled over some bits of timber that we managed to ignite, and waited for the dawn. The rest did us good, and we reached the saddle before the sun was up. From there back to our cave in the Mackinder valley was mostly downhill, but it seemed a very long way.

Masede was pleased to see us, but he was not greatly concerned. It is no longer possible to surprise the East African negro by the inexplicable follies of the White Man. For our part we were in no mood for conversation. We got into our sleeping bags, a ten-pound Cheddar cheese and a bottle of pickled onions between us, and ate and ate until we fell asleep. We awoke in the evening and ate again, and then slept until late the following morning.

I still regard the traverse of the twin peaks of Mount Kenya as one of the most enjoyable climbs I have ever had – a perfect and wholly satisfying episode, shared with an ideal companion.

We still had nearly a week left. The weather held, and we climbed several more peaks. One of these was Point Piggot, which gave us a superb view of the west face of Batian. The sky remained clear most of the day, and we lay for a long time on the summit basking in the sun and gazing contentedly across at the west ridge. Another long day was spent walking all the way round the foot of the central peaks. Immediately below one of the glaciers we found the skeleton of a wild buffalo, which had evidently broken its leg by slipping between the great boulders that formed the slope. Others had been found before, and it would be interesting to know why these creatures should wish to stray from the pleasant country below. It cannot be to escape from the heat, and the glacial regions offer them nothing to feed on but lichen. There was the skeleton of a leopard near the summit of Kilimanjaro.

Our last climb provided an adventure which came too near to disaster to be pleasant. We set out to climb the lovely, slender spire of Midget Peak. We had examined it in passing on our journey round the peaks, and it seemed to us that it might be possible. It would certainly provide rock climbing of a high standard, but on clean granite there is no knowing what you can do until you try. To get to the peak we had once more to cross the high saddle near Lanana and go down the Lewis glacier past Point John. The clouds came up in the usual way, and apart from the fact that the two previous days had been brilliantly fine, there was nothing to suggest that we were in for a spell of bad weather. Once on the peak the climbing, which was difficult and exposed, occupied all our attention. About two-thirds of the way up we found ourselves in a sort of cave the only exit from which was by way of a narrow, slightly sloping ledge that jutted over a considerable overhang. There was no handhold, and it was simply a matter of standing on the ledge and edging along it. It was only about three yards long, and led to a comfortable platform. Above this there was a steep and narrow gully.

After some more hard climbing we reached the summit. We were sitting there feeling rather pleased with ourselves when snow started to fall in large, soft flakes. This was a nasty shock. What had been pleasantly difficult on the way up would be decidedly unpleasant on the way down with the holds covered in snow. We hurried off the summit and began climbing down as fast as we could. The rock was still reasonably dry when we reached the top of the narrow gully. Here there was a large rock bollard. While I hitched the rope round this and paid it out, Tilman climbed on down the gully and soon disappeared from view. The rope continued to go out for a while, then it stopped and I guessed that he had reached the beginning of the sloping edge. Suddenly there was a sickening jerk, and the rope stretched down the gully as taut as a wire hawser from a dragging ship. I waited for a moment hoping to get some instructions as to whether I should hold fast or lower away, but nothing happened. I shouted, but could get no reply.

What was I to do? Possibly the wisest thing would have been to make the rope fast and to climb down the gully to investigate the situation. But it is not good to leave an unconscious man dangling in mid-air for long, as he might easily suffocate. Of course I could not be sure that he was dangling, but judging by the strain on the rope and my memory of the cliff below it seemed very probable. It was quite impossible to haul him up owing to the friction of the rope against the rock; and in any case if he were dangling he would have got stuck under the overhang. The only alternative then was to lower away and hope for the best. Foot by foot the rope went out, and still no slackening of the strain. So far all the weight was taken by the bollard, but soon the rope was finished, and there was nothing for it but to take it off the bollard. Here I made a stupid mistake. I should have done this while there was still sufficient rope to put over my shoulder. I thought of it too late, and of course I could not pull the rope back again. So, instead of taking the strain from my shoulder, I had to start climbing down with it dragging from my waist. Now the friction of the rope against the rock was my ally, acting as it did as a slight brake to the downward movement. On the other hand, whenever I bent I could not straighten myself again except by stepping downwards, and I had to think out my movements very carefully. Fortunately the gully was very narrow, and I could brace my arms against either wall.

To my great relief, before I had gone very far down the gully, the strain lifted, which meant that Tilman had come to rest on a ledge. I hurried on down to the platform below the gully, and looked over the edge. He was sitting on a ledge looking up at me. I thought he looked a bit queer, though he answered my questions rationally. He seemed to be unhurt. I discovered afterwards that he was still only half conscious, and had not the least idea of where he was. I asked him if there was a way on down from where he was sitting. I could not see because of the overhang. He said there was a way, and I decided to join him.

By climbing a little way down to the right I reached a place from which the doubled rope would reach the ledge below. Then hitching it over a bollard I slid down it. To my dismay, when I reached it I found that Tilman's ledge was quite isolated, and that there was no possible means of getting on down. The next ledge below was far beyond the range of our rope. The only thing to do was to climb back again up the rope.

Tilman was recovering rapidly. I do not know when he started remembering things again, but I believe it was not for quite a while after this. To this day he cannot remember anything that happened between his slip and our safe arrival in the cave beyond the sloping ledge. How he contrived to climb up the rope to the platform above, I cannot imagine. At the best of times a climbing rope is not very easy to swarm up, as it is too thin; now our fingers were cold and the rope was wet from its contact with the snow. I found it about as much as I could do. However, we were beginning to get somewhat desperate, and that can account for a lot.

Back on the platform we still had to cross the sloping ledge which now had a thick layer of snow on it. It was impossible to climb carefully along it as one's foot would certainly have slipped. There was only one way to deal with it. Firmly belayed by Tilman against the possibility of a repetition of the contretemps we had just experienced, I placed one foot as far out on the ledge as I could reach, and, with a combination of a spring and a dive, I leapt forward.

The manoeuvre succeeded, and I landed sprawling on the lip of the cave beyond. Tilman repeated the performance, and the worst of our troubles were over.

By now all the ledges and cracks in the rock were deep in snow, and climbing in the ordinary sense was impossible. We could only proceed by a series of *rappels*. This is a method of 'roping down' which has been referred to before. It is a simple dodge employed either to save time or to get down an otherwise unclimbable place. The rope is doubled and fixed to a rock bollard (if there is none available, an iron spike hammered into a crack in the rock will serve) and the two ends are allowed to dangle evenly down. By letting the rope slide between the legs and over one shoulder, by holding the upper part of the rope with one hand and the lower part with the other, and by steadying oneself with one's feet against the rock it is possible to slip comfortably without much muscular effort. So as to retrieve the rope when one is at the bottom, it is generally necessary to pass it through a separate sling which is itself attached to the bollard, then, by pulling one end, and with reasonable care, the rope slips through the sling and is recovered. The slings are generally made by cutting a short length (varying according to the size of the bollard) from the main rope.

I forget how many *rappels* we did that day, but by the time we reached the foot of the peak our rope, which had started as a 120-foot length, was reduced to about forty feet.

Large soft snow-flakes were still falling steadily as we trudged slowly up the Lewis glacier through the deep, new snow. I did not know how Tilman felt, but I was mighty glad to be on firm ground again. It was dark by the time we reached our cave.

The next morning it had stopped snowing and I took Masede up to show him a glacier at close quarters. He was politely interested, but what he was really curious to know was how much the Government would pay us for our activities of the last ten days. He just would not believe me when I told him that we had done it for our own amusement and that the Government would not pay us a cent for all our hard work. Like a skilful barrister he kept trying to trap me into an admission, and it began to rankle that he could not prove me a liar. However, on our way back through Nairobi I happened to go to lunch with Major Dutton at Government House. When I came out Masede met me with a smirk on his face. It was quite clear to him that I had gone there to collect our money. In face of such evidence it was useless for me to argue further, and so long as I knew him he never again believed anything I said.

5   Mountains of the Moon

Whether Ruwenzori, Kenya, Kilimanjaro or the group of volcanoes of Kivu are Ptolemy's 'Mountains of the Moon', is an open question. Nor is it of great importance, for the ancient tradition of the Nile rising in a system of lakes fed by snow mountains, though true, seems to have been more in the nature of a lucky guess than a result of actual geographical observation. However, as Ruwenzori alone fulfils the ancient tradition, it has come to be labelled with that romantic title. Its mystery, invisibility and remoteness, surrounded by thousands of miles of tropical swamp and vegetation, and the fact that, unlike its rivals, it is a *range* of non-volcanic mountains, perhaps make it the more worthy of the distinction. The origin of the name Ruwenzori is very doubtful, and it is not used by any local natives in speaking of the mountain range.

Nevertheless, it is remarkable that the ancients should have believed in the existence of these snow mountains, as it was not until 1888, some thirty years after the discovery of the Victoria Nile by Speke, that Stanley discovered the existence of snow mountains in Central Africa; this despite the fact that many explorers had been travelling for a number of years in the neighbourhood of the range, and Stanley had himself camped for months at its foot without so much as suspecting the existence of vast glacier-covered mountains. To those who have experienced Ruwenzori weather, this is not so surprising!

During the next eighteen years various attempts were made to penetrate to the glaciers, but it was not until 1906 that a large expedition led by HRH the Duke of the Abruzzi explored the peaks and glaciers of the range and reached the summits of the highest peaks.

In 1926, G.N. Humphreys led two remarkable expeditions, during which he explored much new country to the north of the range, and carried out some very good work amongst the peaks. During the second expedition he reached the summits of Margherita and Alexandra for the first time since the Duke's expedition.

In spite of the opening of good motor roads through Uganda to Fort Portal and beyond to the foothills of Ruwenzori, very few Europeans ever penetrated far into the mountains, and, since 1926, the ascent of the high peaks had not been repeated. In recent years Humphreys had explored much of the country, but there was a great deal still to be discovered. Tilman and I had decided to go to Ruwenzori at the earliest opportunity. Our interest was centred mainly upon the high peaks, for we had not yet realised that fascination of unexplored valleys.

In 1931 I was invited to join Smythe's expedition to Kamet, and it was not until early in 1932 that we had the chance of further African ventures. We travelled the 500 miles from Turbo in Kenya to the foot of the mountains in Tilman's car. We had no difficulty whatsoever in collecting porters to establish us. Our requirements were very small as we proposed to establish any high-level camps ourselves. We started with twelve porters, and one man cut a path through the forest. All porters' food had, of course, to be taken with us.

The porters were of the Bakonju tribe, who live on the lower slopes of the range. They were delightful people, with a ready grin, even in adverse circumstances, and they were generally cheerful and willing. One of their chief characteristics was the way they balanced up and down formidable slopes, or from one tree trunk to another, with fifty-pound loads on their heads – a feat to be envied by even the most practised mountaineer.

Three marches took us to the forest. It was difficult going as the vegetation was everywhere dense and perpetually wet. Sometimes we went for half an hour at a time without touching the ground, walking over thickly-matted branches. The sides of the valley were steep and broken, and progress was infinitely laborious. We found rock shelters at frequent intervals; these were very useful as camping sites, for it was always raining. In the evening, sitting before a fire, sheltered from the rain, it was good to watch the clouds driven wildly about the craggy foothills of the range, or clinging to the gullies in the enormous rock precipices; to listen to the roar of a hundred torrents; and, after dark, to see the flickering of lightning towards the high peaks. One afternoon, while still in the forests, the weather cleared, and we saw the great ice peaks of Stanley and Speke – a startling sight indeed, seen from such very tropical surroundings. It is easy to realise with what excitement those early explorers first set eyes on these snow peaks after travelling for many months through the swamps of Central Africa.

At an altitude of about 10,000 feet we came to very strange country. A fantastic tangle of rotting vegetation – giant groundsel, lobelia and giant heath – all thickly covered in moss. Moss was everywhere; we waded feet deep in it and walked through tunnels of it. The very air seemed to be tinged with an eerie green light. All the streams were hushed and a strange silence reigned.

Two more days were spent in reaching the Bujuku Lake, at the foot of the Scott-Elliott Pass, where we made our base camp in a cave. Moving about in the high valleys was exasperating. We were either in swamp, groundsel forest, or struggling through a vile growth known as 'helichrysum', which is a sort of juniper growing to a height of about seven feet, and so dense as to be at times impenetrable. The giant groundsels found on Mount Kenya grow singly and far apart. In the Ruwenzori they grow close together in dense forests, their rotten trunks lying about in a thick tangle on the ground. These, though stout, were rarely strong enough to bear our full weight, so that when we stepped on them they snapped helplessly in mid-air. Apart from the great labour needed to make any headway, it was almost impossible to go more than a few yards in any direction without getting wet to the hips – even if it did not happen to be raining or snowing. Again, above the limit of the helichrysum the rocks were covered with thick moss, which peeled off as soon as any weight was placed on it. This rendered any but the simplest approaches very dangerous.

But when all is said, Ruwenzori, like our Lakeland, would lose a great deal of its beauty, mystery and charm were it deprived of its continuous cloud and damp. Nor did we go there for comfort or freedom of movement.

We discharged two porters *en route*, and from the Bujuku camp we sent down another five. The remaining six were installed in a cave, and waited there with food and fires until we returned down the mountain. We went on alone with a light bivouac camp to the glaciers of Mount Stanley. All the time we were in thick mist and, with our heavy packs our progress was slow for we became involved in many difficulties by not being able to see more than a few yards ahead. Eventually, however, we reached the plateau of the Stanley glacier and, by accident rather than by design, camped right on the summit of the main divide. Though when we stopped we had no idea where we were.

At sunset that evening the mists cleared, and we looked straight down to the Congo. In the foreground was a sheer precipice of broken glacier, from which angry clouds strove to detach themselves. Beyond, like a hazy map beneath us, stretched the plains of the Congo across which the Semliki River coiled like a silver snake. To the south was the huge expanse of Lake Edward. The whole scene was flooded in the deepest blue – a blue so vivid that it coloured everything around us, becoming more and more intense the farther one gazed over the Congo, until swallowed up in a blazing sunset.

For the next twenty-four hours it snowed almost continuously. The following morning we set out in the vain hope of finding our way about the glaciers, but we spent a fruitless day losing ourselves in snow flurries, as our tracks were immediately blotted out by the driving snow. However, late in the evening, we managed to reach the foot of the south ridge of Alexandra. The next day, 19 January, we climbed the ridge to the summit of that peak. There was one difficult cornice to be overcome and a fair amount of step cutting on the ridge. This, I believe, was the route taken by the Duke of Abruzzi's party. We found a cairn on the summit. The mist cleared for a few moments while we were on the top, but we could see very little.

We were four and a half days on the glacier. There was a high wind most of the time, and snow fell all night and most of the day. But each evening at sunset the weather cleared for a moment and gave us superb views over the Congo. On the 20th we became hopelessly involved in a maze of crevasses while attempting to reach the east ridge of Margherita. At last, on the 21st, after repeated efforts, we managed to strike it at a point where the cornice was small, and could be cut through without great difficulty. From there we had little trouble in making the third ascent of the highest peak of Ruwenzori.

The snow and ice formations on these peaks are remarkable. Strong, cold winds, blowing newly fallen snow against any irregularity, produce the most fantastic shapes and forms. Practically no melting seems to take place, and gigantic cornices are formed. The snow surfaces have a very curious feathery appearance which is most beautiful.

When our food was finished we started an undignified descent to our base. We slid and slithered on moss and lichen-covered rocks, and spent most of the time sitting down heavily on the ground. Our packs were far heavier than they had been when we left our base camp, owing to the fact that tent, sleeping-bags and all our kit were water-logged. But our real troubles began when we got amongst the helichrysum and rotting giant groundsel. At last, floundering through swamp and black mire, we reached the luxury of our cave by the Bujuku Lake.

We allowed ourselves a whole day to recuperate from this battering and to dry our sodden garments and bedding. It was a mystery to me how the porters continued to keep a fire going, still more to light it in that perpetual wet. But it did not seem to present any problem to them and two furnaces raged day and night at the mouth of the cave.

The Bakonjus of Ruwenzori have a remarkable method of carrying fire about with them. Straw, thatched tightly in the shape of a cigar about 18 inches long forms a receptacle in which the fire lies dormant. They carry these curious objects strapped to their shoulders and when they want a light they just take off the end of the cigar and blow. It is said that fire can be carried in this way for a month without renewal.

We set out for Mount Speke in thick weather on 23 January, and after a further tussle with swamp and drenching vegetation, reached a glacier. A short clearing enabled us to see that we were almost directly above the Stuhlmann Pass. We climbed to the crest of a ridge and followed it to the summit of Vittorio Emmanuele Peak without encountering any mountaineering difficulties. There was a biting wind and we were wet to the waist. We waited for three hours hoping for a view, stamping about in a vain attempt to keep the circulation moving in our legs. At about 1.30 p.m. the mists lifted for a short time. We raced along the long ridge to the north, and, after crossing three intervening peaks, reached the unnamed peak which was climbed by Humphreys in 1926. It is the highest point of Mount Speke.

One of our principal objects was to force a route direct from the Bujuku valley to the highest peaks of Mount Baker. With this in view, we left our camp at dawn on 24 January. We had hoped to make the attempt direct from the

Scott-Elliott pass, but the vicious ice-clad slabs and ice-filled cracks and gullies of the ridge above the pass looked impossible, so we decided to attempt the face about half a mile farther down the valley. The lower part of the face was covered in thick moss and lichen, and required extreme care. Above this the steep rocks were covered with ice and snow which, together with the rottenness of the rock, produced an exasperatingly false appearance of simplicity. It was difficult in the thick mist to make a good choice of route. After some hours of this sort of climbing we were faced by a formidable line of overhangs guarding this side of the east ridge of Baker. But after several attempts we overcame these and gained the ridge at 11 a.m.

Turning to the west, we followed a long easy ridge leading over several minor peaks to Semple Peak, which we reached at about 1p.m. From there we turned south and climbed to the summit of King Edward Peak, the highest point of Mount Baker.

Shortly before reaching the summit, the whole range of high peaks cleared and we had a superb view of Mount Stanley. Having been surrounded by impenetrable fog for many days, the effect of such a sudden and complete clearing was indescribably wonderful; it felt as though a great load had been removed from one's mind. Subjects of considerable speculation and heated argument suddenly became clear. Our flounderings amongst the glaciers of Mount Stanley were at once revealed, and it was difficult to understand why we should ever have been at a loss to know where to go; though no doubt we would have been in exactly the same state of perplexity had we found ourselves again on the Stanley glacier wrapped in cloud.

With the sudden clear weather we decided to complete the traverse of Baker, disregarding the painful prospect of the weary return to the Bujuku valley by way of the Scott-Elliott Pass. We allowed ourselves about half an hour's rest on King Edward Peak, to examine our first real view of the range as a whole. Far below, the valleys, now bathed in sunlight, looked mild and beautiful, and we almost forgot our struggles amongst their vile vegetation and swamp. Their intense green contrasted superbly with the crags surrounding them. Here and there deep blue lakes nestled in emerald beds. The neighbouring ice peaks, with the fantastic shapes of the twin peaks of Mount Stanley, completed this wonderful scene. Boiling masses of cloud still hung over the lower valleys.

The descent south towards Freshfield Pass was easy, though we had to be careful as the snow was inclined to avalanche. About half-way down the ridge we turned west and descended the steep glacier, on which there was a layer of unstable snow covering the ice. Once off the glacier we again encountered rocks with a treacherous coating of moss. At first it was so sparse as to be hardly perceptible, which made it the more dangerous, as our feet were apt unaccountably to slip off the most secure ledges. This direct descent was something of a step in the dark as we could not see what was below us. Lower down when we reached the upper line of the helichrysum, we became involved in a series of difficult crags. There the helichrysum in part atoned for its previous behaviour, as without its assistance the crags would have been impassable and a return to the summit ridge unavoidable – a matter of many hours' toil. Even as it was, the descent of the line of crags, which we were lucky enough to strike in the only feasible place, proved a difficult struggle, during which Tilman lost his watch and I succeeded in spraining my right shoulder. We reached the valley close by a small lake, and then toiled wearily towards the Scott-Elliott Pass. When at last we reached its foot, we were delighted to find that the vegetation gave place to scree, up which we could walk in a normal position. The clouds had long since enveloped us again, and we were fortunate in reaching the pass at a point from which a descent could be made on either side. Most of the way down was through a narrow gully, at the foot of which we were exasperated to find more giant groundsel and helichrysum. During the descent Tilman suffered the further loss of his camera. It was getting dark when we reached the Bujuku valley once more, and we spent a long time before reaching camp, floundering knee-deep in vile-smelling black mud by the lake.

Long into the night we sat before a blazing fire of groundsel wood in our cave and in turn forgave this plant some of its atrocities, taking back a few of the unmentionable names we had called it. Even when damp (which is always) it makes excellent firewood.

On the following day we started back. Progress was almost as bad as on the ascent, except that there was no cutting to be done. But the porters were anxious to reach their homes, and consented, with some persuasion, to a double march each day.

Climbing on Ruwenzori was a memorable experience, and well worth the discomfort and the exasperating toil. When at length we left the rain-forest it felt as though we had emerged from a world of fantasy, where nothing was real but only a wild and lovely flight of imagination. I think perhaps the range is unique. It is well named 'Mountains of the Moon'.

6   Everest 1933 – 1

During the nineteen-twenties and thirties the repeated attempts to climb Mount Everest bulked large in the thoughts of mountaineers. The idea of climbing the mountain was a natural one for those interested in such things, and it is probable that the project had been considered ever since 1852 when the height of Mount Everest was computed, showing it to be the highest known peak in the world. From the nineties of the last century several definite plans for the exploration of the mountain were formulated. But Mount Everest lies on the borders of Nepal and Tibet and both these countries are for the most part closed to foreign travellers. It was not found possible to overcome these political barriers and the plans came to nothing.

However in 1920 Sir Charles Bell, who was a personal friend of the Dalai Lama, visited Lhasa and succeeded in obtaining the permission of the Tibetan Government for an expedition to approach Mount Everest through their country. The Royal Geographical Society and the Alpine Club jointly undertook the organisation of an expedition, a Mount Everest Committee was formed from these two bodies, and in the spring of 1921 the first Mount Everest Expedition was sent out under the leadership of Lieutenant-Colonel C.K. Howard-Bury.

This was undoubtedly one of the finest exploratory expeditions of the century. Its main objects were to explore the approaches to the mountain, to find a route by which it could be climbed, and to collect as much scientific data as possible in the fields of physiology, zoology, botany and geology. For these purposes experts were selected, and when the expedition reached its field it was divided, as all well-regulated expeditions should be, into self-contained parties each engaged upon its particular task. In this way a tremendous amount of ground was covered. The surveyors mapped 13,000 square miles of unexplored country, some of it in great detail, some more roughly, and the scientists brought back a mass of valuable results. The expedition was conducted with admirable economy and efficiency.

Mallory and Bullock were entrusted with the task of reconnoitring the mountain, and of finding a route by which it would be possible to climb it. It had been seen from a distance that the only hopeful line of approach was from the north. They made their way up the Rongbuk glacier, so called from the monastery of that name. The upper basin of this glacier was found to lie directly under the north face of Everest. To climb straight up this face, which rose in one continuous sweep of 10,000 feet above the level of the glacier, was out of the question. The face was bounded by two main ridges which joined at the summit. One ran down to the north-west and the other to the north-east. Both of these obviously presented great difficulties, but from about half way along the north-east ridge a subsidiary spur ran down to the north to a high saddle between Everest and a peak which came to be known as the North Peak or, translated into Tibetan, Chang Tse. The saddle was called the North Col, or Chang La. This north-east spur provided the only easy route to the upper part of the mountain. The problem then was to reach the North Col at its foot. It was possible to do so from the Rongbuk glacier, but Mallory judged that the route was too difficult to be undertaken with laden porters, and if possible an alternative must be found from the east.

Four miles above the snout of the Rongbuk glacier an inconspicuous defile enters the main valley from the east. Farther up, this broadens out into a wide glacier combe which curls round the spurs of the North Peak and has its origin below the north-eastern face of Everest. It offers a perfectly easy route to the eastern foot of the North Col. But Mallory attached no significance to this valley, and only discovered his mistake when, after many weeks of arduous travel, he reached its head by crossing a 22,000-feet pass from the distant Kharta Valley. By this time winter was approaching, but he and his companions succeeded in reaching the North Col, and so set foot on Mount Everest for the first time.

The following year, 1922, another expedition was sent out, this time under the leadership of Brigadier-General the Hon. C.G. Bruce. It was a very different type of expedition from the first one. The way had been found, and the job now was to climb the mountain. For a mountaineer this was a thrilling enough task though it lacked the wide horizons of a journey through unknown country. Little was known about climbing at great altitudes. The highest point that had ever been reached on a mountain was 24,600 feet – on Bride Peak in the Karakoram by the Duke of Abruzzi. Many scientists believed that it would be impossible to climb much higher without an artificial supply of oxygen.

The 1922 party consisted mainly of expert mountaineers, though there were a few scientists and transport officers attached. The party was equipped with a number of portable oxygen apparatuses for use above the North Col. But there was considerable dissension among its members concerning the use of oxygen. One group held that their task was to climb the mountain by their own unaided efforts, and that to use an artificial means of breathing in the rarefied atmosphere at high altitudes would be to overcome by unfair means Everest's principal weapon of defence. The opposing school of thought argued that their instructions had been to climb the mountain by every available means; that they were mountaineers and therefore principally interested in the mountaineering difficulties; that, in fact, the climbing of Mount Everest was not just a stunt to see whether their lungs could or could not sustain life at an atmospheric pressure of ten inches of mercury, but an interesting piece of geographical and mountaineering exploration. They pointed out, moreover, that the term 'unaided efforts' was meaningless. Were not ice-axes and ropes aids? Would moral principle forbid the use of thermos flasks? If science could produce oxygen in tabloid form instead of in heavy, cumbersome cylinders, would it then be acceptable to the purists?

But apart from this moral aspect of the case it is by no means certain that the use of oxygen as it has hitherto been provided is, in fact, an aid to climbing Mount Everest. In the first place the apparatus weighs about thirty-five pounds, which is an awkward burden to carry on one's back while climbing over difficult ground. Then, any sort of mask over the face produces a feeling of claustrophobia, and must impede the climber's sense of balance and his general efficiency. Again the oxygen contained in such an apparatus only lasts for about eight hours, and it is probable that the sudden cutting off of the supply when one has become used to it would produce a state of collapse. There is also the possibility of a breakdown in the working of the apparatus. No one has yet produced a satisfactory answer to the objections by actual demonstration, and the debate continues.

It was thought that the best time of year for an attempt on the mountain was between the middle of May and the middle of June. Before that period Tibet is swept by violent northerly gales which make life very unpleasant and would render climbing, or even existence, on the exposed north face of Everest quite impossible. In June the warm, moisture-laden monsoon winds would start blowing up from the south, and though life at high altitudes might be more comfortable, masses of snow would be deposited on the mountain which would make climbing very difficult, if not impossible.

The 1922 expedition established its Base Camp (16,800 feet) in April, a mile or so below the snout of the Rongbuk glacier, and from there started working slowly up the glacier by establishing a series of camps. Camp I (17,700 feet) was put at the entrance of the valley branching off to the east. The glacier contained in this valley came to be known as the East Rongbuk glacier. Camp II (19,800 feet) was placed about four miles up this glacier, and Camp III at an altitude of feet in the upper basin, and in full view of the North Col. Camp IV was on the North Col, some 23,000 feet above sea level. Thus far, the same procedure has been followed more or less by all the subsequent expeditions. The camp on the North Col has formed a sort of advanced base from which the real climb begins.

In 1922 two climbs were made above the North Col. Mallory, Norton, Somervell and Morshead established their Camp V on the north-east spur at an altitude of 24,500 feet. Morshead was suffering severely from exposure, and had to remain behind there while the other three climbed on up the spur and reached an altitude of 26,985 feet. (I have never understood why this figure is always quoted with such precision. In the first place no height on Everest can be estimated with greater accuracy than to the nearest fifty or 100 feet; secondly, even this degree of accuracy could only be achieved by theodolite observations from a dozen miles away, and such precise identification from this distance of the spot reached would hardly be possible.) The second attempt was made by Finch and J.G. Bruce using the oxygen apparatus. They put their Camp V at feet, and after weathering a storm, succeeded in climbing to 27,300 feet.

Both these parties suffered very severely from the cold and the deadening effects of altitude. As far as they had gone they had encountered no great mountaineering difficulties, and the sloping, tile-like rocks forming the upper part of the mountain presented a foreshortened effect, and led them to suppose that the rest of the way would be similarly devoid of serious obstacles. It was thought that the altitude, the severe cold and the wind constituted the real problem. In this they were very much mistaken.

After their tremendous effort, all those who took part in these two climbs returned in a state of great exhaustion, several of them suffering from frost-bite and badly dilated hearts. By the time a further attempt could be organised the monsoon had broken. In attempting to reach the North Col again the party was involved in an avalanche, and seven of their Sherpa porters were killed.

Two years later, in 1924, another expedition went out, again under the leadership of General Bruce. Unfortunately Bruce became ill and had to retire. However, Norton, who had played such a distinguished part in the 1922 attempt, took his place as leader. With the lessons learned on the previous expedition, the party were confident of success. It had been proved that men could spend more than one night at 25,000 feet. It seemed reasonable to suppose that it would be possible to climb to 29,000 feet. It was clear that the chief problem was to put a camp considerably higher than Camp V had been placed before, and this would necessitate porters spending the night at Camp V and carrying yet another camp farther up the mountain. It would be no small task to induce them to do this.

In May a series of terrible storms overtook the party while they were engaged in the task of establishing Camp IV. A party of porters was marooned on the North Col for several days, and, only after the most desperate efforts by the climbers were they rescued. 'Desperate efforts' are not made above 22,000 feet without great exhaustion, from which it is not possible wholly to recover without a prolonged rest at a very much lower altitude. So, by the time the weather improved, the strength of the climbers was seriously impaired.

On 1st June, Mallory and J.G. Bruce set out from the North Col for the first attempt. They established Camp V at 25,900 feet, and spent the night there with their porters. But they were met by a hurricane and forced to return. Norton and Somervell took their place at Camp V with a fresh lot of porters, with whom they succeeded in establishing Camp VI near the place where the north-east spur abuts against the north face at a height of 26,800 feet. The next day they set out for their final attempt on the summit. Somervell had to give up before Norton, who continued alone to a point estimated at about 28,100 feet, before he was forced, partly by exhaustion and partly by the difficulty of the ground, to abandon the attempt.

A few days later Mallory and Irvine came up the north-east spur for one more attempt, this time with oxygen. They set out from Camp VI on a fine, calm morning (8th June) and never returned. What happened to them we can only guess. We should all like to think that they reached the summit and that they died on the way down, but I for one consider that to be improbable. On the day of their attempt Odell came up to Camp VI in support and returned to Camp V in the evening, as there was not room for three to spend the night at the upper camp. He came up again later and found Camp VI still empty. Though he scoured the mountain side above he could find no trace of the missing climbers.

Taken together and told in detail, the story of these first three expeditions to Mount Everest is an inspiring one that cannot fail to move even those who can see no reason for wishing to climb the highest mountain in the world. From almost every point of view it was sad that they were not crowned with the success they so richly deserved. Not only would this have rounded off a fine epic of mountaineering, but, in my opinion it would have induced a healthier outlook towards Himalayan exploration in the years that followed. I say 'almost every point of view' because there are some, even among those who have themselves attempted to reach the summit, who nurse a secret hope that Everest will never be climbed. I must confess to such feelings myself.

Ten years is an epoch of almost infinite length when it spans one's 'teens and early twenties. I was still at my preparatory school when the first Mount Everest Expedition took place, and not being in the habit of reading The Times, it passed me by unnoticed. As a result of this I came to regard the three expeditions as ancient history, something that had always been discussed, like Scott's journey to the South Pole, or the Spanish Armada. There was always a good deal of talk about the attempt being renewed, but I was not very well up in those circles, and as the talk never seemed to come to anything it appeared that the idea was buried in the past. I regarded participation in one of these expeditions as an impossible dream upon which it was not good to dwell for long, since it made me feel that nothing else in the world was worthwhile.

One day in the autumn of 1932 while I was peacefully occupied with problems of manure, soil erosion and farm politics, I received a note from a neighbour who had a wireless set, saying that he had just heard that Lhasa had consented to allow another expedition to go to Mount Everest, and that this was being organised under the leadership of Mr Hugh Ruttledge, and would set out early the following year. This news was deeply disturbing, and a storm that carried away a long job of terracing that I had completed passed almost unnoticed. It seemed that I might have some claim for consideration, and I could think of nothing else. I had an Irishman staying with me at the time who became almost as excited about it as I was, and certainly a good deal more optimistic about my chances. But as the days passed and nothing further happened I tried to resign myself to disappointment.

A little time later, however, when I was returning home from a job at the other end of the farm, I was met by my friend brandishing a bit of pink paper. This turned out to be a telegram which read 'mount everest committee invite you join expedition subject medical approval please reply goodenough'.

Admiral Sir William Goodenough was at that time president of the Royal Geographical Society. To save time, and mistaking Sir William's name for a kind of code word, my enthusiastic friend had sent the telegraph boy back with the cryptic reply 'Goodenough-Shipton'. I managed however to intercept the message.

The need to collect equipment seemed to provide sufficient excuse for coming home, and I secured a third-class passage on a German ship sailing from Mombasa on 1 November, and reached England on 1 December. Wyn Harris, who had also been invited, came home a little later. Seven of us sailed for India towards the end of January, 1933: Hugh Ruttledge, C.G. Crawford, L.R. Wager, J.L. Longland, T.A. Brocklebank, Wyn and myself. We travelled First Class P&O, which I found a pleasant contrast to my voyage of a few weeks before. Of the other seven members of the expedition Frank Smythe and Raymond Greene came out on a later ship, Hugh Boustead came to India from the Sudan where he was commanding the Camel Corps, and W. McLean, the second medical officer, from Jerusalem. Shebbeare, who had been transport officer with the 1924 expedition, Bill Birnie and George Wood-Johnson were already in India.

We had two main occupations on the voyage out. One was to learn Khaskra, a language spoken by the Sherpas. For this we had a teacher in Crawford, who had been in the ICS for twelve years in North-East India, in a Gurkha regiment in the last war, and a member of the 1922 Everest Expedition. I am afraid we were reluctant and most inept pupils. As far as I remember, Longland was the only one who learnt enough to be of any use. Ruttledge, of course, spoke Urdu fluently, which was far more use than a smattering of Khaskra, Wyn conversed happily in Swahili which certainly seemed to be as effective as anything else, and Wager remained content with English.

Our second occupation was much more congenial: an endless discussion of how the mountain should be climbed. As far as the North Col it was all fairly plain sailing, and we had only to follow the practice of our predecessors and to organise the transport of sufficient supplies and equipment to stock the three glacier camps and Camp IV on the North Col. Though of course this task was of fundamental importance, its accomplishment was a matter of straightforward organisation and much hard work, mainly on the part of the porters.

The first real problem was the establishment of the high camps. It was clear that we must aim at getting a camp considerably nearer to the summit than Camp VI had been placed in 1924. Would it be possible to do this with only two camps above the North Col? Camp V, at 25,500 feet, was already a tremendous carry from the North Col, and could not be placed very much higher. But to attempt to establish a third camp above the col would involve serious difficulties. In the first place it would mean increasing the size of Camp V enormously, to accommodate the extra number of porters necessary to carry the food and equipment for those porters who would have to sleep at Camp VI which would itself have to be very much bigger. It was by no means certain that a platform could be found wide enough to accommodate either of these enlarged camps. This difficulty might be partly overcome by a system of relay, but it would not be easy to find many porters to go far above the North Col, and it was most unlikely that more than a very few could be induced to make the trip twice. Again, would any of them be willing to stay the night at Camp VI and carry still higher? Norton and Somervell had experienced the greatest difficulty in persuading them to go above Camp V after the exhaustion and discomfort of a night spent there. Also the longer any individual party spent above the North Col the greater the risk of encountering a storm which would force them to retreat, probably in a state of such exhaustion as to render them incapable of further effort.

The next question was the route to be followed, and this matter was debated over a large photograph of the north face of the mountain. After the 1924 expedition, it was realised that the climbing on the upper part of the mountain was not so easy as had at first been supposed. Between the North Col and the top of the north-east spur there were, in good conditions, no real difficulties. The upper 2,000 feet of the mountain was built of three horizontal bands or strata. The first of these, composed of a light-coloured rock, was about 800 feet thick and lay between 27,200 feet and 28,000 feet above sea level. This was known as the 'Yellow Band'. Above this was a stratum of dark rock called the 'Black Band'; on this again was superimposed another layer which formed the summit cap or 'Final Pyramid'. The surface of the Yellow Band was composed of a series of overlapping slabs set at a fairly steep angle and sloping outwards like the tiles of a roof. The surface of the Black Band was considerably steeper, and, as the rock strata were also tilted towards the north, they formed a series of overhangs. The Final Pyramid, though steep, was more broken and appeared to offer several relatively easy routes.

From the purely mountaineering standpoint, then, the crux of the climb was clearly to get past the Black Band. At first sight the obvious route to follow from the head of the north-east spur seemed to be along the crest of the main north-east ridge. This could be seen in profile from the Base Camp, and its general angle was very gentle. But ridges, and particularly Himalayan ridges, are apt to be deceptive and often turn out to be knife-sharp. Climbing along such a knife-edged crest is a slow and laborious business, and any serrature might present a formidable obstacle. Also, by the intersection of the north-east ridge, and the Black Band two steps were formed. The 'First Step' did not appear to be very formidable, but the 'Second Step' was vertical, and its height was estimated at some 200 feet. A third objection to the ridge route was the fact that the climber would be exposed to the full force of the wind, which, if at all violent, might blow him clean off the mountain.

The alternative to following the crest of the north-east ridge was to traverse diagonally across to the head of a conspicuous gully that ran down the north face from a point below the Black Band, a few hundred yards beyond the Second Step. This gully was known as the Great Couloir. It was flanked on the west by a prominent ridge which formed the only breach in the wall of the Black Band. Norton had chosen this route and had reached the Great Couloir, but had failed to cross it, largely on account of physical exhaustion, but partly, too, because of the treacherous nature of the tiled slabs over which he was climbing. Mallory had favoured the ridge route, and his views were supported by the rock-climbing experts of our party, of whom Longland was the recognised ace.

The question of weather we took very much for granted. The original hypothesis had been confirmed by the experiences of the 1922 and 1924 expeditions, and it appeared that we could count on a break of at least a fortnight between the end of the spring gales in May and the beginning of the monsoon precipitation in June. The great thing to avoid was the exhaustion of the party's strength by battling against the early blizzards.

The real bone of contention was how long the climbers should stay at high altitudes. The opposing factors were 'Acclimatisation' and 'Deterioration', and as we had very little data from which to argue the debate waxed exceeding fierce. It was recognised that men could only climb to great altitudes by allowing their bodies gradually to acclimatise themselves to conditions of low atmospheric pressure and lack of oxygen. If a man is lifted rapidly from sea level to a great height he will lose consciousness at altitudes varying, in normal cases, between 20,000 and 22,000 feet. The experiment is easy to make in a decompression chamber, and has been done hundreds of times. A peculiar thing is that the patient does not realise that he lost consciousness, and often hotly denies it when he is brought back to normal conditions. The best method of convincing him that he did in fact 'pass out' is to make him write while the experiment is conducted.

This difficulty is quite easy to overcome in flying, by supplying the airman with oxygen. But it is clearly impossible to supply all the members of a climbing party with oxygen all the time, and whether or not oxygen is used as an aid in the final assault, some degree of acclimatisation is obviously necessary. The question is, how much? For although the lungs, blood and heart have the power to adjust themselves to a reasonable lack of oxygen, above a certain altitude the body begins to lose strength very rapidly. These two processes are going on at one and the same time, and the problem is to strike the optimum mean between them. What then is the altitude at which this physical deterioration begins; how long does it take a man fully to acclimatise to a given altitude; how quickly will he deteriorate at that altitude? Unfortunately no definite answer can be found to these questions, except perhaps the first. Each individual varies in his reactions to altitude; one man acclimatises quickly, another slowly, some deteriorate more rapidly than others; I have known men with robust constitutions who have failed altogether to acclimatise even to quite moderate elevations. The whole process appears to be analogous to sea-sickness about which predictions are impossible. Indeed one of the party advanced the ingenious theory that bad sailors acclimatised quickly, though I suspect that the only evidence he had to support it was his own dislike for rough seas.

Obviously upon the conclusion adopted on this weighty matter rested the whole question of tactics to be followed in the attempts to climb Mount Everest; and we had lamentably little to go on. Those in favour of long acclimatisation made much of the experience of Odell in 1924. He had gone very badly at first, but when at last he did acclimatise he accomplished some remarkable feats. From this slender evidence it was assumed that all slow acclimatisers would go well later. On Kamet two years before, on the other hand, although we had talked a lot about acclimatisation, actually we had gone from the Base Camp at 15,000 feet to the summit at 25,450 feet in a fortnight, which was considerably quicker than the quickest of the plans for attempting Everest. Nor had we had the advantage of a long journey across the high Tibetan plateau. We had not suffered seriously from the altitude while climbing the peak, though on the other hand in that short time we found, when we arrived back at the Base Camp, that we had suffered considerable physical deterioration.

It seemed odd to be discussing earnestly such problems as these as we sat deep in deck chairs, listening to the gentle swish of the sea, a cool drink within reach and with the comfortable prospect of a large lunch and a sleep to follow. In these circumstances gasping toil, blizzards and the like were hard to visualise in true perspective. No one, I think, doubted for a moment that we would succeed. Indeed it was solemnly debated whether, in the most probable event of the first 'assault party' reaching the top, it would be permissible for others subsequently to climb the mountain.

Three very pleasant weeks were divided between Darjeeling and Kalimpong; we spent busy days recruiting porters and sorting out, numbering and arranging in eighty-pound loads, suitable for animal transport, an enormous mass of stores that had been sent out from England. The real starting point was Kalimpong, and here we enjoyed the perfect hospitality of Mr and Mrs Odling in their delightful home. We left there in two parties; the first on March 3rd and the second a week later. There were seven of us in the first party. Our departure must have been very amusing to watch. We were given a tremendous send-off by the 600 children of Dr Graham's St Andrew's Homes. Our ponies, which were very fresh, entered into the spirit of the thing, and, scared by the noise of the cheers, charged off down the road at a breakneck speed, entirely out of control. Every hundred yards or so we were ambushed by a batch of yelling children which maddened our ponies still more. Most of us had very little idea of how to ride. Wager led the field clinging grimly to his pony's neck. He tore round the wrong corner, and the rest of us followed, crashing down towards the forest-filled valley where we seemed destined to meet an ignominious end. Eventually we succeeded in pulling up, though how I never knew. Our return to the right road provided something of an anti-climax.

The march from Kalimpong to the Rongbuk valley took us some six weeks. It can be done in considerably less, but in the first place we were in no hurry and had purposely left early so that we could take it in easy stages; in the second place the formidable number of transport animals (between three and four hundred) required to carry all our baggage caused some delay. The same animals could not be taken right through and they had frequently to be changed. It was no easy job for the authorities of the small towns through which we passed to produce enough yaks or donkeys. For the first eight stages the way was through pleasantly wooded foothills and over the 14,000 feet Natu La into the Chumbi valley in Tibet. Before crossing the border we halted for a few days by a little lake at a place called Tsomgo. Beyond the Chumbi valley we halted again to allow the main body to catch up. After that we left the trees behind and climbed up on to the great tableland of Tibet.

From here, most of us had expected to encounter severe conditions. For the first two days our expectations were realised. The temperature dropped to 36degrees of frost and a continuous gale blew from the north-west. But after that the weather was so mild and pleasant that soon some of us began to wonder if we had come to the right place. The only hardship we had to bear was the dust, which was at times rather unpleasant. Apart from that nothing could have been more delightful than riding along at a comfortable speed of about fifteen miles a day through that lovely land. Tibet is a very beautiful country – at least the part of it through which we were travelling; rather bleak perhaps in the early spring, but even that was mitigated by the clear, blue sky, the sharp detail of the distant ranges and the lovely colouring of the nearer hills. To the south was the sparkling white barrier of the great Himalayan range. The peaks themselves did not look their best owing to the gradual lift of the plateau towards a nearer range of rounded mountains, but they formed a lovely background to the wide, frozen rivers and lakes, teeming with Brahmini duck and bar-headed geese. The large majority of us had never been to Tibet before, and we found the people with their strange way of life, their art and architecture a source of constant interest and delight.

Each of us had a large Whymper tent to himself, and a big marquee served as a mess tent. We had not yet had time to become irritable or tired of each other, and, with the wide diversity of professions in the party, the talk was good and varied. This was spoilt at times by a natural tendency to talk shop. To a layman it would have seemed amazing that, in a simple matter like the climbing of a mountain, we could have found so much to argue about. Each of us had his own pet theory on every aspect of the problem and aired it with monotonous regularity and lamentable disregard for opposing points of view. I was certainly one of the worst offenders in this respect, and despite my frequent resolves to conduct myself in a more gentlemanly fashion, I could never refrain from joining the fray. But we were saved from serious dissension by the wise and balanced judgment of our leader, who refused to be drawn into taking sides.

We were all rather ridiculously self-conscious about our acclimatisation. The average altitude of the plateau over which we were travelling was about 13,000 feet and several of the passes we crossed were 18,000 feet high. We used anxiously to count our heart beats and watch our breathing, while the doctors examined the reaction of our blood-pressures and counted the red corpuscles in our blood. All this tended to produce a state of hypochondria and a sense of rivalry, which Ruttledge did his best to discourage. His was no easy task with such a large party of mountaineers – temperamental and individualistic creatures at the best of times – each passionately keen to justify his selection, and we owed a great deal to his sympathetic understanding. On the whole we kept our sense of proportion remarkably well, on the march out anyway. Crawford's acute sense of the ridiculous kept us from taking ourselves too seriously; Greene's remarkable gift for anecdote was always fresh – I never grew tired of listening to him; Shebbeare's deep knowledge of natural history was a constant source of delight; each contributed something. I have very pleasant memories of that march.

At each of the big towns we were entertained by the Dzongpen, the administrative head of the district. From these parties we often emerged in a pleasantly intoxicated condition, as it was impossible to refuse the large quantities of Chang provided by our hosts. Chang is the Tibetan equivalent of beer. It is brewed from barley, has a greyish-white appearance, an acid taste and varies greatly in quality and potency. Good Chang is an excellent drink. I also developed a great liking for Tibetan tea. This is made from Chinese brick tea and is properly prepared in a large bamboo churn, with the addition of butter and salt. The butter is not generally rancid as is popularly supposed. The tea has a soft, delicate flavour, and is remarkably refreshing; badly made it is disgusting. Our contact with the Tibetan people was made easy and pleasant by our Tibetan interpreter, Karma Paul.

We arrived at Rongbuk on April 16th. The next morning was occupied with the ceremony of receiving the blessing of the Abbot of the Rongbuk Monastery. This old man was a great character. He was then close on seventy years of age, had a tremendous sense of humour and he took a kindly interest in our project. The blessing ceremony consisted in each of us bowing before the Abbot in turn, receiving a sharp tap on the head from his mace and repeating after him 'Om Mani Padmi Hum' (Hail, the jewel in the Lotus). Most of us had to repeat the formula several times before we got it right, to the great amusement of the Abbot. We were each given a little packet of pills to take when we felt in need of spiritual sustenance. The Sherpas conducted themselves with far greater dignity and savoir-faire than we did. The same afternoon we went four miles farther up the valley where we established the Base Camp, which was to be our haven of rest, our coveted metropolis, for nearly three months.

The Rongbuk valley is a grim and desolate place, a waste of stones shut in from all pleasant prospects, flanked by shapeless, disintegrating walls of rock. Its upper end is dominated by the huge mass of Everest. Seen from the top of the surrounding peaks, this northern face of the mountain has a fine simplicity of design and a certain grandeur, though even then it cannot compare with the magnificent architecture of the eastern and southern aspects. But from the Base Camp it appears stunted and deformed, a mere continuation of the graceless forms about it.

The features of the upper part of the north face were so well known to us from our prolonged study of photographs that it seemed as though we had been looking at it most of our lives. But it was exciting to see at last all the obstacles we had discussed so endlessly – the Second Step, the Great Couloir, the Yellow Band. We spent hours gazing at them through a powerful astronomical telescope. It was tiresome to reflect that many weeks must still elapse before any of us could make their close acquaintance.

Before the arrival of the monsoon, the north face of Everest is, for the most part, swept clear of snow by the violence of the northerly winds. Very little melting appears to take place at great altitudes, and, but for these winds, which probably blow more or less continuously throughout the winter, the snow would accumulate to a great depth, the pressure of its weight would form ice and the north face of Everest would be covered by a glacier sheet resembling those on its far steeper eastern and southern slopes. The mountain might then be much easier to climb.

The establishment of the lower camps was a leisurely business. In the first place we were in no hurry, because the severity of the conditions would forbid operations on the mountain for several weeks; secondly, slow progress was necessary for our acclimatisation, and thirdly, we had so much stuff to transport up the glacier that even with our vast army of porters (forty-six more joined us later from Solu Khombu which brought our total strength up to about one hundred and seventy), many relays were necessary to establish each camp. The distances between these were fairly even, and it took about three or four hours of very easy going to go up from one to the next, and about half that time coming down. The porters carried forty pounds each; we carried nothing, the theory being that we must conserve our energy for higher up. Though it is a debatable point, there is certainly something in this argument. At high altitudes (in my opinion above 21,000 feet) the wastage of muscle tissue is so rapid that it is well to start with a fairly large reserve of flesh. A man highly trained in the athletic sense is liable to be worn down much more quickly than one less finely drawn. On the other hand we had too little to do. We fell over each other in our efforts to secure the few jobs that were going. It is not enough to say that a man of intelligence should find sufficient interest in his surroundings, in reading or in playing chess. We were all intensely keen about the expedition and could not be expected to remain satisfied with a purely waiting role, particularly knowing as we did that only a very small proportion of the party could be chosen to go high. On the whole people were remarkably good about disguising their feelings, but that did not remove the feelings themselves. We made a great show of reconnoitring the route and 'escorting' parties of porters; but no one but a blind man could have failed to find his way up the East Rongbuk glacier, there were no more difficulties than one would expect to encounter in a country walk at home and the porters certainly needed no escorting.

One of the most tiresome things about an Everest Expedition was the amount of time one had to spend in bed. It was not usual to spend more than six hours on a job, so that the day's work was generally done by three o'clock. In the spring, at any of the lower camps the sun would disappear at about four o'clock; it was too cold to sit outside after that, so from four o'clock until about nine o'clock the next morning was spent in our sleeping-bags. That was in good weather; on the frequent days of bad weather we usually spent twenty-four hours in bed.

In 1933 it was all new to us and interesting. When we were not engaged in walking from one camp to another we climbed up the sides of the valley for practice and to get a wider view of our surroundings. But our main pre-occupation was in keeping ourselves reasonably fit. This was no easy matter for we were constantly assailed by influenza and throat troubles. It has been the same on each of the four occasions that I have been to Everest. It appeared that the party became infected on the march across Tibet, and that the lowered resistance of the individual, due to altitude, made it impossible to throw off the disease once above the Base Camp. This bugbear contributed largely to our general weakness which was a potent factor in our failure to reach the summit. The valiant efforts of the doctors had little effect. We consumed enormous quantities of antiseptic tablets and were forever gargling and douching our noses. Already, at the Base Camp, several members of the party had been ill, Wyn Harris and Wager with 'flu and Crawford with bronchitis. Nor were the Sherpas exempt. Ondi developed double pneumonia, for the treatment of which the oxygen supply came in handy. We all had our troubles in varying degree. I lost my voice completely for six weeks, which, though a considerable boon to my companions, was certainly a handicap to me.

The glaciers on the northern side of Mount Everest were different from any I had seen before. They were divided into four distinct zones. Firstly there was the usual upper *névé*, or snow basin, from which the glacier rises. Then followed a section of smooth ice, free from a covering of permanent snow or moraine deposits. Below this the ice-stream merged gradually into a forest of fantastic pinnacles of all shapes and sizes. Some of these pinnacles have been measured and found to stand more than 300 feet high, though usually they do not exceed 100 feet. Farther down they increased in size and decreased in numbers, until a few isolated towers were left standing out of the lower section of the glacier, which was so covered with gravel and boulders that very little ice could be seen. Moraine-covered troughs, caused by the junction of tributary ice-streams, ran down through the pinnacled areas, and provided easy roads up the glacier. I have never heard a satisfactory explanation of why these pinnacles occur. Camp II on the East Rongbuk glacier was situated in this zone which was very beautiful.

7   Everest 1933 – 2

The work of carrying loads up from the Base Camp began on 19 April and on 2 May and we established and occupied Camp III in the upper basin of the East Rongbuk glacier at a height of 21,000 feet. We were now in full view of the North Col. At last we were confronted with a real mountaineering proposition which would require some concentration of energy and skill. The prospect was a good one. Pleasant and intensely interesting though the journey had been, most of us I imagine had been keyed up by the anticipation of the toughest climbing of our lives. So far it had all been make-believe, and it was difficult to avoid the question, 'When are we going to be called upon to do a job of work; when will we have something really to bite on?'

The eastern slopes of the North Col are composed of steep broken glacier and rise about 1,500 feet from the level of ice below to the crest of the col. As the glacier is moving slowly downwards the slopes present a different appearance from year to year. Our task then was to find a way up them, to make a ladder of large, safe steps to fix ropes to serve as hand rails all over the difficult sections, so that it would be possible for laden porters to pass up and down with ease and safety.

We started the work almost at once. It was about an hour's walk from Camp III to the foot of the steep slopes below the col. The ice of the upper basin had been swept clear of snow by the wind. It was rather like walking on an ice skating rink and required some little practice to avoid sitting down heavily. But fortunately the slopes above were composed of hard snow, for it would have been a tremendously laborious task to cut steps all the way up in hard ice, and also very difficult to fix the ropes. As it was it was very hard work. Even at that height any physical exertion left one gasping for breath. We took turns of about twenty minutes each at cutting the steps. Even that seemed an eternity and it was a great relief to be told that the time was up. We climbed about a third of the way up to the col on the first day.

There followed days of storm and wind which rendered work impossible. Below, we had experienced fairly severe conditions, but Camp III was much more exposed to the weather, which deteriorated a good deal during the fortnight after our arrival there. I gathered from the Sherpas who had been with the 1924 Expedition that the conditions were very similar to those experienced in that year. But we had an additional item of equipment, which added enormously to our comfort and rendered us impervious to the buffeting of the wind. This was a large, double-skinned, dome-shaped tent of a type that had been used by Watkins in the Arctic. It had a circular floor about fifteen feet in diameter, and was built round a bamboo frame, the outer skin fitting over the frame while the inner skin hung from it, so that there was an air space about a foot wide between the two. It was difficult to erect, but once up it was as snug as a well-built log hut.

As soon as there was a lull in the wind, we resumed work on the slopes below the col. We found that the steps we had already cut had been swept away, and that not a trace of them remained. So as to take advantage of brief periods of fine weather, we put a camp (III A) at the foot of the slopes. This was a bleak and comfortless spot, and even more exposed to the wind than Camp III, which was situated on rocks close under the cliffs of the North Peak. The new camp was pitched on hard, smooth ice on which it was difficult to anchor the tents. One night, during a particularly violent storm, one of them broke loose from its moorings causing a certain amount of excitement. But the new position was a great help, and from it we were able to make progress. But our advance was very slow, and as we set out day after day I began to wonder if we should ever reach the col. The most difficult part was about half way up. This consisted of an ice wall about twenty feet high, topped by a very steep ice slope. We had a lot of fun getting up it, and succeeded largely owing to a fine lead by Smythe. We hung a rope ladder down it for subsequent use.

At last, by the 15 May, the road of steps and fixed ropes was complete, and we established Camp IV on an ice ledge, some twenty feet wide, about 200 feet below the crest of the col. The ledge was formed by the lower lip of a great crevasse, the upper lip of which, forty feet above, almost overhung the ledge. The camp was well sheltered and quite comfortable, the only disadvantage being the danger of small snow avalanches falling from above.

For the next four days the storm was continuous, and we could do nothing but lie in our sleeping-bags. Nor was any communication possible with the camps below. But on the evening of the 19th, the wind dropped and Smythe and I climbed up the last 200 feet. Apart from the ice wall this was by far the steepest part of the North Col slopes. When we reached the narrow crest of the col we were met by a most glorious view to the west, over range after range of giant peaks, draped by dark cloud banners, wild and shattered by the gale. The mighty scene was partly lit by an angry red glow, and rose from a misty shadow lake of deep indigo that often appears among high mountains in the evening after a storm.

The next day Wyn Harris, Birnie and Boustead started up with ten porters, intending to reach 25,500 feet to choose a site for Camp V. But they were forced to retreat from 24,500 owing to the wind. Actually there was some difference of opinion about the wisdom of this decision, and a hot-tempered argument raged most of the succeeding night, by the end of which the subject under debate had become rather confused. Nerves were already frayed, and we were all liable to lose our tempers at the slightest provocation, and to take our silly grievances sorely to heart. This seems to be a common manifestation of the effects of life at high altitudes. In our case it was undoubtedly aggravated by the rough handling we had received from the weather, and by having been forced to spend so much of our time during the past month cooped up in a tent with too little to do and too much to anticipate. Being unable to speak above a whisper, I found it difficult to quarrel with anyone, and it would have been too exhausting to attempt to pull my opponent's beard. Had I been psycho-analysed at the time, I would no doubt have been found to be suffering from some fierce repressions.

We were very comfortable at Camp IV. Cooking and breathing soon produced a pleasant fug in the tents: we had large double eiderdown sleeping bags, and our snow beds were soon made to conform with the shapes of our bodies. The crevasse provided a convenient latrine, though it required a strong effort of will to emerge from the tent. It was only at the upper camps that the cold compelled us to use a bed-pan in the form of a biscuit box. So long as we did not have to do anything, the time passed pleasantly enough. Lethargy of mind and body was the chief trial. Once one got going it was not so bad, but the prospect of toil was hateful. At the higher camps, of course, this lethargy increased tenfold.

Eating, however, was the serious problem, and one which, to my mind, did not receive nearly enough attention. This was entirely the fault of the individual, for we had more than enough food, and its quality and variety could not have been better. The trouble is that at such an altitude the appetite is jaded, and unless a man forces himself to eat regular and sufficient meals he does not consume anything like enough to maintain his strength. Melting a saucepan full of snow for water and bringing it to the boil took so long that people tended to delude themselves that they had eaten a hearty meal. Over and over again I saw men starting for a long and exhausting day's work on the mountain with only a cup of cocoa and a biscuit or two inside them; the cold and the wind discouraged eating during the climb, and they were generally too tired to eat anything much when they returned. This state of affairs contributed largely towards the rapid physical deterioration of the party. There was endless talk about rations, and certainly these were carefully and efficiently planned beforehand; but in actual practice we ate whatever we wanted and whenever we felt inclined. Sweets were the easiest kind of food to swallow, but it is doubtful if haphazard sweet-eating is as beneficial as the taking of regular substantial meals, which it certainly discourages. In most cold climates people develop a craving for fat, which has a higher calorific value than any other food. Unfortunately at high altitudes fat of any kind is particularly repugnant.

On the 21 May, Smythe and I climbed some 1,500 feet above the North Col for exercise. We both felt extremely fit, and without undue effort we maintained an average speed of 1,000 feet an hour, which would not have been a bad performance had we been at sea-level. Individuals differ very widely in their physical reactions to the effects of high altitudes; some vomit a great deal, some suffer from blinding headaches, some cannot sleep, while others can hardly keep awake, some gasp and pant even when at rest. I used not to suffer much from any of these maladies; my particular trouble was physical lethargy which grew progressively more intense the longer I remained at a high altitude. For example, in 1933 I made three climbs up the north-east spur above the North Col. On the first occasion, after six nights at Camp IV (about 23,000 feet), I felt very strong, and as though I could go on indefinitely; the second time, after eight hours at Camp IV, I was weaker, though I still went fairly well; on the third occasion, after two nights spent at Camp V (25,700 feet) and twelve at Camp IV, I only reached Camp V, for my second sojourn there, after a hard struggle. Smythe and I reacted to the effects of altitude in very much the same manner, though in 1933 he deteriorated considerably less quickly than I did. For men with no previous Himalayan experience, and considering that they had spent a whole fortnight laid up at the Base Camp while the rest of us were working slowly up the glacier, Wager and Wyn Harris acclimatised remarkably quickly. Longland was slow in adjusting himself, which made his subsequent performance all the more remarkable. Crawford and Brocklebank were at their best when it was too late for further attempts on the mountain, and thus were robbed of the chance of going high, though they spent weeks of the monotonous but vital work keeping the North Col route open.

Weather conditions now appeared to have reached that state of comparative quiet that we had expected just before the arrival of the monsoon. Wireless messages received at the Base Camp spoke of an exceptionally early monsoon in Ceylon and its rapid spread over India. This news was confirmed by the appearance of great banks of cloud from the south which, however, were still far below us. Obviously the critical moment had arrived. On the 22nd of May, Birnie, Boustead, Greene and Wyn Harris, with twenty porters carrying twelve pounds each, established Camp V at 25,700 feet. The plan was for these four climbers and eight of the porters to stop the night at Camp V and to carry Camp VI as high as possible on the following day; Birnie and Boustead would then return to Camp V with the porters, while Wyn Harris and Greene would stop at Camp VI and attempt to climb the mountain by the 'ridge route'. Meanwhile Smythe and I would follow up to Camp V on the 23rd, take the place of the first party at Camp VI on the 24th, and make our attempt on the summit on the 25th, choosing our route in the light of the experiences of the first pair. Greene unfortunately strained his heart during the climb to Camp V, and his place was taken by Wager who had accompanied the party for exercise.

It was hard to believe that the time for the supreme test had arrived. Waiting at the North Col on 22 May, I felt as I imagine an athlete must feel just before the boat-race, Marathon or boxing contest for which he has been training for months. It was difficult to keep one's mind from the nagging questions, 'Will the weather hold long enough to give us a decent chance?' 'How will I react to the extreme exhaustion that must inevitably accompany the final effort?' 'What is the climbing really like on that upper part?' 'For all our previous optimism, is it, in fact, possible to climb to or even to live at 29,000 feet?' Three more days, seventy-two hours!

It was a great relief when, the next morning, the moment to start arrived. We had the whole day before us, and there was no need to hurry. The basis of all mountaineering is the conservation of energy by the three fundamental principles – rhythmic movement, balance and precise placing of the feet. As far as possible, steps should be short so that upward motion appears as a gentle sway from the hips rather than a strong thrust by thigh muscles. It is better to use a small nail-hold at a convenient distance than a large foot-hold involving a long stride. If a long stride is necessary, the balance must be adjusted by lateral pressure by the hand or ice-axe. A practised mountaineer is, of course, in the habit of observing these principles even on the simplest ground; his ability to maintain them on difficult and complicated terrain determines in large measure his quality as a climber. Nowhere is perfection of technique so important as at high altitudes where the slightest effort takes heavy toll of the climber's reserves of strength; nowhere is it more difficult to achieve.

Above the North Col we were met by a strong wind, which increased in violence as we climbed. I have no idea what the temperature was. On the glacier below a minimum of twenty degrees Fahrenheit was observed. I doubt if we experienced less than that on the upper part of the mountain. Judged by winter temperatures in the Arctic or Antarctic, such cold is not considered severe. But at great altitudes it is a very different matter. Due to lack of oxygen, the various functions of heart, lungs and circulation are most inefficient, lost heat is difficult to restore, and there is danger of frost-bite even at freezing point, particularly when there is a wind blowing: one has constantly to watch for its symptoms. If a foot loses feeling it is wise to stop to remove one's boot and bang and rub it to life again. This is one of the greatest difficulties we have had in dealing with the Sherpas at high altitudes; it was most difficult to induce them to take these precautions.

We were not altogether surprised, when at about four o'clock we reached Camp V, to find that the whole party was still there. Though by now the wind had dropped, it had been even more fierce at Camp V than it had been below, and it had been impossible to move on up the ridge. There was no room for two more at Camp V, and, though we offered to go down again, it was decided that Smythe and I should change places with Wyn Harris and Wager, in the hope of being able to push on up the mountain the next day.

The site of Camp V was composed of two platforms, one about four feet above the other. Each was sufficiently large to accommodate two 'Meade' tents pitched end on. The tents themselves were about six feet six inches long by four feet wide by four feet high, made of light canvas and weighed about sixteen pounds each. The 'Meade' tent is really a smaller edition of the 'Whymper', and is named after the well-known mountaineer C.F. Meade – I have asked him why, but he could not enlighten me.

I doubt if anyone would claim to enjoy life at high altitudes – enjoy, that is, in the ordinary sense of the word. There is a certain grim satisfaction to be derived from struggling on upwards, however slowly; but the bulk of one's time is necessarily spent in the extreme squalor of a high camp, when even this solace is lacking. Smoking is impossible; eating tends to make one vomit; the necessity of reducing weight to a bare minimum forbids the importation of literature beyond that supplied by the labels on tins of food; sardine oil, condensed milk and treacle spill themselves all over the place; except for the briefest moments, during which one is not usually in a mood for aesthetic enjoyment, there is nothing to look at but the bleak confusion inside the tent and the scaly, bearded countenance of one's companion – fortunately the noise of the wind usually drowns the sound of his stuffy breathing; worst of all is the feeling of complete helplessness and inability to deal with any emergency that might arise. I used to try to console myself with the thought that a year ago I would have been thrilled by the very idea of taking part in our present adventure, a prospect that had then seemed like an impossible dream; but altitude has the same effect upon the mind as upon the body, one's intellect becomes dull and unresponsive, and my only desire was to finish the wretched job and to get down to a more reasonable clime – with strong emphasis on the latter part of the programme. I found that I could sleep pretty well, providing I was reasonably comfortable, but the slightest irritation, such as a jagged rock sticking into my back was enormously exaggerated, as it is when one is suffering from a high fever. At Camp V we had a fairly comfortable place to lie on.

All that night and most of next day a blizzard raged, and it was impossible to move either up or down. Fine snow driven in through the thin canvas of the tent, covered everything inside and filtered in through the opening of our sleeping-bags. Being on the crest of a ridge we received the full force of the gale. There was a continuous and mighty roar, and it seemed that the tents could not possibly stand up to such a hammering. At one point one of the guy ropes of our tent broke loose. Smythe struggled outside to deal with the situation, while I had the soft job of acting as ballast inside to hold the tent down.

Smythe was only out for a couple of minutes, but when he returned we spent hours rubbing and thumping his limbs to restore the circulation.

On the evening of the 24th the wind dropped, and there was a great calm. We opened the tent flap and looked out. Such cloud as there was, was far below us. The magnificence of the view penetrated even my jaded brain. The summit, greatly foreshortened, seemed close above us. Smythe and I discussed seriously whether it would not be better after all to make our attempt from Camp V. We were still fairly active, and all this delay at high altitudes was certainly doing us no good. Anyway, there was no need to decide yet; we could start out with Birnie and Boustead and the porters who would be going up to establish Camp VI, and judge our condition then. That we could have discussed such a hopeless proposition shows how we were feeling.

But while we were preparing to start next morning, the gale began to blow again. Standing outside the tents the icy wind made us feel supremely helpless and foolish. The others had spent three nights at Camp V; already the Sherpas were nearly exhausted by the storm, and some of them were frostbitten. Had the weather been calm it is doubtful if they would have been able to go far; any advance under the present conditions was out of the question. Nor could we ask the porters to stay at Camp V yet another day and night, even if we had been willing to do so ourselves. There was nothing for it but to retreat to the North Col. It was a bitter blow, for all the time we were losing strength, and none of us could hope to be really fit for another attempt.

In the meantime a good deal of snow had fallen on the North Col, and Camp IV was in danger of being buried by a snow avalanche. The following day, the 26th May, was spent moving the tents and stores to the crest of the col, while Ruttledge, Greene, Crawford and Brocklebank escorted the exhausted porters down to Camp III. Some of them were very weak, and required assistance over every step of the descent.

Birnie who was chiefly responsible for handling the porters, now had a difficult job in finding more men who were fit and willing to go up the ridge for the all-important task of establishing Camp VI. He was helped a great deal in this by the remarkable courage and loyalty displayed by two of the old gang, Angtharkay and Kipa, who volunteered to go up again. It must be remembered that the Sherpas could not be expected to have the same feeling about the job that we had. These two had already done as much as could reasonably be expected of them. Their example was an inspiration to the other porters – and to us.

On 28 May, Birnie, Longland, Wager and Wyn Harris went up to Camp V, with the eight porters. Smythe and I followed on the 29th. This time there was less wind than there had been before. We reached Camp V after five hours' climbing, and we were relieved to find that things had gone according to plan. Birnie was there insole occupation. For the next few days his was the thankless job of remaining at Camp V in support of the parties attempting the summit. During the afternoon the gale returned with something of its old violence, and we were much relieved when Longland and the porters arrived from above. They had fought a tremendous struggle with the blizzard during the last two hours. Two of the porters were almost exhausted, and Longland had a difficult job in getting them down. Poor, gallant Kipa was in a bad way. It was already clear that he was out of his mind. For a long time he remained firmly convinced that he was dead. In consequence it was most difficult to persuade him to move, for, as he argued with perfect logic, dead men could not walk, even downhill. Even when, after several weeks it dawned on him that he was, in fact, alive, he still clung to his original hypothesis and attributed his phenomenal recovery to Green's magic. Such temporary madness or hallucination is not uncommon at high altitudes.

Longland brought us the splendid news that Camp VI had been established at 27,400 feet; 600 feet higher than it had been placed in 1924, and only 1,600 feet below the summit. This was a magnificent achievement on the part of the porters and those that were leading them. Their feat gave us a fine chance of climbing the mountain. Wyn Harris and Wager were now at Camp VI, and would start the next morning on their attempt to reach the summit.

By now the force of the gale had slackened, and after we had provided them with a mug of tea each, Longland and six of the porters went on down to the North Col. The other two porters stayed the night with us.

The next morning was beautifully fine. Not a breath of wind disturbed the stillness, no cloud obscured a single detail of the vast panorama beneath us. To the east was a fantastic tangle of ice and jagged rock, each fold a mighty peak, now dwarfed to insignificance; to the north the desert ranges of Tibet, calm and soft, stretched away into the violet distance. The sun was well up before Smythe and I left Camp V. In spite of a fairly good night I felt far from well. I was suffering from slight diarrhoea which accentuated the weakness due to the physical deterioration that was now becoming only too apparent. Every movement was a great effort, and I found myself counting each step and wondering when I could decently suggest a halt. At first the climbing was fairly difficult over a series of outward sloping buttresses, but after a while it became easier. We followed the ridge until, in a little hollow, we found the remains of the 1924 Camp VI – a few broken and bleached tent poles with some tattered wisps of canvas clinging to them. From there we traversed diagonally across the face of the mountain, climbing slowly up towards the Yellow Band.

The climbing was very easy, and it was possible while moving along to examine the features of the upper part of the mountain. The Second Step looked very impressive. It now appeared almost end-on, and I saw that on its southern side there was a steep ice slope. Suddenly I noticed two dots, one above the other, on this slope. The day was so still that Smythe, who was about ten yards in front, heard my excited whisper, 'There go Wyn and Wagers on the Second Step.' We sat down to watch. Yes, they were moving, but very slowly, probably cutting steps in the ice. But after a while we were not quite so sure; we got up and went on. After a quarter of an hour the dots did not appear to have moved, and we gradually realised that they were rocks sticking out of the ice. When we came closer we saw that they were a great deal larger than human beings. For all our knowledge of the features gleaned from photographs and distant study, we were greatly surprised by the scale of things up there; certainly everything was very much bigger than I had imagined. Longland had described the position of Camp VI, and as we approached we had no difficulty in spotting it – a little dark patch against the yellow limestone.

Before reaching the foot of the Yellow Band we had a prolonged struggle, first with a short ice slope which required stepcutting, then in powder snow into which we sank to our knees. I thought we would never get through it. That was followed by 200 feet of difficult rock climbing, each sloping ledge laden with snow. I found this less unpleasant; to have a technical difficulty to grapple with, which required delicate balance rather than dull plodding, was somehow stimulating. All the same, we were both very thankful when we crawled into the tiny tent that was Camp VI. I believe it was somewhere about one o'clock.

Camp VI was no luxury establishment. A tiny recess at the head of a gully and some loose stones had enabled the others to build a rough platform, perhaps three feet wide, on which to pitch the tent. The platform sloped downwards, and one side of the tent hung over the edge, forming a pocket. But at least it provided somewhere to lie down. After a rest we set about the task of melting a saucepan of snow. At the other camps we had used Primus stoves, but these did not work above a certain altitude, and at Camp VI we used little tins of solid fuel known as Tommy Cookers. Even these were most inefficient at that height, and it took us an hour to provide two miserable cups of tepid water slightly coloured with tea. Then we brewed some more against the return of Wager and Wyn Harris.

They arrived about the middle of the afternoon, showing every evidence of the tremendous effort they had made. They had tried to reach the ridge just below the Second Step but had met a continuous line of overhanging rock, so they had traversed along below the Black Band, and had reached the Great Couloir. This they had managed to cross, but had found the rocks on the other side laden with powder snow, which about 12.30 had forced them to abandon the struggle. How far this decision had been induced by sheer exhaustion and how much by the difficulty of the ground, on which the slightest slip must have been fatal to both, it is difficult to determine. Wager has since told me that he has found it impossible to assess the real position in which they found themselves. At that altitude mental processes are so sluggish and inefficient that it is most difficult to retain a clear memory of what has actually occurred.

In any case their decision was absolutely right; there was not the slightest chance of their reaching the summit and to have persisted much farther would most probably have involved them in disaster.

Just below the crest of the north-east ridge they had found an ice-axe. This can only have belonged to Mallory or Irvine and throws some small light upon their fate. It seems probable that they fell from the place where the axe was found. It may be that one of them slipped, the other put down his axe to brace himself against the jerk of the rope but was dragged down. Certainly the axe cannot have fallen, for had that happened, there was nothing to prevent it from bounding down at least to the foot of the Yellow Band.

I had gone so badly that day that I offered to change places with one of the others, and let him try again with Smythe. But they had both had more than enough. Wager was gasping for breath in a most alarming manner and Wyn looked terribly tired. So after a short rest and a cup of our home-brewed nectar they went on down to Camp V.

That night and the one which followed were by far the worst that I had spent on the mountain. I had the lower berth and kept on rolling off the ledge into the pocket formed by the tent floor. Smythe spent the time rolling on top of me. From sheer self-preservation, to prevent myself from being suffocated, I had to kick him with my knee or jab him with my elbow. This I did over and over again, hoping vaguely that the action would not reveal the temper that was undoubtedly behind the blows. I did not sleep at all and I do not think Smythe fared much better. Several hours before dawn we gave up the unequal struggle and started to prepare for the climb.

But before it was light snow started to fall, and presently a strong wind was driving the flakes against the side of the tent. It was no use thinking of starting in those conditions, and there was nothing for it but to resign ourselves to spending the day at Camp VI. I think we both realised then that our slender chance of reaching the summit had now vanished. In the first place the snow that was falling would, at the lowest estimate, increase the difficulties enormously; secondly, our physical deterioration due to lack of oxygen, sleep and appetite must now be very rapid. Indeed we were worried, so far as we were capable of worrying about anything, by the question of how long it was possible to live at 27,400 feet. Would the danger line be apparent? Or would one suddenly find oneself incapable of moving? Or perhaps just die in one's sleep? Nobody had ever tried the experiment of a prolonged sojourn at such an altitude.

It was a dreary day. The wind dropped in the afternoon. Looking out of the little window at the back of the tent, we could see the summit. Very little of the intervening ground was visible, and it looked ridiculously close. Well, 1,600 feet was not far; without the powder snow on the rocks and in sea-level conditions one could climb it comfortably in an hour! An ambition of a lifetime and we were too weak to reach out to grasp it! Fortunately our dulled intellects lessened the sting of this thought, but it was sharp enough.

The next night was a repetition of the first, tossing, kicking, panting. At about three o'clock in the morning we started melting some snow, to make a brew of something – Cafe-au-Lait I believe it was called, though everything tasted much the same. Thawing our boots was the longest job; they were like lumps of rock. We had intended taking them to bed with us to keep them soft, but, like so many good resolutions made below, this had not been done. But by holding them over candle flames we managed to make the uppers sufficiently pliable, and, with a tremendous effort, to force our feet, already encased in four or five pairs of socks, into them. For the rest we each wore two pairs of long woollen pants, seven sweaters and a loosely-fitting windproof with a hood that went over a balaclava helmet. Our hands were protected by one pair of thick woollen mitts covered with a pair of sheep-skin gauntlets. I felt about as suitably equipped for delicate rock climbing as a fully rigged deep-sea diver for dancing a tango. It was quiet outside and we waited for the dawn.

It must have been about 7.30 when we started. It was a fine morning, though bitterly cold. I had a stomach ache and felt as weak as a kitten. We started climbing diagonally up towards the head of the Great Couloir, taking the lead in turns of about a quarter of an hour each. The ground was not exactly difficult nor particularly steep. But it was rather like being on the tiles of a roof; one had to rely largely on the friction of boot-nails on the shelving ledges. A slip might have been difficult to check. The more exposed parts of the Yellow Band had been swept clear of snow by the wind, but in the little gullies and cracks there were deep deposits of powder snow which obscured all foothold. We were not climbing quickly, but our progress was steady and fast enough. After about two hours I began to feel sick and it appeared to me that I was approaching the end of my tether. In such a condition I would certainly have been no use to Smythe in an emergency; also it was a firm rule among us that one simply must not go on until one collapsed altogether, as that would have placed one's companion in a most awkward position. So I decided to stop and let Smythe go on alone.

By now it was fairly warm in the sun. I sat down and watched Smythe making his way slowly along the slabs and wondered if I might follow him at my own pace. But then it occurred to me that, seeing me coming, he might wait for me, so I reluctantly gave up the idea, and after waiting a little longer started back to Camp VI.

It was about 1.30 when Smythe returned. He had reached the Great Couloir, but had found masses of new snow on the rocks beyond and had been compelled to return from much the same place that the previous party had reached. The height at this point was estimated at 28,100 feet. The altitude of all the major features on the north face of Mount Everest had been determined (to within a hundred feet or so) by theodolite observations from below, and it is from these computations that we were able to judge with reasonable accuracy the height of any point on the upper part of the face. The readings on an aneroid barometer at that altitude would be hopelessly inaccurate.

Smythe was so exhausted by his effort that he was reluctant to move farther down that day. To give him a chance of a good night's sleep, and also to relieve the anxiety of the unfortunate Birnie, it was decided that I should go down to Camp V and that Smythe should come all the way down to the North Col on the following day. With the tent to himself and two sets of sleeping-bags he would be fairly comfortable. I left Camp VI at 2.30. By now we were enveloped in cloud. To avoid the difficult pitch below the camp I traversed along towards the north-east shoulder as the other descending parties had done. For some distance the way was along a sloping terrace that provided fairly easy going, but near the north-east shoulder, the terrace petered out into steep rocks that were now laden with powder snow. At one point I nearly came to grief by lowering myself on to a ledge of snow which promptly slipped away and left me hanging by my fingers.

I had scarcely reached the easier rocks below when I was met by a tremendous blast of wind. I have never known anything like the suddenness of those Everest storms. They arrived out of perfect stillness, without any warning, and at the full height of their power. This was the fiercest gale I had encountered on the mountain – at any rate while out of shelter. I found it impossible to stand up against it even for a moment, and all I could do was to cower against a rock with my back to the wind. Luckily this did not maintain is maximum velocity for long and after a time I was able to proceed in short rushes. But presently I found that I had lost all sense of direction. The cloud was thick and I could see no more than a few yards ahead of me. It was no use going on down, for if I missed the top of the north-east spur I should get myself into a hopeless mess. I sat down helplessly and waited. For those who wish to achieve complete philosophical detachment, there is perhaps something to recommend life at high altitudes. The mind appears to be quite incapable of strong emotion of any sort. To be lost on a mountain side in such circumstances would normally be an unpleasantly exciting experience to the calmest of men. I found it neither unpleasant nor exciting, and was blissfully resigned to whatever the fates chose to do with me. I have no idea how long I waited, but eventually a sharp spire appeared through the driving mist and snow. I remembered having seen this before and made towards it. Presently a window opened, and far below I saw the summit of the North Peak, a rock in a storm tossed sea. Soon I reached the little hollow of the 1924 Camp VI which provided a welcome refuge from the storm.

I almost enjoyed the rest of the descent to Camp V. I felt gloriously careless as I bumped and slithered down from ledge to ledge; the wind provided a mad confusion that matched my state of mind. When I arrived I found that Birnie had made a tremendous brew of hot liquid; I think it was tea, but whatever it was it was excellent. He, poor chap, was very weak. He had spent longer above the North Col than any of us, his feet were frost-bitten and the altitude had taken a severe toll of his strength. He had had none of the interest of the attempts on the summit; only a long, lonely vigil and anxiety. But I found his cheerfulness even more warming than his tea. It was nearly dark before I had the strength of mind to go out into the storm again to collect a sleeping-bag from the other tent. I found this to be full of snow and though I tried for a quarter of an hour, my fingers were so lifeless that I could not undo the fastenings. I tried to tear the canvas open with no more success, and finally I gave it up. Birnie gave me half his sleeping-bag and we spent a miserable night huddled together in a tent half filled with snow, listening to the crazy raving of the storm. This had partly spent itself by morning and when the sun was up we made our way slowly down to the North Col.

Here we found Longland and McLean. While the former went off up the ridge to meet Smythe, the latter ministered to our needs. The large dome tent which we were now housed seemed to us the height of luxury and spacious comfort. McLean insisted on our relaxing completely, while he undid our boots, massaged our limbs and provided endless supplies of food and drink. Smythe came in some hours later.

It took us a very long time to get down from the North Col the next day. Immediately after we had started, McLean became ill. He could hardly walk and had to be nursed carefully down the slopes. When we reached the bottom we found that a party had been sent up from Camp III to meet us with tea. When we had assembled to drink this I suddenly found that I was suffering from aphasia and could not articulate words properly. For example if I wished to say, 'Give me a cup of tea' I would say something entirely different – may be 'tram-car, cat, put'. It was a most aggravating situation and reminded me of the fate of the banker in 'The Hunting of the Snark', though I was spared the more spectacular symptoms of his malady. As in my normal speech I was still confined to whispering, my peculiar complaint did not attract attention at first. But I could not conceal it for long and I had to suffer the pitying looks of my companions who were obviously thinking, 'Poor old Eric, now he's gone bats'. In actual fact I was perfectly clear-headed; I could even visualise the words I wanted to say, but my tongue just refused to perform the required movements. At length, from sheer exasperation I got up and ran off down the glacier so fast that I arrived at Camp III a long time before any of the others. There however my case was even worse, for everyone was naturally eager to hear news of our attempt, while all I could do was to talk drivel. Poor Ruttledge was most concerned at having another lunatic on his hands. The cause of my complaint was attributed either to sunstroke or to the blizzard. I think it was a form of migraine, a theory that is supported by the blinding headache from which I suffered throughout that night. However I was well again in the morning.

The whole party retreated down the glacier quickly or slowly, each according to his physical condition. Birnie had to be carried most of the way, and McLean required the support of a strong arm. The Base Camp was now very different from the bleak comfortless place we had left seven weeks before. It was still no beauty spot, but there was grass, the soft, warm smell of earth and growing things, blue poppies brought the sky to earth and primulas peeped from behind the rocks. After a week of delicious rest and luxury we returned up the glacier to Camp III, in the night expectation of renewing our attempt on the mountain. But it soon became obvious that this was impossible. The monsoon had broken and though it was much warmer and more comfortable than before, the slopes of the North Col were too dangerous, and masses of snow had fallen on the upper part of Everest.

Before retreating again some of us visited the Rapiu La, the saddle at the foot of the north-east ridge of Everest, and climbed a small peak above it. From the top we had a view that could not be imagined by those who have not seen the fantastic country that lies to the south-east of Mount Everest – the colossal ramparts that join Everest with Lhotse, the delicately fluted ridges of purest ice, a hundred peaks of exquisite form, deep, wooded valleys; what a contrast to the bare, unlovely slopes of rubble about the East Rongbuk glacier!

8   Large Expeditions

In 1933 I formed a deep conviction of the fallacy of tackling Mount Everest with such a huge organisation. In the first place no expedition had in practice launched more than two attempts on the summit; it was agreed that the best number for an attempt was two, therefore it seemed improbable that in any expedition more than four men would be required to make the actual attempts. Why then should a party consist of fourteen climbers? It was argued that there must be reserves in case some of the climbers went sick. But in no case had a man, who was known to be capable of climbing to great altitudes and who had been relied upon to take part in the final climb, actually succumbed to sickness before the attempt. It seemed clear, then, that this risk was insignificant compared with the enormous chances against any one expedition finding the mountain in a climbable condition. Reserves yes, but not three reserves to every one man who was expected to go high. Again, this question of sickness should surely be regarded against a background of individual experience. In all the dozens of expeditions and climbing holidays that I have done I do not recall a single occasion on which sickness of any member of the party has prevented us from reaching our objective. I believe that most climbers can say the same, or at any rate will agree that such a misfortune is a rare occurrence. Further, when a man is sent on an important job during which he has to live, perhaps for years, in a bad climate the appointment is not duplicated in case he goes sick. Why, then, this extraordinary expectation of disease and accident on an Everest expedition? I refer of course to the approach and not to the final attempt on the summit.

Another reason given for the inclusion of a large number of Europeans in the party was the alleged necessity of having experts to deal with the problems of transport. This may or may not be true of a giant expedition; I have never had the job of running one. But it is certainly not the case with an expedition of moderate size. The organisation of transport to Mount Everest is peculiarly easy – a far simpler matter than in any other part of the Himalayas that I know. Animal transport can be used all the way to the Base Camp and even beyond; the passport issued by the authorities in Lhasa includes an order to all Tibetan officials along the route to supply the transport required, a luxury that I have met nowhere else; supplies of fodder can be obtained all along the route; on the wide, open plains of Tibet, over which lies the majority of the way, one is blissfully free from the danger of landslides, a constant menace in other parts of the Himalayas, which may cut the road for weeks; the Tibetan interpreter deals efficiently with the problem of language and the settling of minor disputes. The rest is a simple division sum: the weight of each load into the total weight of baggage to be transported equals the number of animals required.

Opinions vary considerably regarding the optimum size of expeditions. I once asked my friend Dr Humphreys for his views on the matter. He replied firmly and without hesitation 'Three constitutes a large expedition, a party of one may be considered a small expedition'. I did not propose anything so drastic for an attempt on Mount Everest, though I have always thought that a party of three climbers would stand almost as good a chance as any large number. The kind of expedition that I visualised was one consisting of six European members all with considerable Alpine experience and all with a proved capacity for going high, and about thirty carefully selected and specially trained Sherpa porters. I advocated a considerable reduction in the quantity of stores and equipment taken per head, and the total expenditure of somewhere between £2,500 and £3,000, as against £12,000 which was the average cost of each of the previous expeditions (except for the first 'Reconnaissance').

Such an expedition would have the advantage of mobility, with a consequent lessening of the risk of a breakdown in lines of communication. Even at the enormously reduced cost, each porter could be provided with much better and more carefully selected equipment. The climbers would get to know the porters individually in a way that was quite impossible when there were 170 of them; this would lead to a greater mutual understanding and trust. The chances of theft of equipment would be greatly reduced. With a huge caravan of three or four thousand animals, varying from powerful yaks to tiny donkeys, which inevitably become spread out over miles of country, it is exceedingly difficult to prevent looting, and vital equipment is as liable to be stolen as are superfluous stores. In 1933 a considerable number of porters' boots were lost in this way; had the theft been larger than it actually was it might have resulted in the complete breakdown of the expedition. Also the provision of a small number of animals would not disrupt the normal life of the country, which is one of the principal objections of the Tibetan officials to Everest expeditions.

But it was mainly on psychological grounds that I was opposed to large expeditions. It is vitally important that no member of a party should at any time feel that he is superfluous, or that he is simply there in case someone else breaks down. Such a state of affairs imposes an intolerable strain on everyone, and is bound to lead to friction and a consequent loss of efficiency. This matter is easily overlooked by a leader who has all the interest of the organisation and is constantly busy with his plans. On a scientific expedition each man is, or should be, absorbed in his particular line of research; the party can easily be split up into self-contained units each with its special task and responsibility. But when the sole object of a venture is to reach the top of a particular mountain, the problem is entirely different. It is merely tactless to remind a man that he is lucky to be there at all, and that there are hundreds of equally good climbers at home who would be only too glad to take his place. You cannot argue an expedition into running smoothly, nor avoid a competitive feeling by appealing for the 'team spirit'. The strongest mountaineering party is one in which each member has implicit confidence in all his companions, recognises their vital importance in the common effort and feels himself to have an equally indispensable part to play. This ideal is no less important to a Himalayan expedition than on an Alpine peak. To my mind it can only be achieved with a relatively small, closely knit party. Only then can you talk (if you must) about 'team spirit'. How is it possible, when at least fifty per cent, of the members are destined to remain in reserve, to avoid a feeling of competition? Only a saint could expunge from deep down in his soul all hope of another man falling sick, that he might take his place. How different from the joyous partnership we have known on other climbs!

For my part I loathed the crowds and the fuss that were inseparable from a large expedition. I always had the ridiculous feeling that I was taking part in a Cook's tour or a school treat, and I wanted to go away and hide myself. Of course this did not apply to the few days or weeks when one is actually doing a hard job of work, but unfortunately such spells occupied a very small proportion of the whole time. The small town of tents that sprang up each evening, the noise and racket of each fresh start, the sight of a huge army invading the peaceful valleys, it was all so far removed from the light, free spirit with which we were wont to approach our peaks. And I believe that spirit plays an important part in the success of any mountaineering venture. Remove, then, the impression that one is engaged in a vast enterprise upon which the eyes of the world are focused, realise that one is setting out to climb a mountain, higher perhaps, but fundamentally no different from other mountains, and one will add greatly to one's chances of success, and, more important still, enjoyment.

Then there is the question of finance. The argument here, as I understood it, was that money for an Everest expedition was easy to raise, so why not spend it if it would help? In the first place the mere spending of money does not in itself increase the efficiency of an expedition; indeed it can, only too easily, be a source of weakness by cluttering up the works with a lot of superfluous junk and obscuring the really important issues. For example it would be of more value to supply all the porters with precisely the same equipment – dome-tents, boots, sleeping-bags – as that used by climbers, than to transport cases of champagne and other luxuries all the way from London to Rongbuk. Secondly, if the money must be spent, there are many profitable ways of doing it. For the difference in cost between a large expedition and one of moderate size, no fewer than a dozen expeditions could be sent to other parts of the Himalayas. These, if properly run, could have a direct bearing upon the main problem of climbing Mount Everest, and could be undertaken during the years when political permission to enter Tibet was not forthcoming. There are hundreds of young mountaineers who would give anything for a chance to go to the Himalayas. How much easier would be the work of the Mount Everest selection committees if some of them could be given that chance. Again, the climbing of Mount Everest is as much a physiological as a mountaineering problem. We are lamentably ignorant of the real effects of high altitudes upon the human body, or of the means by which these may be countered. Physiologists have been working for years upon these problems; they have been handicapped by lack of opportunities and subjects for their experiments. It would be possible for a small party of trained physiologists and climbers to camp for a month on the summit of Kamet. The results of their experiments would be as valuable to science as to those who wish to climb the lofty peaks of the Himalaya.

Finally, the disadvantage of large expeditions lay in the fact that the necessity of raising big funds made it difficult to control publicity. The expeditions became invested with a glamour foreign to the fundamental simplicity of the game. It was quite natural that mountaineers should wish to climb the highest peak in the world, or at least be interested in the project. But unfortunately Everest's supremacy among mountains appealed to the popular imagination of a record-breaking age, and gradually the expeditions began to receive a press publicity out of all proportion to the value of the undertaking, and certainly out of keeping with what used to be regarded as 'the best traditions of mountaineering'. It was claimed that the enterprise symbolised the spirit of modern youth, and that its success would represent a triumph of humanity over Nature. In fact, of course, the first part of the venture was an intensely interesting piece of geographical exploration, and the second an absorbing mountaineering problem – no more, no less; both were on the same plane as any similar project.

I knew a man with a strong claim for a place on the expedition, who said that he wanted to climb Everest so as to make a big name for himself, which would enable him to use his influence in the cause of world peace. A worthy ambition no doubt, but surely it would have been more profitable to devote his energies to the study of political economy rather than to proving himself a mountaineer with an exceptionally large lung capacity, or whatever it is that enables a man to climb to great altitudes. This is one example among many of an extraordinary distortion of values which has its roots in the opening of a short-cut to fame. Were it not so laughable it might well be resented by those who find in mountaineering a deep aesthetic pleasure.

It was perhaps difficult for those actually engaged in the expeditions not to be carried away by this flood of notoriety, and it needed a good deal of sober introspection to trace the origin of the nasty taste that began to appear in the mouths of the more sensitive. But I think that the feeling of a large section of mountaineers was summed up by the remark that a friend of mine (not himself a member of the expeditions) once made: 'For heaven's sake climb the wretched thing and let us get back to real mountaineering.' It seemed a pity that so simple a project should have led to such a feeling.

One of the most unfortunate effects of the Mount Everest expeditions was their influence upon Himalayan mountaineering. In consequence of their elaborate scale, it came to be thought impossible to achieve anything in the Himalayas without an enormous and costly organisation. Many of the expeditions – Italian, German, French, international – which followed the early attempts to climb Everest, were run with an extravagance that made the Everest expeditions appear modest by comparison. Fantastic equipment was evolved, dynamite brought to blow away obstacles, aeroplanes used for dumping supplies on the mountain, all the delicacies known to culinary art were provided to sustain the exhausted climbers, whole populations were uprooted from their homes to carry this stuff up the glaciers – with the consequent risk of famine the following year due to the neglect of agriculture. Needless to say these tactics met with very little success, and not one of the peaks attacked with such ferocity was climbed. But the sad thing was that the lessons taught by the great pioneers of Himalayan exploration – Longstaff, Conway, Kellas, Godwin Austin, Freshfield, the Schlagintweits – who achieved so much by the simple but hardy application of their art, were forgotten or ignored.

It is perhaps unfair to blame this cult of mighty Himalayan campaigns entirely on the Everest expeditions, but from talks I have had with the organisers of one of these foreign expeditions, in which I tried in vain to persuade them to adopt a less elaborate plan, I am sure that they based their ideas largely upon the Everest precedent.

These observations are made in no unfriendly spirit, and I hope that they will be regarded as constructive criticism. It was sincerely believed that the job could best be tackled by employing all the resources that money could buy. There are still those who hold this view, though I am narrow-minded enough to believe that they cannot have themselves experienced the enormous moral and material advantages of the small compact expedition. One day men will again turn their eyes towards the Himalayas; I hope that then this other point of view will be kept in mind.

When all is said, the Mount Everest expeditions have been a good adventure, and I think that most of those who were lucky enough to take part in them have gained much by the experience. For my part, much as I disapprove of large expeditions, I would not have foregone a single friendship that I made in 1933.

9 Small Expeditions

One cannot wander far from the normal trade and tourist routes without being impressed by the enormous area of the earth's surface still unexplored. It is a pleasant discovery to make. The superficial observer is too apt to suppose that, because the South Pole has been reached, the mysteries of the Antarctic Continent are all revealed, or to imagine that if Everest were climbed then there would be nothing more to discover in the Himalayas. In fact, of course, the journey to the Pole disclosed no more than a thin strip of country on either side of the route followed; the climbing of Everest would tell us nothing that we do not already know about the earth's surface. Certainly there are no more continents to be found; it is doubtful if we will ever see falls more magnificent than Victoria and Niagara; lost civilisations beyond the ranges exist only in the imagination of romantic novelists. But the detailed exploration of the world is very far from complete; huge areas are still untrodden by the foot of man, unmapped and unknown; a school atlas will show with dotted lines that many of the mighty rivers of Asia are unexplored in their upper reaches; within the last twenty years the largest glacier known to exist outside the polar regions was discovered. Besides, geographical exploration means more than the discovery and survey of country; even a well-mapped area may be *terra incognita* to the botanist, the geologist, the zoologist, the archaeologist. There is no end to it. Start, with a spark of interest, to look into the matter, and your head will soon begin to reel with the mass of fascinating problems crying out for investigation. It is a virulent bug, this desire to see what lies round the next corner. An energetic life-time spent in the pursuit will leave you as far from complete satisfaction as you were at the start.

Mountain climbing has its roots in mountain exploration, and it is not unnatural that in little-known ranges the mountaineer should tend to revert to the basis of his pursuit. It would be difficult for anyone with an interest in strange country to go all the way to Mount Everest without feeling some desire to leave the route and wander off into the labyrinth of unmapped ranges that stretch away on every side. On the way back to India in 1933, Wager and I left the main party and made our way across a small strip of unexplored country to the south, and crossed into Sikkim by a new pass. My chief interest was in climbing peaks. Wager, on the other hand, as a geologist, had a wider view. He had already tasted the joys of serious exploration in Greenland, and his main enthusiasm was for the country itself. Though I disputed the matter hotly at the time, I gradually became converted to his way of thinking. Something of my early feeling for mountains began to revive.

Then the thought occurred to me, 'Why not spend the rest of my life doing this sort of thing?' There was no way of life that I liked more, the scope appeared to be unlimited, others had done it, vague plans had already begun to take shape, why not put some of them into practice? It was a disturbing idea, one which caused me much heart searching and many sleepless nights. The most obvious snag, of course, was lack of private means; but surely such a mundane consideration could not be decisive. In the first place I was convinced that expeditions could be run for the tithe of the cost generally considered necessary. Secondly if one could produce useful or interesting results one would surely find support; and as experience grew, so too would the quality of the results. No, lack of money must not be allowed to interfere. The fact that I had no training in any particular branch of science was a more serious obstacle. But might not this defect be remedied as one went along, or in spare time between expeditions? Also there is much to be said against the organiser of a scientific expedition being himself a specialist; firstly because he would tend to take a narrow view of the work of the expedition, and secondly because the running of an expedition is in itself nearly a whole-time job. For I did not expect to have to hunt alone – I anticipated no difficulty in finding men willing to join me on an attractive project.

I do not know how much I fought the temptation. I certainly suffered qualms of conscience, but they were due more to the mere prospect of such exquisite self-indulgence than to the fear of the consequences of abandoning the search for an assured future, provision for old age and other worthy ambitions. I had always rather deplored the notion that one must sacrifice the active years of one's life to the dignity and comfort of old age. Also the less conservative of my monitors assured me that things had a way of panning out so long as one knew what one wanted. So the decision was taken, albeit with a faint heart.

Beginnings must be small. I could hardly expect much backing at first, and it looked as though my theories regarding small expeditions would receive a pretty severe test. Of the dozens of fascinating projects that presented themselves, the one that appeared to suit my purpose most admirably was the exploration of that remarkable geographical phenomenon, the Nanda Devi basin. First, because there were no political obstacles to be overcome, and secondly, I had already had experience on the Kamet expedition of that part of the Himalayas. I first became interested in the problem after hearing Ruttledge talk about it. He had made four attempts to enter the basin, and had given me an enthusiastic description of them, and a vivid picture of the strange sanctuary. The spark was rekindled by a conversation with Dr Longstaff.

Here was a famous peak, 25,660 feet high, completely surrounded by such a formidable mountain barrier that no one had been able to penetrate to the country lying at its foot. The only breach in this barrier was on its western side, where the Rishi Ganga river had carved a tremendous gorge some twenty miles long. Since W. W. Graham and his two Swiss guides, Emil Boss and Ulrich Kauffmann, had tried to force their way up the gorge in 1883, repeated attempts had been made by explorers to reach the sanctuary. Every angle of approach had been tried without success. Dr Longstaff, with his usual generous enthusiasm for the projects of younger men, advised me to try the gorge once again. Although he himself had tried to find a way up it, he had not been able to press home his attempt, but he was convinced that there was a way.

At first it looked as though it might be difficult to find anyone who would fall in with my apparently heretical ideas of extreme frugality. Most fortunately, however, Tilman arrived in England at just the right moment. I had a letter from him announcing that, after indulging in a little gold-mining in Kakamega, he had bought a push-bike and had ridden it right across Africa to the west coast where he had picked up a cargo ship which had brought him home. He asked me to go with him to climb in the Lake District for a week or two. I replied with the counter proposal that he should come with me to the Himalayas for seven months. He agreed that this was the better plan, and came to London immediately to discuss my project.

I also asked Dr Humphreys to come. He had wide experience of mountain exploration in Africa, and was a great believer in travelling light. Besides being a doctor, he was an expert surveyor and botanist. He was tremendously keen on the idea, but unfortunately, just before I asked him he had undertaken to lead an expedition to the Arctic. But his sympathetic advice and encouragement were invaluable. Our 'expedition' was lamentably short of scientific qualification, though we did manage to acquire some small knowledge of survey.

Money, of course, was our first concern. Try as I would, I could not bring my estimates to below £150 each, if we were to allow ourselves the rather important luxury of three Sherpa porters, and spend the whole season in the field. I had managed to raise a little money by the distasteful business of lecturing during the winter, but not as much as that. Tilman, however, in spite of his gold-mining was rather more affluent, and he thought he could put up his share. The chief item of the budget was the passage to India. The cheapest return fare by passenger steamer was £50. The romantic notion of working one's passage is difficult to put into practice, for few ship's masters are willing to sign on hands who have every intention of deserting half way through the voyage. Tilman's idea of bicycling to India was turned down. For some weeks the issue hung in the balance. In the meantime I went off to lecture in Norway. When I came back I found that Tilman had fixed up return passages by cargo steamer for £30 each return from Liverpool to Calcutta, including our modest baggage. This put the project just about within our grasp, though even then Tilman had to advance some of my share against uncertain security.

We set sail on the 6 April, 1934. The voyage took a month. We had nothing much to do, but the tedium was lightened by the extremely pleasant company of the ship's officers. We had collected all the available literature about Nanda Devi, and before long we knew the whole story by heart. I taught Tilman what little Urdu I knew, and then we spent a weary hour each morning supplementing this from Hugo. We passed a considerable part of each day throwing a medicine-ball at each other and skipping. In spite of this we became so liverish that by the time we reached Aden we felt compelled to supplement the ship's food with extra fruit. In its purchase I nearly succeeded in ruining the finances of the expedition. All the cash we had with us was one £5 note, which had rashly been entrusted to my care. After some difficulty we found a local financier who was willing to provide us with change. This consisted mostly of shillings and sixpenny pieces which took a long time to count. It was very hot, and we were hard pressed on all sides by shouting pedlars, all eager to take their share of our wealth. When the count was complete, and our pockets and hands were laden with silver, our banker not unnaturally demanded his £5 note. This had vanished. In a frenzy I emptied each pocket in turn, spilling coins all over the place; it was nowhere to be found. Then suddenly I noticed a screwed-up bit of white paper reposing in a basket of oranges. To my intense relief, and the chagrin of the slow-witted owner of the basket, this turned out to be the missing note.

The only other incident of importance during the voyage happened a few days later, when I broke a toe by jumping onto an awning that had been rigged up to provide a swimming-bath. However, the purser performed a painful but successful operation, and in time the toe resumed its normal appearance.

Before leaving England I had arranged with Karma Paul to engage the services of three of the Sherpas who had been with us on Everest the previous year – Angtharkay, Pasang and Kusang – and to send them down from Darjeeling to meet us in Calcutta. At Vizagapatam we sent him a wire informing him of the date of our arrival, but we had to wait for two days before the Sherpas appeared. Our budget contained no provision for hotel bills, but fortunately the captain of our ship was kind enough to allow us to remain on board.

The journey from Calcutta to Kathgodam took thirty-six hours – the hottest I have ever known. I suffered from a raging thirst, but Tilman was a stern task-master and would not allow me to squander our slender reserves on tea or soda water. Every piece we spent had to be accounted for in a little notebook, and each day's expenditure was carefully scrutinised. My discomfort was increased by watching Angtharkay, who travelled in our compartment, quaffing cup after cup of tea at every halt. I had not quite the face to sponge upon him, and bore my torment in silence. The last fifty miles of our journey to Ranikhet were completed by lorry, and at last we had relief from our suffering as we took deep gulps of cool, pine-scented air, deliciously sweet after the appalling heat and dust of pre-monsoon India.

We reached Ranikhet at about noon on 9 May, and put up at the government rest-house. A day and a half was sufficient to complete our simple preparations. We had worked out everything beforehand and knew exactly what we wanted. Within a couple of hours of our arrival we had engaged twelve Dhotial coolies to carry for us across the foothills, and had sent them off to meet us at Baijnath, the terminus of the road, fifty miles farther on. Then each of us was issued with his allowance of kit, which consisted of a suit of light, windproof material, sweaters, woollen pants, a woollen helmet, puttees, socks, a double sleeping-bag, a pair of climbing boots and an ice-axe. Survey instruments, cameras, ropes, two small Meade tents, Primus stoves, two tins of kerosene oil, candles, lanterns, matches and the food we had brought out from England were packed into 80-pound loads. We collected from the local bank the money we would want for the next five or six months, most of it in silver. A lorry was chartered to take us and our baggage to Baijnath. The surplus clothing which convention had thus far imposed upon us was packed away and deposited with the secretary of the local club. All was set by the evening of the 10th, and we started early on the morning of the 11th.

It all seemed too easy. I had been told so often before leaving England that my budget was ridiculously inadequate, and that though we might reach Ranikhet we would certainly not get much farther; there had been so much talked and written about the vast amount of organisation required for an expedition, that I had begun to suspect that there must be some hidden snag. There was no snag. These widespread beliefs were simply founded upon a confusion between necessity and luxury; this great bug-bear of cost and organisation was largely due to the attempt to carry the amenities of civilisation into wild places. In most parts of the world travel is as simple or as complex as you care to make it. As it was, in our ignorance, we had brought many things that we could well have done without. On the other hand there was not a single item of equipment or food which we needed and had not brought; nothing that in the smallest degree could have aided us in the achievement of our plans, or increased our enjoyment.

The Dhotials were waiting for us when we arrived at Baijnath at about noon. Without any fuss they shouldered their loads and started on the first stage of the march. Their regulation load is 80 pounds, 20 pounds more than the usual load carried by Himalayan porters. Like the Sherpas they support the weight with a head-strap; indeed this seems to be the method employed by most of the best load carriers throughout the world. I have tried it myself but without much success, though I could see that if one acquired the knack it would be very much less tiring than the usual shoulder-strap method.

Though it was only about ten miles, I found that first march a great trial. I was suffering from the usual complaint of newcomers to the Indian hills, known as 'hill diarrhoea' and which is due either to mica in the water or to a chill induced by the change of climate. My broken toe was still painful, and I had to wear a tennis-shoe with the toe-cap cut off. Baijnath was only about feet above sea-level, and it was a very hot, sultry afternoon. It was uphill nearly all the way. The path was dusty and I suffered from a fearful thirst. In the evening we reached Gwaldam, 7,000 feet up on a wooded ridge overlooking the deep valley of the Pindar River, cool and lovely. I satisfied my only desire – to drink and drink and drink. Instead of any supper I took a huge dose of castor-oil.

It was a typical start and I have made many such. But two or three days of easy marching produced a wonderful change. Fatigue and stiffness left us; feet were no longer sore; having left behind the filth of semi-civilisation we could drink freely from frequent springs; we marched in the cool of the morning and lazed in the shade of the oak and pine woods during the heat of the day; we became fit and gloriously alive. The weather was perfect, the country magnificent. Our way led over ridge after ridge of forest-clad hills; not the oppressive rain-forest of the Eastern Himalayas, but gentle wooded slopes interspersed with grassy glades, moss and bracken and splashing streams. The rhododendrons were in bloom, and many kinds of Alpine flowers. Above were the sparkling white peaks of Trisul and Nanda Ghunti. The soft music of running water, the murmur of a light breeze in the trees, the summer note of the cuckoo, these were the sounds we awoke to each morning. With such a small party, we could camp far from the dusty villages, wherever we chose. We rarely bothered to pitch a tent, but lay, instead, on a luxurious bed of deep grass, beside a huge log fire. We lived with a sense of perfect freedom and deep physical and mental well-being. We wanted nothing.

Our food was very simple. It consisted mainly of flour, rice and ghee (clarified butter) which we bought as we went along. We had brought various luxuries to supplement these; sugar, tea, lentils, a number of 10-lb. Cheddar cheeses sewn up in cloth, and some tins of pemmican. Except for the pemmican we rarely tasted meat. Tilman favoured a vegetarian diet, largely because he had recently had most of his teeth knocked out by a fall from a horse while steeplechasing, and I was quite willing to fall into line. For the first few days I found our diet a bit hard, but as I became fit my appetite grew and I ate my meals with great relish. I certainly found this simple fare far more satisfying than a diet of tinned food, which soon becomes dead and tasteless. There cannot have been much wrong with our diet for we never lacked energy. The supply of Vitamin 'C' presents no problem anywhere in the Himalayas for it is always easy to find edible plants such as chives and wild rhubarb.

The bulk of our time was spent in uninhabited country, and for this we collected supplies of flour from the last village through which we passed. And here was yet another advantage of travelling light. For our small party we rarely experienced any difficulty in obtaining food for several weeks. Most of the flour was converted into tsampa by the simple process of roasting it. Tsampa is almost universally used in the high regions of Central Asia, particularly by travellers in Tibet and by shepherds grazing their flocks in the mountains beyond the reach of fuel. Its great virtue lies in the fact that it can be kept almost indefinitely without going bad, and it can be eaten without any further cooking. Our breakfast generally consisted of tsampa mixed in mugs of tea, for supper it was usually boiled into a thick porridge with a sauce of lentils strongly seasoned with chillies and other spices.

The simplest method of working out the amount of food required for a given period is to allow two pounds per man per day, and to divide the total suitably between the various commodities available. Then with a small spring balance it is easy at any time to take stock of the food situation. I have nearly always found this way infallible; for months at a stretch one is rarely out more than a day or two either way. For us the task of estimating the food we needed was a matter of a few minutes' work with pencil and note-book. It went something like this:

Food for five men for six weeks:
$45 \times 5 \times 2 = 420$ pounds

Flour, 210 pounds
Rice: 60 pounds
Ghee: 40 pounds
Cheese: 30 pounds
Pemmican: 10 pounds
Sugar: 40 pounds
Lentils: 30 pounds
Total: 420 pounds

Such things as tea, salt and spices were not included in this weight, and were calculated separately. Provided most of the food is dry, two pounds a day is liberal allowance, and men can do hard physical work on quite a lot less for short periods. The normal Arctic sledging ration is something like twenty-seven ounces, but it contains a very high proportion of fat. In the Himalayas fat is difficult to procure locally, expensive to import, awkward to carry and very indigestible at high altitudes. Fresh meat does not keep long, and is wasteful in weight as it contains a high proportion of water and bone. Tinned meat is also very wasteful in weight. Dried meat, similar to the original Canadian pemmican, is better than the modern tinned pemmican, but it is not easy to procure and is very expensive. The great advantage of a carbohydrate diet in the Himalayas are that it can most easily be procured locally and that it can be carried in sacks. But it is necessary to supplement it with a small proportion of fat and some form of protein, though most Asiatics seem to be able to get along very well without these additions.

The word 'march' with its associations of discipline and routine seemed scarcely applicable to that blissful saunter over the foot-hills. Beyond setting a time-limit, we had no fixed plan. The distance we covered each day was limited by the pace of the heavily laden Dhotials, and it rarely amounted to more than three or four hours walking, which even in our untrained condition was not very tiring and gave us plenty of time to bathe in pools, to climb a hill for a more extensive view or to practise rock climbing on boulders. One of the things that I enjoyed most was the opportunity of getting to know the Sherpas intimately, which was impossible on either of the two previous Himalayan expeditions I had known. Sharing with them the same life, the same camp fire, the same food and, later, the burden of load-carrying, we soon came to regard them as fellow mountaineers rather than servants and they felt with us the excitement of anticipation and the joy of success. We were admitted to their endless jokes and their occasional philosophical talk. We relied upon their judgment as much as upon our own.

Much has been written about the Sherpa, and he certainly deserves the praise he has been given. Besides a natural mountaineering skill, toughness and an ability to carry heavy loads, which are shared by most hill people, the peculiar qualities that make him such an admirable companion on an expedition are his inexhaustible humour and love of nonsense, his individuality, his great sense of loyalty, his willingness and ability not only to undertake but to seek out a job that needs doing and a pride that does not turn easily to sophistication. His trust in his employers is, I think, an acquired rather than a natural virtue, and I have known it to break down.

But for all their lovable qualities, it is as well to remember that there are good and bad among the Sherpas as among all other people, and not an unusually large proportion of good. This fact has very often been overlooked. Many expeditions coming out from Europe, have sent word to Darjeeling to order so many Sherpas to be sent to meet them at their particular starting point, just as one might order pack-mules. Often they have received very inferior material, either raw lads with no real mountaineering experience or the riff-raff of the Darjeeling bazaar. These unfortunates have then been called upon to tackle severe climbing propositions and to undertake responsibility that was wholly beyond their capacity, sometimes with disastrous results. Even among the good Sherpas each man has his own peculiar characteristics. One may be a superb load-carrier, and very agile on difficult ground, but lacking in intelligence; another may be intelligent and reliable in normal circumstances, but very highly strung and liable to break down under stress; another may be a born leader and a bad mountaineer, another only able to give his best under the influence of a strong personality among his companions. There is no end to the variety of these combinations. The Sherpas are essentially individualists, and they do not take kindly to mechanical discipline.

Mrs Townend, the secretary of the Eastern Section of the Himalayan Club, has done a great deal towards the organisation of the Sherpas. Every man who has taken part in serious expeditions has been given a little book in which is entered his past record together with a note written by each of his employers. But this cannot be expected to act as a wholly reliable guide. The leader of an expedition employing hundreds of men cannot have much insight into the character of each of them; further, anyone with experiences of references will realise that employers are not always honest in what they write; moreover a man who has performed a prodigious feat of endurance in 1924 might be a drunken sot by 1934. When employing Sherpas on an expedition involving serious mountaineering, or long periods when any kind of crisis may arise, one is not justified in asking any one of them to undertake responsibility without a pretty shrewd knowledge of his physical and moral capacity. This may seem a heavy demand from someone without previous experience of the Himalayas. But actually, so long as not more than, say, half a dozen Sherpas are employed, it is not difficult to get to know them well if one is prepared to take the trouble. The first thing, of course, is to obtain as much really reliable information about them as possible before starting, and not merely to accept a few eulogistic references; then to make a point of becoming on intimate terms with them on the march; and then to study them closely in the early stages of the climb. The personal element is by far the most important on any climbing or exploratory expedition. In difficult circumstances, the presence of one weak member in the party is a far more serious handicap than any lack of equipment.

If possible, it is a good plan to find one good Sherpa, whose judgment is absolutely reliable, and to give him a large share in the choice of his companions. In this I may have been exceptionally lucky, and admittedly I have based the theory largely on one outstanding example.

The development of the Sherpas has a long way to go before even the best of them become guides in any way comparable with those of the Alps. Personally, much as I like and admire them, I cannot envisage this. Their environment and their temperament are so totally different; the Himalayas are so vast and the opportunities for practice of really difficult mountaineering so rare, that they can never achieve anything like the same standard of technical excellence as a first-rate Alpine guide. But for unselfish loyalty, for strength and endurance, for sureness of foot and steadiness of head, for resourcefulness in all kinds of conditions, and as delightful companions, the best of them are unbeatable.

It was more by luck than by good management that Tilman and I had such a remarkably good trio in 1934. Pasang I knew fairly well as he had acted as my private servant during the march across Tibet in 1933. He was tall and slim, with fine, aristocratic Mongolian features. He was really a Bhotia (Tibetan) from Shigatse, but there is so much intermingling between the Sherpas and Bhotias that I think of them all as Sherpas, who, in fact, have formed the large majority of the men employed by expeditions. The Sherpas proper came from two districts, Sola and Khumbu in the north-east corner of Nepal, though many of them have recently migrated there from Tibet. Pasang was highly-strung and temperamental, sometimes absurdly sentimental and often moody. When he was on form nothing could stop him, when depressed he required tactful handling. Luckily on this occasion he had two very steady companions, which helped to maintain a balance. He was a beautiful mover on difficult ground, and consequently rather a brilliant rock-climber. He had been among the eight who carried Camp VI to 27,000 feet on the 1933 Mount Everest Expedition.

I had chosen Angtharkay for his remarkably fine performance in weathering the storm at Camp V and then volunteering to carry to Camp VI. Beyond that I knew nothing about him. He was small even for a Sherpa, but very well built. We soon learned to value his rare qualities, qualities which made him outstandingly the best of all the Sherpas I have known. He had a shrewd judgment both of men and of situations, and was absolutely steady in any crisis. He was a most lovable person, modest, unselfish and completely sincere, with an infectious gaiety of spirit. He has been with me on all my subsequent journeys to the Himalayas, and to him I owe a large measure of their success and much of my enjoyment.

I had intended to have another Camp VI man, Rinzing, to complete the party, but he was engaged elsewhere and Angtharkay had brought Kusang in his place. The latter had joined the 1933 Expedition from Sola Khumbu, but as he had only been employed on the glacier, I do not remember having seen him. He was by far the youngest of the trio, and very raw. He hardly spoke any Urdu. He was not remarkable for his intelligence, but he was very strong, quite imperturbable, and, under Angtharkay's leadership, absolutely reliable. To us it seemed that he was rather put upon in the matter of work. But the performance of domestic chores seemed to be his chief delight, and he was never idle – tending to the fire, fetching wood, scrubbing pots and plates, darning socks, greasing boots, washing clothes. In spite of our strict censorship of his personal belongings, he somehow contrived to smuggle with him some cakes of soap. When occasion demanded he could carry a prodigious load, and he always took more than anyone else.

One of the most delightful things about the Sherpas is their extraordinary sense of comradeship. During the six months we were together, I never once detected the slightest sign of dissension among our three. There are few Europeans who can live in close proximity to each other for long without an occasional quarrel or divergence of opinion. Often, on the numerous occasions when I was irritable and quarrelsome, I was made to feel thoroughly ashamed of myself by the example of the Sherpas. This quality of theirs is due largely, I imagine, to their robust sense of humour. It hardly ever failed. Each enjoyed jokes against himself as delightedly as those which he perpetrated. Two of them would conceal a heavy rock in the load of the third, and when, after an exhausting climb, this was discovered, all three would be convulsed with mirth. I do not consider it a compliment that they did not try out this one on us, though I was glad they did not. They were forever laughing and chatting together as though they had just met after a prolonged absence.

Nine leisurely days took us from Gwaldam, across the Kuari Pass, with its magnificent views of the great peaks of the Central Himalayas, to the valley of the Dhauli River at its junction with the Rishi.

10 Nanda Devi

Lovely though our ten-day march across the foot-hills had been, we were glad when it came to an end. We had been speculating for so long upon the nature of our curious problem that we were most anxious to get to grips with it. The idea of this stupendous gorge that had guarded for so long the secret shrine of Nanda Devi was fascinating, and filled us with a pleasant mixture of eager anticipation and fear for what we should find. The unbroken series of fine days too, had worried us, for although we had the whole summer before us, we knew that once the monsoon broke towards the end of June our chances of success would vanish; and we wished not merely to reach the sanctuary but to explore it.

The gorge of the Rishi Ganga, about twenty miles long, is divided into three sections. The lowest of these is so formidable that no one has yet succeeded in forcing a way through. Graham and his guides tried in 1883, but they were forced to retreat after they had covered some four miles. Later however they out-flanked this section of the gorge by crossing a pass to the north and following a track used by the local shepherds. In this way they succeeded in reaching a point some sixteen miles up the valley before they were forced to abandon their attempt. In May, 1907, Longstaff, Bruce, Mumm and their three Alpine guides attempted this route again, but the pass was still blocked by winter snow. Rather than waste time waiting for this to clear they explored the country still farther to the north. They found their way up the Bagini glacier which flowed down from the peaks forming the north-western 'rim' of the Nanda Devi basin. From the head of the glacier they crossed a very difficult pass (Bagini Pass), about 20,000 feet high, which they hoped would lead them into the basin. They found instead that it led them into a valley (Rhamani) which curled round to the south and joined the Rishi Ganga at about the point that Graham had reached. After making their famous ascent of Trisul, Longstaff and his guides tried to find a way along the northern side of the upper gorge. They failed, however, and had not sufficient food with them to explore the southern side. But Longstaff was convinced that there was a way and had advised us to concentrate all our efforts on this southern side.

In this way we had an enormous advantage over our predecessors. All the preliminary work had been done, and the problem was fined down to a single line of possibility. Nor were we likely to be tempted from the gorge by the hope of discovering another entrance to the basin. In the first place repeated attempts had been made from every side to find a way in, and secondly it would have taken us many weeks to make our way round to the north, east or south sides of the amphitheatre.

Our first objective, then, was to reach the junction of the Rhamani and Rishi rivers with sufficient food to give us time to find a way through the upper gorge, and, if we were successful, to explore the country beyond. It was not much past the middle of May, and we knew that masses of snow would still be lying on the pass we must cross into the middle section of the Rishi Ganga. But to have waited for this to clear would have left us with too little time before the arrival of the monsoon. We had intended to engage eighteen men in the Dhauli valley to accompany us as far as the Rhamani junction, who would then leave us there and return. These men, as well as providing local knowledge, would be more adept at travelling over difficult country than the Dhotials who earned their livelihood by carrying loads along well-made paths in comparatively civilised country. But ten of the Dhotials were so tremendously keen to come on with us that we agreed and decided only to take eight local men. This was a lucky decision, for after the first day the local men deserted us. This produced a serious crisis, and the situation was only retrieved by the gallant Dhotials who agreed to carry most of the abandoned loads as well as their own. I am sure they had no idea what they were in for, and many times in the days that followed they refused to go any farther. Moreover, our obvious lack of knowledge of the country made it difficult to inspire them with confidence. However, the prospect of receiving the wages of the deserters in addition to their own turned the scale in our favour.

For the best part of two days we fought our way through soft snow up to our knees, our waists and occasionally up to our armpits. Tilman and I, lightly laden, went ahead to flog the trail, while the others struggled along behind with their enormous loads. Twice, after exhausting effort, we reached a saddle which we hoped was the pass, only to find a sheer drop of several thousand feet on the other side. The third time we were lucky.

Once in the valley beyond the pass we descended below the spring snow-line, and life was more comfortable. But the huge scale of the country made route-finding very difficult, and over and over again we reached an impasse and were forced to retreat to try another line. This was terribly disheartening for the Dhotials, but they stuck to it splendidly. As we went, their loads became lighter by the amount of food that was eaten, and by the dumps of tsampa which we left each day for their return journey.

It was a most magnificent place. The southern side of the valley was built up of tier upon tier of gigantic, steeply inclined slabs, which culminated 10,000 feet above the river in a multitude of sharp rock spires set at a rakish angle, while beyond them stood great ice peaks. The northern side, along which we were travelling, was broken up into a series of glens. Some of these contained little alps, each a fairy garden of birch and pine trees, deep grass and drifts of flowers, aflame with colour, each secluded from the savage world outside by precipice and crag.

Unfortunately we had little 'time to stand and stare', for now we had a fresh reason for haste. The Dhotials had to be fed, and each day we spent in getting to the Rhamani junction meant that we would have three days' less food for the work beyond. We were by no means certain of inducing them to go as far. As we advanced, 'the valley grew narrow and narrower still', and its sides became steeper and steeper. The Dhotials liked the look of it not at all. Their protests became stronger and more difficult to overcome. Mercifully the weather held; a single day of mist, rain or snow would have stopped us, and we would have been faced with the laborious task of relaying the loads the rest of the way to our base by ourselves. Actually, in spite of our many mistakes and setbacks and by driving the unfortunate Dhotials through all the daylight hours, we covered the distance in the time allotted – six days from the Dhauli River – and arrived at the Rhamani junction by nightfall on the 28th of May. To emphasise our good fortune, a storm which had been brewing for some time past, broke five minutes before we had found a suitable site for our base camp, and heavy snow fell throughout the night.

The next morning we paid the Dhotials the reward they had so richly deserved, and parted with them on the best of terms. They expressed reluctance at leaving us alone in such a fearsome spot, and we for our part were very sorry to see them go, for they had served us well, and we had become very fond of them.

I have never been able to decide whether, in mountain exploration, it is the prospect of tackling an unsolved problem or the performance of the task itself, or the retrospective enjoyment of successful effort which affords the greatest amount of pleasure. Each provides emotions so widely different; each has its particular limiting factor – restless uncertainly, fear and fatigue, or regret for an enchanting problem that is no more. Certainly no situation has provided me with greater happiness than that in which we found ourselves at the mouth of the upper gorge of the Rishi Ganga. Four miles of canyon, one of the mightiest in the world, separated us from the untrodden country beyond. We had sufficient food to last us for five weeks. Whether we succeeded or failed, nothing but a bad accident could deprive us of some of the best weeks of our lives.

Our base camp was on a narrow strip of shore, covered with birch jungle, on the southern side of the river. The cliffs, undercut by the action of water, provided us with a snug cave. It was a very pleasant spot for temporary residence; though the lack of sunlight, the sense of confinement and the thunder of the river, amplified by echo, might have become irksome had we been forced to stay there long. The immediate prospect was far from encouraging. A few yards beyond the strip of shore the river issued from a perfect box-canyon, whose vertical sides were smooth and almost unbroken. However, a little gully above the camp enabled us to climb beyond the overhanging cliffs to easier ground. Two thousand feet above the river we reached the first of a series of broken terraces which ran along the side of the gorge.

It took us nine days to find a way and to relay our food and equipment through the remaining four miles of the gorge. It was exhilarating work, for until the last moment the issue was in doubt, and each section of our route appeared to rely for its practicability upon the slender chance of a rock fault. Apart from the immense scale of the precipices, the weight of our loads precluded any really difficult climbing, except in short vertical sections where the baggage could be hauled up on the rope. The last mile of the gorge looked so unpromising that we tried to force our way up the river bed itself by zigzagging from side to side. This attempt provided our most exciting adventure, as the force of the current was terrific. It was perhaps fortunate that it did not succeed, for later, as the ice of the glaciers started to melt more rapidly, the river became very swollen, and we would certainly not have succeeded in getting back that way. Defeated there, Pasang and I then tried to find a way along the northern side of the gorge, while Tilman and Angtharkay explored the remainder of the southern side. We failed to make any headway, but the other two discovered the last frail link of the chain, and we entered the Nanda Devi basin with enough food for three weeks.

We set about our task of exploring the basin with a feeling of great exultation. After the confinement of the gorge, the freedom of movement about wide open country was a delicious contrast. The exquisite joy that any mountaineer must experience in treading new ground lent a special charm to everything we did and saw; even our clumsy toil with the plane-table yielded deep satisfaction as a form of self-expression. It was glorious country; gentle moorland grazed by herds of bharal (wild sheep), and in places gay with Alpine flowers; small lakes that reflected the surrounding mountains; deep lateral valleys holding glaciers, enclosed by a hundred magnificent peaks of clean, strong granite or glistening ice and snow. Out of the centre of the basin rose the wonderful spire of Nanda Devi, 13,000 feet above its base, peerless among mountains, always changing and ever more lovely with each new aspect, each fresh effect of colour and cloud.

Three weeks was not long enough to explore the whole of the basin, so we decided to concentrate upon the northern half, and to return to survey the southern half in September when the monsoon should be over. This plan had an additional advantage, as we wished to find another way out, over one of the ranges that formed the 'rim' of the basin; to have done so now would have interfered with our programme for the monsoon season in the Badrinath range to the north. We had many more fine days than bad, and the weather seldom hindered us. We rarely bothered to pitch a tent as we found it so much pleasanter to sleep in the open, even at our higher camps. It seemed somehow to provide a continuity between rest and action, to deepen the sense of harmony between ourselves and our surroundings, which even the thin canvas walls of a tent can destroy. In the lower parts of the basin there was a plentiful supply of juniper wood, and there we had the luxury of huge camp fires. Higher up we had to be more economical though we generally managed to carry some wood up with us so as to avoid using a stove. Though we were concerned mainly with exploring and mapping the country, we were able to combine this with some mountaineering on the higher peaks. We reached three saddles on the western and northern 'rim' of the basin, each more than 20,000 feet high. We climbed a peak of 21,000 feet, and made an unsuccessful attempt to climb another of about 23,000 feet. On each occasion we had wonderful views of the basin itself and over the great ranges outside it.

The monsoon came gradually towards the end of June, and its arrival coincided with the exhaustion of our food supplies. Meagre dumps had been left at various places in the Rishi Ganga. We returned down the gorge in torrential rain; tussles with the swollen waters of the river and of side streams provided the main excitement. The gorge was even more impressive in foul weather than in fair. Particularly I remember one night of heavy storm. I was snugly wedged in a little recess between two boulders listening comfortably to the hiss of the rain outside, and to the thunder which, echoing along miles of crag, maintained an almost unbroken roll. Lightning flickered continuously upon the grim precipices and upon cloud banners entwined about buttress and corrie. The sense of fantasy was heightened by the semi-consciousness of a fitful sleep. At one moment it seemed that I was perched on an eagle's nest above an infernal cauldron of infinite depth, at another that I was floating with the mist, myself a part of an unearthly tempest.

July and August were spent in exploring the range of mountains which forms the watershed between the three main sources of the Ganges. It is a country full of romantic legend. Most of this is rather difficult to follow without a deep study of Hindu mythology, but mountain legend is always fascinating. Our chief object was to link up the three main affluents of the Ganges, the rivers Alaknanda, Bhagirathi and Mandakini, by passes leading across the range direct from one to another.

The determination of the actual source of a great river is often a matter of conjecture, since the choice may lie between streams with various claims to the title. First there is the traditional source, ascribed by ancient history or local legend. An example of this kind is to be found in Ptolemy's remarkable statement that the Nile was born of two small, bottomless wells situated in the 'Mountains of the Moon' – a statement made nearly two thousand years before any recorded visit to the upper reaches of the Nile. Dr Humphreys discovered in Ruwenzori two tiny lakes of immense depth which gave rise to a stream which formed part of the head-waters of the great river. Some Hindu mythology ascribes the source of the Ganges to a beautiful waterfall which forms a tiny tributary of the Alaknanda river. Modern geography demands a more concrete claim: the stream which rises the farthest in a direct line from the river's mouth; the stream whose waters travel the greatest distance; the source that supplies the greatest volume of water.

There is nothing in my experience more fascinating than finding and crossing an unknown pass across a mountain range. The more important the watershed, geographically speaking, the more satisfying is the achievement, but even the crossing of a minor pass can be an exciting experience. To my mind it is mountaineering at its best, for it combines in even measure so many branches of the craft: accurate appreciation of the country as a whole, judgement of difficulty, anticipation of unknown factors, technical skill and disposal of resources. Then there is the eager speculation upon the difficulties of the other side, the thrilling moment when these are revealed and the enchanting descent into the new world beyond. The view, too, from a pass is often much more satisfying than that from a high peak, for, though less comprehensive, it reveals the surroundings more in their true perspective: the mountains are not dwarfed, and there is not the same mass of jumbled detail.

Our first plan was to cross the range from Badrinath to the Gangotri glacier, the largest in the Central Himalayas, to explore its unknown upper reaches and to work our way down to the source of the Bhagirathi at its foot. In 1912, C. F. Meade and his two Alpine guides had reached the watershed from the Bhagat Kharak glacier, but they had not descended to the other side of the range. This was therefore the obvious way of approach. But when we reached its foot we judged that the route to Meade's saddle was in danger of being swept by ice avalanches from the peaks above. In this I think we were mistaken. However, as there seemed to be no alternative route across the main watershed from the upper basin of the Bhagat Kharak, we crossed a series of passes to the north. This led us eventually into the glacier system above the Arwa valley, where we had spent a fortnight after climbing Kamet, three years before. From there we crossed the main watershed and descended a long tributary which joined the Gangotri glacier only two or three miles above its snout. We went on down to the source of the river, and then returned over the range to Badrinath.

These activities occupied us during most of July, and at the beginning of August we started on the second half of our monsoon programme. This proved to be considerably more exacting than the other. Our plan was to cross the range, this time from Badrinath to Kedarnath, another famous Hindu shrine. No route was known to exist across the range between these two places, but among the many legends of the country was a story that many hundred years ago there was no high priest of Kedarnath Temple, and that the high priest of Badrinath used to hold services in the temples of both places on the same day. The tradition of the Lost Pass is a common one in mountains of Central Asia.

From the head of the Satopanth glacier we reached a saddle, 18,400 feet high, on the crest of the main watershed. We arrived there in thick mist and falling snow, but on the following morning there was a brief clearing which revealed a discouraging view of the other side. The glacier forming our saddle descended in a steep ice-fall for about a thousand feet, then it flattened out into a fairly level stretch of ice before heeling over for a final tremendous plunge into the blue depths of a gorge 6,000 feet beneath us. We began to have a healthy respect for our reverend predecessor.

After some search we managed to find a way down through the first ice-fall on to the terrace. But the next part of the problem was much more formidable. The angle of the ice below increased steadily, and it soon appeared that we were on the upper part of a hanging glacier. We worked over to the right and descended for a few hundred feet before we were brought up by an impassable crevasse. Then we tried on the left, and on the following morning succeeded in roping down into a narrow gully between the ice and the containing rock wall of the glacier.

The forest-filled valley below appeared very enticing from the icy steep above, but when eventually we reached it we soon changed our opinion. The undergrowth in the forest was so dense and the sides of the valley so steep that we could rarely cover more than a mile a day. Side streams, too, caused us a lot of trouble, for they were generally at the bottom of deep ravines and always in spate. One of these held us up for two days before we found a place at which we could bridge it. It rained incessantly and with considerable vigour, so that our loads soon became waterlogged. This precipitated a crisis in the food situation. We had already spent longer over the job than we had anticipated, and now our small supply of tsampa had become as sodden as everything else, despite the fact that it was packed in canvas bags. It went bad, and we suffered such acute stomach-ache when we ate it in this condition that we jettisoned the remainder. To add to our troubles, a falling rock hit Pasang on the foot and, I think, broke a small bone, so that he could only just get along without a load, and from then on was no more than a passenger.

The main concern of the Sherpas was their fear of bears. Having no experience of Himalayan bears, Tilman and I were able to take the menace more calmly. Actually we only encountered one of the creatures at close quarters, and he ambled off as soon as we came upon him round a corner. That we did not meet more was probably due to the din the Sherpas made as we went along, designed to scare them away, for their spoor was everywhere. But the bears were a nuisance in that they were our rivals in the difficult matter of feeding.

We owed our salvation, or at least the fact that we did not land ourselves in a considerably worse mess, largely to the woodcraft of the Sherpas. First and foremost they provided us with food by their knowledge of edible plants. Our staple diet was bamboo shoots. This delicacy only occurs in its edible form for a short season of the year, and it was fortunate for us that it was then in season. The shoots were anything up to 8 feet long, but only an inch or so below each notch was edible. However, except where a hungry bear had forestalled us, it was fairly easy to collect a pot-full of the little green cylinders, which, boiled, constituted our evening meal. It was quite a good dish; with a little imagination, not unlike asparagus. But, though the shoots could also be eaten raw as we went along, they were insubstantial food to sustain the long hours of heavy physical labour that our progress demanded. Once we found a fairly large quantity of an edible forest fungus. Boiled, it had the negative taste of over-stewed meat, but it was pleasantly satisfying.

Each night Angtharkay and Kusang displayed considerable skill in constructing a bamboo shelter under which we could light a fire. On the first night this appeared to me an impossible undertaking, but it was not beyond the ingenuity of the Sherpas. By pounding some sodden sticks of dead bamboo with a stone, and holding the pulp over a series of lighted matches it eventually took the flame. This was fed by more dead bamboo until there was a sufficient blaze to dry and ignite logs of wood, and in a couple of hours we would have a good fire. Fortunately we had a large supply of matches that had been safely stowed in a pair of sheep-skin gauntlets. We halted at about five o'clock each evening so as to give ourselves time to construct a platform if necessary, to build the shelter and light a fire under it and to collect bamboo shoots and fuel. After that we would strip off our sodden garments and roast our naked bodies by the fire until we went to sleep.

The work during the day was rather exasperating. An endless succession of rocky, bramble-filled gullies made the going exceedingly slow and laborious, so that frequently it took us an hour to cover twenty-five yards. In some places a cliff or ravine would force us to climb many hundreds of feet. We had to maintain our altitude so as to avoid getting out of bamboo zone. But in other places the going was good, and the day's toil generally yielded about a mile of progress.

Apart from the problem of food, which was worrying, it was not on the whole an unpleasant experience; the days were full of vital interest, the nights warm and comfortable, and the forest was wild and beautiful. Anyway, whatever discomforts and anxieties were our portion, these were amply repaid when at length we reached a tiny hamlet consisting of three houses and some fields. The hamlet provided us with a dry billet in a barn, four pounds of flour, a cucumber, some dry apricots and the happy knowledge that our struggle with the forest was at an end and that a well-worn path would lead on down the valley to the Kedarnath pilgrim route.

In September we went up the Rishi Ganga again. The difference between this and our previous journey was even more striking than the difference between the first and second ascents of a peak, for the size of the valley had laid more emphasis upon the problem of finding a route than upon actual difficulties. We had covered the ground so often in the process of relaying loads and knew so exactly what lay round each corner and how long each section would take, that now it was hard to believe that we had experienced any difficulty on the first occasion. For once I was keeping a day to day diary, and it was interesting to read over the entries made on the first occasion. This time we were only two days getting through the upper part of the gorge from the Rhamani junction, and we took local men with us right through into the Nanda Devi basin before we discharged them and sent them back. By then the monsoon was spent and we had a long spell of fine weather.

The geography of the southern section of the basin was simple and our rough plane-table survey of it did not take long. First we set out to climb a peak (since named Maiktoli), 22,320 feet high, and situated on the southern 'rim' of the basin. We pitched a camp at 20,000 feet, but just before we reached this point Tilman became ill with 'mountain sickness' and had to return with Pasang. The following day, Kusang, Angtharkay and I climbed the peak from which we had a most magnificent view. Even the gigantic southern face of Nanda Devi was dwarfed by the very extent of the panorama. The Badrinath peaks, Kamet, the Kosa group, Dunagiri and the great peaks of the northern part of the Nanda Devi basin, all mountains amongst which we had been travelling for the past four months, served merely as a foil to set off the stupendous ranges lying beyond Milam and across the borders of western Nepal. What a wonderful field of exploration lay there – the heritage of some future generation.

Tilman, for all his strength and mountaineering competence, appeared to be quite unable to acclimatise to high altitudes. It seemed that his ceiling was about twenty or twenty-one thousand feet, and on the several occasions when we went above that altitude he became ill. Though he was supremely fit, he was no better in this respect at the end of the season than he was at the beginning.

One of the chief interests on our second visit to the basin, was to find a route by which Nanda Devi could be climbed. The northern side, which we had seen on our first visit, was utterly impregnable and the great western ridge scarcely less so. This left two alternatives; firstly an ascent of the east peak of the mountain from the south, and thence along the crest of a tremendous curtain of rock, two miles long, to the main peak; secondly a route up the great south ridge of the main peak. The former we ruled out owing to its immense length, and to the appearance of the connecting ridge, which was serrated and probably knife-sharp, and which maintained an altitude of some 24,000 feet throughout. But the south ridge, though formidable, was by no means hopeless. It swept up in a great curve from the floor of the basin at about 17,000 feet to the summit, 25,660 feet. Though steep it maintained a fairly uniform angle and was broad enough to allow the choice of alternative routes up its difficult sections. Its great advantage was that there was no long and complicated approach, and that its base was within easy reach of juniper fuel so that it could be reached by porters without special high-altitude equipment.

With only two tents, one Primus stove and very little kerosene, our boots full of holes and now almost devoid of nails, we were obviously in no position to make a serious attempt to climb Nanda Devi. But we could at least climb some way up the ridge and get a pretty good idea of the nature of the difficulties. We camped near its foot on a little alp covered with grass and snowy edelweiss, and on the following day climbed some three thousand feet up the ridge. We would have had time to go farther, but Tilman again felt the effects of the altitude and began to vomit. But we had gone far enough to see that the ridge was practicable. We had encountered no serious difficulties, and though there might be plenty ahead, the uniform angle of the ridge and its width made it unlikely that any of these would prove to be insurmountable by a thoroughly competent party. It would be no easy task, and in my judgment, not one for a large, heavily organised expedition. But what a prize! There is no finer mountain in the world. Its graceful beauty from every aspect was a source of inspiration and wonder as the Matterhorn had been to Alpine mountaineers in the middle of the nineteenth century. And what finer setting than a hitherto inviolate sanctuary?

Finally we set about the achievement of our long cherished ambition, to find an exit from the basin over some portion of its 'rim'. The southern segment offered us two alternatives. One was a saddle reached by Longstaff and his guides in 1905 in their attempt to reach the basin from the east, the other was a depression on the southern 'rim', which Ruttledge and his guide Emile Rey had attempted in 1932. Both these ways were likely to prove extremely difficult. At first we were inclined to favour 'Longstaff's Col', for he had proved the practicability of its farther side by climbing it from that direction; also it was the lower of the two. But its western aspect looked so formidable that we decided to attempt the Sunderdhunga Col, as the southern saddle was called. We had seen that we could reach it easily from the north, but Ruttledge's description of its southern aspect was far from encouraging: 'Six thousand feet of the steepest rock and ice ... Near the top of the wall, for about a mile and a half, runs a terrace of ice some two hundred feet thick; in fact the lower edge of a hanging glacier. Under the pull of gravity large masses constantly break off from this terrace and thunder down into the valley below, polishing in their fall the successive bands of limestone precipice of which the face is composed. Even supposing the precipice to be climbable, an excellent mountaineer may be acquitted on a charge of lack of enterprise if he declines to spend at least three days and two nights under fire from this artillery. An alternative is the choice of three knife-edge arêtes, excessively steep in their middle and lower sections, on which even the eye of faith, assisted by binoculars, fails to see a single platform large enough to accommodate the most modest of climbing tents.'[1]

I had seen something of this precipice from the summit of Maiktoli which stood immediately above the saddle, and the view confirmed Ruttledge's description. But it is a very different matter to get down such a place carrying a small quantity of food, and to force a way up it with the prospect of being cut off for weeks from further supplies. We should be able to move much more rapidly over the danger areas, and to rope down ice-cliffs and other obstacles that might otherwise have been impossible or very difficult to climb; though of course we should be handicapped in the choice of a route. Anyway, we decided to give it a trial, and leaving a dump of food in the basin against our probable failure, made our way to the saddle.

We reached it one morning and spent the rest of the day trying, in bad visibility, to find a point from which to start the descent. First we tried to reach the rock arêtes or ridges that Ruttledge had referred to as being out of range of the ice avalanches from the hanging-glacier terrace. We could see the top of the first one through the mist on our left, but we could not reach it. Then we tried to the right but were brought up short on the brink of the ice terrace overhanging the ice-polished limestone cliffs that plunged out of sight. It was a fine spectacle. Every now and then enormous masses of ice would break away from the cliffs on which we were standing and crash with a thunderous roar into the cloudy depths below. It is not often that one has the opportunity of watching a display of ice avalanches from so close, and rarer still to see them breaking away from the very cliffs on which one is standing.

Our only alternative now was a narrow ice-fall lying between the terrace and the three arêtes, and of which we could see no more than a few feet of twisted and riven ice. There was nothing to do but to go straight for it and worry our way down by a tedious process of trial and error. However, we had plenty of food with us, and so long as we could keep out of the line of bombardment from the terrace we could afford to take several days over the job if necessary. It was strenuous work trying line after line without success, but as the evening wore on our energy seemed to increase – a phenomenon I have often noticed in mountaineering. A series of slender ice-bridges suspended over space by some conjuring trick of nature would lead us downwards to the brink of an impassable chasm. Then a wearisome retreat by the way we had come, to try a

---

1 *The Times*, 22 August 1932.

new and perhaps equally futile chance. The farther we went the more complex became the precipitous maze we were in.

The next morning we waited until the sun was up before starting again, as our clothes had become sodden in the soft snow of the previous day and an early start would probably have resulted in frost-bite. It was a most lovely dawn. In the right and left foreground were the icy walls, steep-sided and grim, enclosing the head of the Maiktoli Valley; in front, beyond the brink of the ice ledge on which we were camped, and immensely far below, was a lake of vivid colour, at the bottom of which we could see the Sunderdhunga River coiling like a silver water-snake, away into a placid cloud-sea which stretched without a break over the foothills and the plains of India.

The day was one of vivid life and heavy toil. Hour after hour we puzzled and hacked our way down, lowering our loads and ourselves on the rope down an ice cliff, chipping laboriously across the steep face of a tower or along a knife edged crest, sometimes hopeful and sometimes despairing. The ice-fall stood out in high relief from the mountain-side, so that we were fairly well protected from the ice avalanches, which started falling again in the heat of the afternoon. Evening found us working on dry ice 3,000 feet down, and it was becoming increasingly clear that we must soon find a way off the glacier which evidently overhung at its base. Beside us to our right was a prominent rock ridge, which, though lying immediately below the higher line of hanging glaciers, offered us a heaven-sent alternative if only we could reach it. We cut steps to the edge of the glacier and from there we looked down a sixty-foot ice cliff into a steep gully of polished slabs. It was obviously a path for ice avalanches, but it was narrow and once in it we could cross to the farther side in a couple of minutes. By chipping away the ice in a circle we fashioned a bollard from which we roped down the wall into the gully. A short race across it took us to a little ledge under an overhang on the ridge, which offered a convenient and well-protected site for a camp. No sooner had we pitched the tents than there came a mighty roar from above and for fully a minute a cascade of huge ice blocks crashed down the gully sending up a spray of ice dust, while a number of ice splinters landed harmlessly on the tents.

The day, begun with the sight of a dawn beautiful beyond description and crowded with lively experience, closed with us stretched luxuriously on our ledge, perched high up amongst the precipitous glaciers of one of the grandest of mountain cirques. Lightning flickered somewhere in the east; the distant thunder was almost indistinguishable from the growl of avalanches. Mists floated stealthily in and out of corries above us forming and dissolving in an ever-changing pattern. Far to the south a placid sea of cloud still stretched over the foot-hills, and the silvery light of a full moon lent to the scene an appearance of infinite depth. It was our last high camp that year, for by the evening of the following day we had reached the foot of the precipice and we slept that night on grassy meadow-land.

Our exit from the sanctuary by way of the Sunderdhunga Col provided a fitting climax to our season of joyous freedom and high mountain adventure – the best five months that either of us had known. We considered the idea of setting out on some new project, but autumn was already well advanced, boots were ragged and funds running low; the break had to be faced sometime, and the perfection of the whole might be spoilt by some minor or uncompleted venture. So we set our course for home.

The march back added a rich store of memories: a struggle to find an exit from the grim gorge in the upper Sunderdhunga valley, into which we had blundered in a heavy mist; our last encounter with a swollen mountain torrent; an enormous feast of wild raspberries and Himalayan blackberries lower down the valley; the generous hospitality of the first villagers we met, and the sweetness of their honey; the sparkling sunlit mornings as we lay sleepily watching the smoke of some distant wood fire mounting straight up into the clear air above the pine forest; a dawn on the distant ice-clad giants whose presence we had just left.

Our venture had met with more success than we had anticipated, and it was sufficient unto itself. But it had a splendid sequel. Two years later, in 1936, a party composed of four British and four American mountaineers came out to climb Nanda Devi. Unfortunately for me I was engaged elsewhere that summer and could not join them, but Tilman was among the party. They agreed among themselves to have no leader, but Tilman with his recent experience naturally played a prominent part in the business of organisation and in the difficult task of reaching the foot of the mountain. He went out to India some months ahead of the others, and after preliminary training in Sikkim, he made the journey to the Rishi Ganga, and, with the help of seven Sherpas and some local men carried the bulk of the expedition's stores and equipment through the gorge. Then he returned to Ranikhet in time to meet his companions. They had a difficult time getting up the gorge again owing to torrential rain, but at length they succeeded in establishing their base camp at the foot of the south ridge of Nanda Devi. Once on the mountain six of the seven Sherpas they had brought proved useless and remained below. This was no one's fault, because the Everest Expedition that had gone out earlier had taken nearly all the good men. The seventh Sherpa, Pasang Kikuli, had a severe attack of snow blindness at the start and was completely incapacitated. So the entire work of carrying the loads up that formidable ridge, on which five camps were established, fell on the climbers. This in itself made their performance unique in the annals of Himalayan mountaineering. Tilman had seen to it that nothing but the barest essentials were taken.

In a climb of this sort the credit for success is shared by each member of the party. Each step of the way calls for a high standard of mountaineering skill and judgment, and the man who reaches the summit owes his achievement as much to the competence of his companions as to his own. Tilman, in a most astonishing manner, found his high-altitude form. This may have been partly due to the psychological result of his responsible position, though I suspect that sheer strength of will had something to do with it. But whatever the cause it enabled him to share with Odell the exquisite pleasure of reaching the summit of that wonderful peak.

In my opinion the climbing of Nanda Devi is the finest mountaineering achievement ever performed in the Himalayas. It was certainly a brilliant example of a light expedition. More daring and desperate feats have been performed and perhaps greater skill displayed, as for example, in the Bavarian attempt to climb Kangchenjunga; but after all success counts a lot. Incidentally Nanda Devi, being some two hundred feet higher than Kamet, is still the highest mountain ever climbed.

Not content with that, Tilman, Houston and Pasang Kikuli, later crossed Longstaff's Col over the eastern rim of the Nanda Devi basin.

After returning from the Everest Expedition that year, I was invited to accompany Major Osmaston of the Survey of India who had been detailed to make a photographic survey of the Nanda Devi basin. We met the party (except Tilman and Houston) in the lower part of the Rishi Ganga on their way out. Peter Lloyd and Graham Brown were a couple of days ahead of the others, and it was from them that we heard the news of the climb. I had met Lloyd many times in the Alps in the twenties, and it was a delightful reminder of old days to see his tattered figure coming towards me and to ask the familiar question, 'Well, did you get up?' Yes, I felt a pang of envy. But it was grand to hear that Tilman had reached the summit.

And there were a hundred other compensations: to revisit the sanctuary and climb again on the surrounding mountains; a swift attempt on the great peak of Dunagiri; the second crossing of the Bagini Pass; the exploration of the beautiful Rinti Nala and the crossing of a pass at its head; to wander among the forests and glaciers south-west of Trisul enchanted by the exquisite autumn colouring, the brilliant monal pheasants rocketing up into the clear, frosty air of late November, the hillsides of long, golden grass moving in the wind ... Oh! but there is no end to it. No life-time is long enough to absorb the wonder of that country.

11 Everest 1935, 1936, 1938

It soon became apparent that Mount Everest was the most immediate barrier to the enchanting plans that had begun to crowd upon my imagination. Having once taken a share in the attempts to climb the mountain, it was hard to stand aside. Although the problem now appeared one of restricted scope, it was no less fascinating. Any one year might yield the right conditions for an unhampered climb up that last, thousand-foot pyramid of rock upon which so much eager speculation had been lavished. It was like a gambler's throw, in which a year of wide opportunity in untrodden fields was staked against the chance of a week of fine weather and snow-free rock. In those days it was not realised how slender was that chance. In 1933 we thought that we had been unlucky with the weather; but never again was it to treat us so well.

When we returned to England in the winter of 1934, Tilman and I set to work at once upon plans for our next venture. He, too, had abandoned himself to a life of self-indulgent freedom. Our plans were well advanced and a grant of money had been obtained, when, early in 1935, permission came for another attempt upon Mount Everest. This time the permission covered two years, 1935 and 1936. It was considered too late to organise a full-dress attempt upon the mountain in 1935, but the Mount Everest Committee invited me to take out a reconnaissance expedition in 1935 prior to the main attempt in 1936, which was again to be led by Ruttledge.

The objects of the 1935 expedition were to try out new men and to give them some preliminary training in high altitude mountaineering, to examine snow and weather conditions on the mountain during the monsoon and to investigate the possibility of climbing it during that season, to experiment with equipment and food, to obtain further data regarding acclimatisation, to train a nucleus of high-altitude porters, and to carry out a sterio-photogrametric survey of the glaciers lying to the north of Mount Everest and of as much of the surrounding country as possible.

At first Tilman did not like the idea of abandoning our plans – I think the idea of travelling with a large party oppressed him – but after a little discussion he waived his objections. Two things attracted me to the scheme: the prospect of being free for several months to wander among the peaks and valleys surrounding Everest, which had not been possible on the 1933 expedition, secondly the opportunity which it offered to demonstrate the possibility of running an expedition at little cost and the advantages of the light over the heavy organisation.

Besides myself, six others were invited to join the party: Edwin Kempson, who had had very wide experience of Alpine mountaineering both in winter and summer; Charles Warren, a doctor with some Himalayan and much Alpine experience; L.V. Bryant, one of the best-known New Zealand climbers; Edmond Wigram, a medical student who had done a lot of climbing in the Alps; Tilman and Michael Spender. Chief among Spender's wide interests was the introduction of sterio-photogrametric methods of survey into England. He had studied the subject for two years in Switzerland and Germany, had taken part in a long scientific expedition on the Barrier Reef and in two Danish expeditions to Greenland, and had worked for some years at the Geodetic Institute in Copenhagen. I budgeted for a total cost of £1,400 – or £200 per head – including travelling expenses to and from India.

We left Darjeeling in May and travelled up the Tista Valley, crossing from Sikkim into Tibet by way of the Kongra La. Our caravan consisted of thirty-five transport animals – seven of which were carrying Spender's delicate apparatus – fifteen Sherpas, Karma Paul the interpreter, and ourselves. From the Kongra La, instead of joining the old route by way of Kampa Dzong, Tengkye and Shekar, we kept south, along the foot of the main range to Sar. We were in no great hurry and had decided to devote a little of our time to the exploration of the Nyonno Ri range which lies to the north of the great Arun Gorge. For this we made our base at Sar where we were most hospitably received by the Dzongpen. We did not reach Rongbuk until about the 6th of July.

While on the march we lived largely off the country. Mutton was easy to procure, though at first the sheep were rather thin. We cooked the meat in pressure cookers and the result was a great success. Where transport presents no problem and fuel is scarce these gadgets are well worth their weight; they overcome in twenty minutes the resistance of even the toughest meat. We could generally get potatoes and onions, though until later in the summer other vegetables were not obtainable. However we had brought out dried vegetables from England, and these provided us with quite a good substitute. Eggs were always plentiful in the villages, and though many of them were rather stale we consumed enormous quantities. Our record was 140 in a single day between four of us, and many times our combined party of seven put away more than a hundred. Tilman could bake an excellent loaf with the local flour and the dried yeast which we had brought as a supply of Vitamin B. Excellent butter made from yak's milk was always available. So food presented no problem while we were in inhabited parts of Tibet; appetites were healthy and no one was inclined to be fussy about lack of variety.

Food for life at high altitudes was a more serious question. I had developed an exaggerated antipathy towards tinned food, largely as a result of two expeditions on which it had been used almost exclusively. There is no doubt that food embalmed in tins, however cunningly, lacks some essential quality, and when one is fed on nothing else one very soon becomes heartily sick of even the most elaborate delicacies. I believe that to be one of the reasons why we had found it so hard to eat enough at high altitudes in 1933. That year I had been given the job of running the commissariat. At first everyone was loud in praise of the fare, and I was always having to emerge from the mess tent to open another tin of this or that to satisfy rapacious appetites. Long before we had reached the Base Camp this enthusiasm had died down; before the expedition had run half its course the complaints against the food were bitter and endless, and to these I had lent strong support. Actually the quality of the tinned food could hardly have been improved; we had every conceivable variety – half a dozen different kinds of breakfast food, bacon, ham, beef, mutton, chicken, lobster, crab, salmon, herrings, cod-roes, asparagus, caviar, foie gras, smoked salmon, sausages, many kinds of cheese, a dozen varieties of biscuit, jam, marmalade, honey, treacle, tinned and preserved fruit galore, plain, nut milk and fancy chocolates, sweets, toffee, tinned peas, beans, spaghetti – I cannot think of anything that we did not have. And it was supplied in such quantities that, rather than transport what was left all the way back from the Base Camp we threw away scores of cases of provisions. And yet, one and all, we agreed that the food was wholly unsatisfying. It seemed to me that the conclusion was obvious – and it was amply confirmed by my subsequent experience. But it was by no means universally accepted, and the majority were inclined to blame the firms that had supplied the food.

In 1935 I went rather too far the other way: it was bad policy to force people who were quite unused to rough food to make such a sudden and complete break with their normal diet. Taken in moderation, tinned food undoubtedly has its uses, particularly when – as on Mount Everest – transport presents no particular problem. But it should be used to supplement fresh, salted or dried food, rather than as the main diet. A perfectly simple compromise is possible on an Everest expedition. If, for example, the party were kept on a diet of fresh food supplemented with untinned ham, bacon and cheese until it reached a point well beyond the Base Camp, such things as tinned brisket of beef and chicken's breasts would then provide a most welcome change of which people would not tire, at least during the critical weeks of the actual climb. I would dispense altogether with caviar, lobster, crab and the like. These are no doubt very delicious when eaten in suitable surroundings, properly served, washed down with the appropriate wine and followed by a comfortable cigar; but I find that they lose all their charm when eaten as a mangled mess out of a battered tin on which someone has probably cut his finger.

I had made a fairly close study of this problem of diet during the previous winter. Dr Zilva of the Lister Institute had very kindly devoted a good deal of time to helping me to devise a suitable diet. I induced each man to keep a simple chart of his daily food consumption so that one could see at a glance how far he was conforming to the balance and quantity prescribed. For the first few weeks, even at the quite moderate altitudes of the East Rongbuk glacier, no one succeeded in consuming more than 1,500 calories a day. This was very far short of the 4,000 calories advocated by Zilva – I doubt if anyone ever approached this figure while we were on the glaciers. However I think the charts succeeded in their main purpose which was to make people watch their feeding and force themselves to eat when otherwise they might have been too lazy or preoccupied to do so. Certainly the party displayed a very satisfactory output of energy throughout the expedition.

We left Karma Paul to amuse himself at Rongbuk and to organise foraging parties to collect a stock of eggs, butter and sheep from the north, and while Spender was busy with his work the rest of us went up the East Rongbuk glacier. Conditions were much more pleasant than when I had been there before, and having had some previous training on the Nyonno Ri mountains we climbed from Rongbuk to Camp III in three days.

About three hundred yards above Camp III we found the body of Maurice Wilson, who had attempted to climb Mount Everest alone the previous year and about whom nothing more had been heard. From a diary which we found on his body and from subsequent enquiries we were able to piece together his curious story. He was a man of about thirty-seven and had served in France during the last war. He had developed a theory that if a man were to go without food for three weeks he would reach a stage of semi-consciousness on the borderland of life and death, when his physical mind would establish direct communication with his soul. When he emerged from this state he would be cleansed of all bodily and spiritual ills; he would be as a new-born child but with the benefit of the experience of his previous life, and with greatly increased physical and spiritual strength. Wilson had fanatical faith in his theory. He believed moreover that he had seen a vision in which he had received divine instruction to preach the doctrine to mankind. Somehow the word 'Everest' had featured in the vision, and he thought that it was intended to indicate the means by which he could achieve his purpose. Obviously if he succeeded in reaching the summit of Mount Everest single-handed, the feat would cause no small stir, and his theory would receive wide publicity.

He knew nothing whatever about mountaineering. At the time, however, the Houston Everest Flight was receiving considerable press publicity. Presumably this gave him the idea that if he were to fly a plane as high as he could and crash it on the side of the mountain he would be able to climb the rest of the way to the summit and return on foot. So with this object in view he learnt to fly, bought a small aeroplane and set out for India. At Cairo he was stopped and turned back by the authorities. But eventually he reached

Purnea in India where his machine was confiscated. He went to Darjeeling where he stayed for four months, training himself and making secret preparations for his journey to Mount Everest. He got in touch with some of the Sherpas who had been with us the year before and they agreed to smuggle him through Sikkim and into Tibet. He then covered up his tracks by paying for his room at the hotel six months in advance so that he could keep it locked with his things inside, and gave it out that he had been invited by a friend to go on a tiger shoot. It was some time before the authorities discovered that he was missing.

In the meantime, by wearing a disguise and travelling at night he had succeeded in passing through Sikkim and into Tibet. There he travelled more openly, but with practically no baggage and by avoiding the big places he and his three Sherpa companions attracted no attention. When they arrived at Rongbuk he told the abbot of the monastery that he was a member of the 1933 expedition and induced him to hand over a few small items of equipment that we had left there. He had evidently made a good impression upon the old man, who, when we visited the monastery in 1935 talked to us a great deal about him. He left the Sherpas at Rongbuk and started up the glacier alone with the complete conviction that he would reach the summit in three or four days. He had with him a small shaving mirror with which he proposed to heliograph to those at Rongbuk from the summit, so as to provide proof that he had actually reached it. He was used to starving himself and intended to live on a small quantity of rice water. It was early in April and he encountered the usual spring gales on the East Rongbuk glacier. He appears to have reached a point somewhere about Camp II before he was forced to retreat, exhausted.

After a fortnight's rest he set out again, this time with the Sherpas. They reached Camp III and the Sherpas showed him a dump of food which we had left about half a mile beyond, and which contained all kinds of luxuries such as chocolate, Ovaltine, sardines, baked beans and biscuits, with which he was delighted. He left the Sherpas at Camp III and went on alone. He had evidently expected to find intact the steps which we had cut in the slopes below the North Col, and he was bitterly disappointed to find nothing but bare windswept ice and snow. Though he had an ice-axe, he did not know how to use it and could make little headway up the slopes. He camped alone on the rocks near the dump and set out day after day to renew his fruitless attempts to reach the col. Though he had plenty of food, he was gradually weakened by the severe conditions. This was clear from the entries in his diary, which became shorter and less coherent towards the end. But he would not give up and still clung to his faith in divine inspiration. The last entry was on 31 May, 1934. He died in his sleep, lying in his small tent. This had been smashed by storms, and all the fragments, except the guy-lines which were attached to boulders, had been swept away.

The Sherpas said they had waited a month for him at Camp III. This is clearly untrue for they would certainly have visited the food-dump from time to time and would have found the body. We had two of the men with us in 1935, but one had been attached to Spender's party and the other had been sent down to fetch some stuff from Camp II on the day that we found the body. We buried it in a crevasse.

It had been generally supposed that it would be useless to attempt Mount Everest during the monsoon. But there was little practical evidence to support this belief. Before 1933 complete faith had been placed in the advent of a fine spell during the few weeks immediately preceding the arrival of the monsoon, and the exploration of further possibilities was thought unnecessary. This faith however was somewhat shaken by our experience in 1933. Some people expressed the opinion that the monsoon season would offer a better chance of success than the late spring. These ideas were, I believe, based largely upon experiences in the Karakoram and those of the Bavarians on Kanchenjunga in 1929 and 1931. One of our jobs in 1935 was to investigate the matter.

There were two factors: the risk of avalanches on the slopes below the North Col and the condition of the snow on the upper part of the mountain. Regarding the former we had little evidence, and of the latter we had none. In 1922 a disastrous avalanche had overtaken the party attempting to reach the North Col in June. In June 1933, Crawford and Brocklebank had reported that the slopes were dangerous (Crawford had himself been involved in the 1922 avalanche). On the other hand in 1921 the North Col had been reached safely in September; but with all respect to Mallory's skill as a mountaineer this may have been due more to luck than to good judgment. In the Alps the study of snow conditions has been reduced to an exact science, but we are still very ignorant about Himalayan snow. It was believed that the dangerous conditions prevailing on the North Col in June were caused by the wind blowing the newly fallen snow from the west side of the col and depositing it at a low temperature on the eastern slopes, thus producing what is known as 'wind-slab', one of the most vicious of all conditions of mountain snow. But it seemed reasonable to suppose that these causes might not be operative later in the summer.

When we arrived there towards the middle of July, 1935, we examined the slopes below the North Col with extreme care. Kempson had had wide experience of winter mountaineering, in the Alps, and by now I had seen a good deal of Himalayan snow conditions. We could find nothing wrong with the slopes. With ten Sherpas it took us three easy days to establish a camp on the crest of the col. On the first of these days we had a slight contretemps with the Sherpas. They had evidently been shaken by the discovery of Wilson's body and regarded it as a bad omen. So half way up to the col they refused to go any further. However a heart to heart talk in camp that evening set the matter right and after that we had no more trouble.

Warren, Kempson and I and eight Sherpas occupied the camp on the North Col with enough food to last us for at least sixteen days. We intended to push on up the mountain at least to 27,000 feet to see what the conditions were like up there. Actually we were in a position to make a strong attempt on the summit if these had proved to be good. The whole of the north face was plastered with snow and very little rock was showing. At lower levels the heat of the sun and the cold nights would have combined in a short time to pack the snow and provide a splendid surface up which one could climb without difficulty. The weather for the past fortnight had been very fine. But it was thought that practically no melting takes place above about 26,000 feet, and that except where it is subjected to great pressure the snow remains powdery. It was our object to prove or disprove this theory. We had seen in 1933 how difficult it was to climb those upper slabs with even a slight covering of powder snow; a blanket of this substance covering the whole face to a depth of perhaps eight or ten feet would present an impassable obstacle. If on the other hand the snow were to consolidate in the normal manner, the mountain would be a great deal easier to climb during the monsoon than at any other season.

The weather deteriorated and we waited for four days on the North Col. One day we climbed some way up the north-east spur for exercise, but it seemed unwise to establish the higher camps until the weather improved. At length we decided to retreat to Camp III and to wait until the bad spell had spent itself. We had the whole summer before us and it would be best to preserve our condition. So we left tents and stores on the col and started down. We were disconcerted to find that 200 feet below the crest of the col the entire surface of the slope had slipped away for a distance of a quarter of a mile and to a depth of six feet. The resulting avalanche had crashed down on to the glacier below. The snow that we had examined with such care, about which we had been quite satisfied and over which we had been blithely working for three days had been completely rotten.

The term 'justifiable risk' is used a good deal by mountaineers, particularly when discussing fatal accidents. It is meant to imply that degree of predictable danger to which, according to the general body of mountaineering opinion, a party is entitled to expose itself. But obviously each man must determine his own standard, and there must be a tacit agreement on the matter among the members of any climbing party. Opinions vary widely according to temperament, between those who regard mountaineering as an exact science whose rules must never be broken and the 'death or glory' attitude of the climbers of the north face of the Eiger. Particular circumstances, too, will exercise an influence; for example, one is likely to accept a narrower margin of safety on the final pyramid of Mount Everest than during a holiday climb on the Matterhorn. There can be few mountaineers who have not at some time run the gauntlet of some obvious danger for the achievement of a particularly enticing goal. Most of us have done it more times than we can remember. But in making a route up a great Himalayan peak the position is altogether different. Each section of the route has to be traversed not once but many times, and generally by slow, heavily laden men, many of whom are not trained to act correctly in a moment of crisis. One may pass beneath a tottering sérac nine times, to be buried by it on the tenth. A competent mountaineer involved in a snow avalanche can often save himself by going through the motions of swimming on his back, but even without an awkward load strapped to his back a Sherpa porter is unlikely to have the presence of mind to do this. I am sure that no one could have escaped from an avalanche such as that which broke away below us while we were lying peacefully on the North Col.

Two things were clear: first that the slopes below the North Col were not safe, and secondly that we were not competent to judge snow conditions at that particular time and place. I am quite satisfied that the avalanche was not caused by 'wind-slab'. The eastern slopes of the North Col form a semi-circular basin, unusually well protected from the wind. The mid-day sun in July, only six degrees from the vertical, beats down with tremendous force upon the stagnant air of this blinding-white cauldron. On occasion I have suffered more from the heat on the snow slopes of the North Col, at 22,500 feet, than I ever have on the plains of India. At night it barely freezes. As a result of these conditions, unusual even in the Everest region, the main body of the snow rots to a great depth, while the surface maintains the appearance of ordinary solid névé. This at any rate was my explanation of the great avalanche and if it were correct it was clear that the slopes would remain dangerous throughout the summer. We decided therefore to leave the North Col alone, for a while at least, and to study snow conditions on other mountains in the vicinity. On these peaks we generally found fairly good snow, presumably owing to better ventilation and lower night temperatures. But on the three occasions when we climbed above feet conditions changed abruptly at about that altitude and we found ourselves struggling in a bottomless morass of soft snow. By the end of August, though the snow on the ridges was still good, the upper glaciers were difficult to negotiate. The ice below the surface was rotten and honeycombed with reservoirs of water.

The more serious work on Mount Everest having been suspended, we devoted ourselves with delicious abandon to climbing peaks, first around the East Rongbuk glacier, then above the main and West Rongbuk glaciers on the Nepal-Tibet watershed, and later we worked our way to the east to the lovely mountains above the Kharta valley. In the meantime Spender worked with tireless energy at his survey and covered a great area of country. We climbed twenty-six peaks, all of them more than 20,000 feet high, many easy, some difficult – it was a glorious orgy. Of these Tilman and Wigram climbed no fewer than seventeen.

But Tilman, in spite of this performance, and although he appeared to have raised his ceiling to perhaps 23,000 feet, was still unable to acclimatise himself to these altitudes. Even to reach 23,000 feet appeared to require an enormous effort; and, as late as the end of August after he had already climbed many high peaks, he became very ill, while he, Wigram and I were making an abortive attempt to climb the North Peak. Bryant took even less kindly to high altitudes. His troubles had begun before we had crossed into Tibet and he became ill again in the Nyonno Ri range. When we reached the East Rongbuk glacier he vomited almost continuously for ten days and could not keep down any solid food. In August he recovered a bit and was able to climb peaks of nearly 22,000 feet. I climbed alone with him for a fortnight above the West Rongbuk glacier: I have never had a more delightful companion – cheerful, humorous and supremely competent. It seemed a tragedy that two men so eminently suited, both temperamentally and technically, to take part in the attempt on Mount Everest, should be debarred from doing so by a slight physical peculiarity. Though they were both bitterly disappointed, neither of them questioned my inevitable decision. Tilman's attitude may be judged from the fact that, later, he subscribed towards the funds of the 1936 expedition in which he was to take no part, although he had other plans of his own. Nothing could have been a more fitting reward than his remarkable achievement on Nanda Devi.

I would have liked to continue with our travels throughout the winter, for besides the intense interest of exploring those ranges there were many questions regarding conditions at high altitudes during the winter months that required (and still require) an answer. But I had promised to return to England to assist in the preparations for the expedition of the following year.

The 1936 Everest Expedition was a bitter disappointment. Camp IV was established on the North Col early in May, but continuous bad weather compelled us to retreat. After a brief rest at Camp I we returned to Camp III. But we were soon forced to realise the almost unbelievable fact that the monsoon was already established. We waited there for some days as though hoping for a miracle. From sheer exasperation Wyn Harris and I set out to climb the North Col. It was a ridiculous thing to do, but we were feeling rather desperate. A strong wind had been blowing from the west for many days, sweeping great masses of newly fallen snow over the col and depositing it on the eastern slopes; there had been heavy night frosts; ideal conditions for the formation of 'wind-slab'. We climbed quickly over a lovely hard surface in which one sharp kick produced a perfect foot-hold. About half way up to the col we started traversing to the left. Wyn anchored himself firmly on the lower lip of a crevasse while I led across the slope. I had almost reached the end of the rope and Wyn was starting to follow when there was a rending sound – 'rrumph' – a short way above me, and the whole surface of the slope I was standing on started to move slowly down like a descending escalator towards the brink of an ice cliff a couple of hundred feet below. Wyn managed to dive back into his crevasse and to drive his ice-axe in to the head and twist the rope round it. I collapsed on to my back and started to perform the frog-like motions prescribed by the text-books, though this was obviously not going to help me much if I were carried over the ice cliff. My principal feeling was one of irritation at having been caught in such an obvious trap. Before it had travelled far the slope began to break up into great blocks. Presently the rope became taut between my waist and Wyn's axe, my swimming was arrested, the blocks began to pile up on top of me and it seemed clear that either I or the rope must break in two. However, before either of these events occurred the avalanche miraculously stopped. It is probable that Wyn's quick action had saved the situation. The slope was not particularly steep, the avalanche had not developed much momentum and the fact that it stopped at that critical instant suggests that the modicum of support afforded by my body held up by the rope was sufficient to arrest it. I was completely winded by the pressure of the rope round my waist, but otherwise unhurt. Having extricated ourselves we went slowly down to the glacier where we met Ruttledge hurrying up with a rescue party. He and the others had watched our inglorious performance through field-glasses from Camp III and were not unnaturally alarmed by it.

Except for a tentative examination of the western approaches of the North Col from the main Rongbuk glacier there were no further activities on Mount Everest that year.

There was another attempt in 1938. This time it was decided to send out a smaller expedition, and Tilman was placed in charge. He decided on a party of seven climbers and budgeted for a total expenditure of £3,000. The weather in 1938 was almost an exact replica of that experienced in 1936. By flogging a way through deep snow in the upper Lachen valley we reached Rongbuk earlier than ever before. With a team of thirty Sherpas, we laid the usual dumps up the glacier and established Camp III about the 20th of April. The usual spring gales were blowing on the mountain and there was every sign that we had struck a 'normal season'. It was clear that until the gales abated there was nothing to be gained by pushing on up the mountain, and everything might be lost. We supposed that our chance would come during the last ten days of May and the first half of June. On this assumption we had a clear month to spare and it was agreed that this could best be employed by improving the health of the party. Every member was suffering in a greater or less degree from the usual coughs, colds and influenza. It was decided therefore to leave the bulk of the stores and equipment at Camp III, and, travelling as lightly as possible, to cross the 22,000-foot Lhakpa La. Then after spending a week or ten days of rest and fat living in the pine forests of the lower Kharta Valley we would return to Camp III about the middle of May. We had already been up the North Col slopes and had found the route to be comparatively easy. Our acclimatisation would last and we would have the enormous advantage of being thoroughly fit and free from bronchial troubles which had always been a great bugbear on Everest. Physiologically the decision was thoroughly sound and the plan is well worth the consideration of future parties. We started to put it into effect on 26 April.

L'homme propose, Dieu dispose. Monsoon conditions were established on the mountain by 3 May, and from that date the north face presented the appearance of a sugar cake that had been our despair in previous years. To avoid any further adventures with 'wind-slab' avalanches we retreated to Camp I and from there made our way up the main Rongbuk glacier to the western foot of the North Col. We succeeded in reaching the col from that side, and in establishing Camp IV, but I doubt if the performance was justifiable in the existing conditions. The narrow combe which led to the foot of the slopes was menaced by avalanches both from the south-east face of the North Peak and from the north face of Everest; a big avalanche had come down from the latter a few days earlier and we camped amidst its debris. The slope leading to the col was of tremendous length, continuously exposed and very steep. Except upon the upper 300 feet, a layer of snow about three feet deep had recently slipped away, leaving a surface of bare ice. Though this was solid enough, it provided no safe anchorage throughout its entire length, and a slip by one of the heavily laden porters would have been almost impossible to hold. To my mind there is no question about the wisdom of Mallory's judgement in rejecting the route.

But we were lucky. The whole expedition reached the col without mishap. It was the beginning of June; we had sufficient resources in men and material on the North Col for three or even four leisurely attempts upon the summit; the weather was pleasant; we were all very fit. The only fly in the ointment – a pretty sizeable one – was the deep blanket of snow that covered the whole north face from head to foot. Still, there was a slender chance that the scientific prophets were wrong and that soon we would find ourselves kicking steps up the dreaded Black Band in good firm snow. We became quite optimistic.

Tilman, Lloyd, Smythe and I went up the north-east spur with about fifteen Sherpas and established Camp V at our old site, at 25,700 feet. Lloyd used oxygen. It was the first time that the much discussed apparatus had received a practical trial on the mountain since 1924. The going, though harder than it had been in 1933, was not altogether discouraging. Smythe and I remained at Camp V with eight Sherpas, while Tilman and Lloyd returned to the North Col with the rest. We stayed for two nights at Camp V owing to a strong wind on the intervening day, and started on up the spur on the second morning.

Above Camp V the conditions rapidly deteriorated. Everything was buried deep in soft, feathery snow into which we sank up to our hips. Little buttresses fifteen feet high, that before had caused us scarcely a moment's hesitation now presented us with really difficult climbing. On one of these I became badly stuck and wasted a lot of time until Smythe found an alternative route. It was terribly heavy work, even for the porters who had merely to follow in the trail we had flogged. It was 4.30 p.m. before we reached the foot of the Yellow Band a little way beyond and directly above the head of the north-east spur. It was high time to stop, so as to give the Sherpas time to return to Camp V before dark. Two of them had collapsed a little lower down, and while a platform was being built and our tent pitched two others went down to retrieve their loads. The only concern of the Sherpas was to put our camp high enough to give us a chance of reaching the summit. Frequently they asked us if we had gone far enough. But they were all terribly tired. Even had there been time it would have been quite impossible to pitch a tent anywhere on the Yellow Band.

The height of our camp was about 27,200 feet. It was considerably more comfortable than our Camp VI of 1933 had been, and we slept very well. We were free from throat troubles and had deteriorated physically very little compared with our state five years before. Nevertheless we experienced the well-remembered feeling of helplessness, of being only half alive.

We started the next morning before the sun had reached the camp and plunged immediately into a morass of powder snow below the Yellow Band. Soon our extremities had lost all feeling and we returned to the camp and waited until about nine o'clock when there was more warmth in the sun. Then we set off again with the intention of reaching the crest of the north-east ridge, now only 300 feet above us. A direct line was impossible and we climbed diagonally up to the right. The conditions were absolutely hopeless. There was no sign that the snow had consolidated anywhere. An hour's exhausting toil yielded no more than half a rope's length of progress. Nor was this by any means the most potent factor. Had it been simply a matter of ploughing a way through many feet of soft snow, we might somehow have contrived to get a large party up to Camp VI and, by working continuously in a series of shifts for a week, to force a way along to the top. But in those conditions the smallest movement even on the moderately steep rocks of the Yellow Band was excessively dangerous. It was the knowledge that we were climbing beyond all reasonable limits of safety that induced us to abandon the attempt. Even if we had been able to reach the Black Band, to have climbed its difficult rocks would have been as impossible as it would have been suicidal to attempt it. We were now completely convinced that when it is covered by its blanket of monsoon snow, the upper part of the north face of Mount Everest is absolutely unclimbable. From where we were, near the top of the north-east shoulder, the peak looked very impressive and very frightening.

We returned to Camp V where we met Tilman and Lloyd on their way up for the second attempt. We were anxious that they should continue, so as to corroborate our evidence. They could make no more impression on the rocks of the Yellow Band than we had. Lloyd used oxygen all the way from the North

Col to Camp VI and on their short climb above. He said that he derived a good deal of benefit from it, but Tilman was going well and the difference in their performance was not sufficient to be in any way conclusive.

We had intended to descend from the North Col by the western route, but Ondi became ill and Pasang, who had also accompanied us to Camp VI, had become paralysed all down his right side. It was obviously impossible to get these two men down by the way we had come, so we were forced to risk a descent by the eastern slopes. Poor Pasang had to be lowered all the way on the end of a rope, or dragged along the horizontal traverses like a sack of coals. He could neither speak nor move. Some months later he recovered his speech and could hobble about, but the paralysis unfortunately proved to be a permanent affliction.

One day Mount Everest will be climbed; of that there can be little doubt. It may be achieved at the next attempt; there may be another twenty failures. From the evidence we have at present it would appear that success will demand a combination of circumstances which in the very nature of the conflicting components is not common. In the spring, northerly gales render climbing on the north face practically impossible. These gales are neutralised by the advent of the monsoon currents blowing up from the south. The monsoon however deposits powder snow upon the mountain which again renders the steep upper rocks unclimbable. This snow neither melts nor consolidates, and the only agent which clears it away is the north wind. We have always relied upon a short period of quiet weather immediately preceding the monsoon precipitation. But was it reasonable to assume that such a period is the rule? Our experiences in 1933, 1936 and 1938 would certainly suggest that this is not the case. From an examination of photographs taken during the attempts in 1922 I should say that there was far too much snow on the rocks to have permitted a crossing of the Black Band. Only once, then, in June, 1924, has the upper part of the mountain been found in a condition which offered any real chance of success. Unfortunately the climbers were then already too exhausted to take full advantage of their opportunity. Nevertheless I believe that the pre-monsoon period is the only possible one.

But there are those who hold that the winter (November, I think, is the month advocated) is the right time for attempting to climb Mount Everest. As far as I know this view is not shared by anyone who has climbed high on the mountain. The risk of frost-bite even in June is deadly at that great elevation. The noon altitude of the sun over Mount Everest in November is only about forty-three degrees, which means that the rocks on the north face would be in shadow for all but a very few hours of the day, and it is doubtful if sunlight ever reaches the upper part of the Great Couloir during the winter months. The cold would be intense, far worse than anything that we have hitherto experienced up there; the slightest breeze would inevitably result in severe frost-bite.

All the Sherpas with whom I have discussed the matter are agreed that October and November are months of heavy wind during which they experience great hardship in crossing the passes from Nepal to Tibet. However it would be foolish to dogmatise. The mountain should certainly be attempted in the winter by those who believe in the plan, so long as they have a clear understanding of what they are up against and are determined not to allow their disappointment to get the better of their sense of proportion, which is very liable to happen on Everest. Actually we had intended in 1938 to stay there throughout the winter, so as to examine the conditions. But we evolved another plan which unfortunately did not materialise.

I believe that the best way of tackling the job would be to obtain from the Tibetan Government permission covering five consecutive years in which to run a series of small expeditions. Each should include four mountaineers with wide Alpine as well as high-altitude experience; its main object would be to attempt the mountain in the usual pre-monsoon period, but it would also have secondary scientific objectives, among which physiological research might well take pride of place. Such a series would not be expensive to run, as the bulk of the equipment could be dumped at Rongbuk on the first occasion for use of the subsequent expeditions. It would not be necessary to have the same party each time, though it would be as well for one man to remain in charge during the whole period, so as to co-ordinate the scientific work and to accumulate first-hand experience of conditions on the mountain. It is probable that at least one of the five consecutive years would provide the fairly late monsoon which appears to be a necessary condition for that period of calm weather and snow free rocks experienced in 1924. Four thoroughly competent climbers with proved ability to go high would be ample to take full advantage of such an opportunity. In addition, with careful organisation, an ambitious programme of valuable scientific work could be undertaken. Winter conditions on the mountain could also be investigated.

With regard to the tactical plan to be adopted on the upper part of the mountain, I am convinced that it is a mistake to keep men for too long on and above the North Col. I believe that in 1933 too much emphasis was laid upon acclimatisation. Admittedly many of us were forced to live above the North Col for longer than had been intended; but the whole policy had been one of slow advance. When we returned to the Base Camp we were terribly emaciated. It was a standing joke that we looked like a collection of famine-stricken refugees. In 1938 we were far fitter both while on the mountain and when we returned. For this reason alone I should be opposed to attempting to establish a third camp above the North Col, and there are many other strong objections. It has been amply shown that the establishment of two high camps can be a simple and rapid operation. No doubt a better site could be found for Camp VI than that used in 1933. I believe that under good conditions the porters could carry from Camp V to the foot of the First Step where Wager and Wyn Harris found a good place for a camp. From there to the Couloir is a very short distance. If in good conditions the climbers could not reach the summit from such a camp it is doubtful if they could ever do so.

The wide interest which the Mount Everest Expeditions aroused among the non-climbing public, the great confidence of each successive expedition in its ability to reach the summit and the fact that several parties have been forced to turn back when success was apparently almost within their grasp, have caused a good deal of perplexity and perhaps have made the repeated failures seem rather foolish. To see the matter in its true perspective it is well to remember that in spite of all the attempts that have been made during the last sixty years upon the giants of the Himalayas by climbers of many nations, not a single mountain of 26,000 feet has yet been climbed. Most prominent among these attempts were the repeated, desperate and sometimes disastrous German efforts to climb Kangchenjunga and Nanga Parbat. There were no fewer than five German expeditions to Nanga Parbat in the nineteen-thirties. On the first of these in 1932, the climbers appeared to come so close to their goal that when I discussed the prospects of the second attempt in 1934 with the leader he appeared to regard its success almost as a foregone conclusion, in much the same way as we had assessed our chances on Everest in 1933. It would seem almost as though there were a cordon drawn round the upper part of these great peaks beyond which no man may go. The truth of course lies in the fact that, at altitudes of 25,000 feet and beyond, the effects of low atmospheric pressure upon the human body are so severe that really difficult mountaineering is impossible and the consequences even of a mild storm may be deadly, that nothing but the most perfect conditions of weather and snow offers the slightest chance of success, and that on the last lap of the climb no party is in a position to choose its day.

In this connection it is not irrelevant to reflect upon the countless attempts to climb the Matterhorn before the summit was finally reached in 1865 – attempts by the best mountaineers, amateur and professional, of the day. Compare the two problems. The Matterhorn could be attempted on any day in each successive summer; attempts upon the summit of Everest have been launched on, at the most, two days of a few arbitrarily chosen years. The upper part of the Matterhorn could be reached in a single day from a comfortable hotel in the valley so that the same party could set out day after day to attempt the climb, gaining personal knowledge and experience of the problem with each successive effort; no man has yet succeeded in making more than one attempt upon the summit of Everest in any one year – few have tried more than once in a lifetime. Climbing on the Matterhorn is an experience of supreme mental and physical enjoyment; life on the upper part of Everest is a heavy, lifeless struggle. The actual climbing on the Matterhorn is no more difficult than that on the last 2,000 feet of Everest. Today the Matterhorn is regarded as an easy climb for a competent party in reasonably good conditions. And yet year after year it resisted all the efforts of the pioneers to climb it; many proclaimed it to be unclimbable. It was certainly not that these men were incompetent. The reason must be sought in that peculiar, intangible difficulty presented by the first ascent of any peak, to which reference has been made in an earlier chapter. How much more should we expect this factor to play a part in the defence of the great peaks of the Himalayas!

No, it is not remarkable that Everest did not yield to the first few attempts; indeed, it would have been very surprising and not a little sad if it had, for that is not the way of great mountains. Perhaps we had become a little arrogant with our fine new technique of ice-claw and rubber slipper, our age of easy mechanical conquest. We had forgotten that the mountain still holds the master card, that it will grant success only in its own good time. Why else does mountaineering retain its deep fascination?

It is possible, even probable, that in time men will look back with wonder at our feeble efforts, unable to account for our repeated failure, while they themselves are grappling with far more formidable problems. If we are still alive we shall no doubt mumble fiercely in our grey beards in a desperate effort to justify our weakness. But if we are wise we shall reflect with deep gratitude that we seized our mountaineering heritage, and will take pleasure in watching younger men enjoy theirs.

12   Shaksgam – 1

The great mountain ranges of Central Asia merge so imperceptibly into one another that it is difficult for the ordinary traveller not to regard them as one stupendous mass extending from the middle basin of the Yangtse-kiang in the east to the Hindu Kush and even beyond into Persia – a continuous stretch of 3,000 miles. Though possibly the conception is geologically unsound, I have always thought of the division of this mountain mass into separate ranges as analogous, on a vastly greater scale, to the groups into which the Alps are divided; each has its peculiar structure and each its climatic conditions, which provide the whole with such an infinite variety of scene and environment.

But in the case of the mountains of Central Asia the appreciation of this division is rendered more difficult, sometimes by the startling contrasts which occur within a single group and sometimes by the great similarity between one range and its neighbour. For example, Mount Everest rises on its various sides from almost every conceivable kind of mountain country; rounded hills and valleys, utterly barren and desolate; pleasant grassy moorland flanked by gentle Alpine peaks; wide sheets of slightly undulating glacier resembling Arctic ice-cap country; mighty peaks of fluted ice standing above dense tropical rain-forests; deep, sunless gorges – all this within a radius of some twenty miles. On the other hand, there is little difference scenically between the Western Himalayas and the Hindu Kush or between the Pamirs and the Kuen Lun.

There is so much exploratory work to be done in these ranges that once one has become involved in the game there seems to be no end to it. Moreover, each expedition suggests half a dozen other equally attractive plans, every one of which clamours for attention. I had hoped that Tilman and I might soon be able to break away from the influence of this strong attraction and chance our arm in the mountain ranges of Alaska, or in the southern Andes, or in the Sierra de Merida of Venezuela, or in the strange mountains of New Guinea. But with the widening of our Central Asian horizon these plans receded into the more distant future. Obviously there were some things that we must do first, before we could claim even a passing acquaintance with our present field. One of these was a journey in the Karakoram, the greatest concentration of lofty peaks in the world. Here, it seemed from all accounts, nature had spread herself on a truly titanic scale. I was told by Longstaff and Bruce that I would never believe in the existence of such country until I had seen it for myself.

Sheer size by itself is no attraction, though it often enhances the value of other characteristics. For example, I have never been very impressed by the feet of precipice forming the north face of Mount Everest, though the wonderful architecture of the south-eastern combe of that mountain owes much of its beauty to its immensity. St. Paul's is beautiful in itself, but an exact model on half the scale would not be nearly so impressive. I find the Eiffel Tower neither impressive nor beautiful.

For some reason I had the impression that the country in the Karakoram was bleak, desolate and colourless; a gigantic stretch of unrelieved austerity, devoid of the soft contrast that I find so essential for the full enjoyment of great peaks; the valleys destitute of trees and grass and flowers, the mountains supported by bare desert hills. So it was not without some misgivings that I decided to go there in 1937. Besides, the more I studied the geography of the country, the more doubtful I became whether the technique for light travel that we had evolved for work in the Himalayas could possibly be applied on the vast glaciers of the Karakoram which were on a scale altogether different from anything I had ever seen, and in country where we would be cut off for many months from any habitation. I was most agreeably surprised when I got there to find that none of these gloomy forebodings was justified.

The most interesting of the many unexplored areas of the Karakoram was that lying in the basin of the Shaksgam river, on the northern side of the main range and somewhere on the undemarcated frontiers of Hunza and Ladakh and the Chinese province of Sinkiang. The first explorer to penetrate this part of the Karakoram was Sir Francis Younghusband. In 1887, at the end of his great journey across Asia, from Peking to India, he crossed the Aghil range by what has since come to be known as the Aghil pass. On the southern side of this pass he discovered a river which his men called the Shaksgam. From there he ascended the Sarpo Laggo glacier and crossed the main Karakoram range by way of the Mustagh pass to the Baltoro glacier.

Two years later he again crossed the Aghil pass to the Shaksgam river, which he followed up-stream for some distance. Then he tried to enter the country to the south-west; but failing to make his way up a great glacier, which he named the Crevasse glacier, he made his way, in the late autumn, down the Shaksgam valley, and so reached the Shimshal pass which lies at the north-western extremity of this area.

The next expedition to visit the region was the one led, in 1926, by Colonel Kenneth Mason and financed by the Survey of India. Mason's object was to cross from the Karakoram pass, which lies at the eastern extremity of the Aghil range, to the headwaters of the Shaksgam. From there he intended to work downstream so as to connect up with Younghusband's route, and to fix the geographical position of the Shaksgam river and the Aghil pass. His way was barred by a large glacier, which, coming down from the northern slopes of the

Teram Kangri range, dammed the Shaksgam river. The ice was so appallingly broken that it was quite impossible for the expedition to cross the glacier and to continue its progress down the river. Mason named the glacier the Kyagar. His party travelled north into the Aghil range and explored its eastern section. There they were faced by the great difficulties of spending, in an entirely uninhabited area, the long time that detailed scientific work demands. In August they found another large river, which at first they imagined to be the Shaksgam itself. They were not able to follow it downstream owing to the enormous volume of water that was racing through its gorges. But they went far enough upstream to realise that the river was not the Shaksgam. Mason named it the Zug – or false – Shaksgam. He was compelled to leave the problem of its course unsolved.

In 1929 a party of HRH the Duke of Spoleto's expedition crossed the Mustagh pass into the Shaksgam valley and followed it upstream beyond the point reached by Younghusband.

In 1935 the Dutch explorers, Dr and Mrs Visser, whose expeditions in the Karakoram have accomplished such a remarkable amount of work, followed Mason's route and succeeded in crossing the Kyagar and in mapping the great glaciers coming down from the Gasherbrum peaks on the main watershed. They were prevented from going farther down the river by the summer floods.

To the west and north-west of the areas visited by these explorers there was still a very large region of unknown country full of interesting geographical problems. It was the exploration of a portion of this area that was our main object in 1937. We had three principal interests. First, the section that lay between the Sarpo Laggo valley and the Shimshal pass, bounded on the north by the Shaksgam river, an area of about 1,000 square miles. Second, the glacier system lying to the north of K2. Third, the portion of the Aghil range west of that explored by Mason's expedition. The two outstanding problems in this area were to find the lower reaches and outlet of the Zug Shaksgam river, and to fix the geographical position of the Aghil pass which had not been revisited by any European traveller since Younghusband's second crossing in 1889.

The most formidable problem in travelling in the uninhabited regions of the Karakoram is that presented by the rivers. After mid-summer the ice of the great glaciers begins to melt in earnest. When this happens the rivers swell enormously and remain continuously in spate until late in the autumn. In this condition they are quite impossible to ford, while the width of the riverbeds precludes the possibility of bridging, even if timber were available. A party that has crossed one of these rivers, say, in June, and has not recrossed it by the time the floods arrive will have its retreat cut off for perhaps four months.

The bursting of the 'Shyok dam' several years ago is a good illustration of the colossal scale of the glacial phenomena in the Karakoram. A subsidiary glacier had advanced across the bed of the Shyok river near its source, thus damming the stream. In time, the weight of the water collected behind the dam burst the ice barrier. Besides causing havoc throughout the length of the upper Indus, the bursting of the dam caused disastrous floods in the plains of the Punjab some six hundred miles away. Similar catastrophes on a smaller scale are common in those parts.

The passes from India to the basin of the upper Indus remain closed until the early summer. This and the winter snow on the far more formidable barrier of the Karakoram range made it virtually impossible for an expedition to reach the Shaksgam early enough to allow a reasonable amount of work to be accomplished before the floods started. Fortunately the bulk of our work lay to the south of the river, though if we were lucky we might snatch three weeks or a month in the Aghil range to the north.

Clearly our best plan was to establish a base somewhere in the middle of the area, so that we would be independent of outside help for the whole period of our stay there, and transport difficulties, once the work was begun, would cause the minimum of delay. The next question was how to achieve this plan. Apart from trying to reach the Shaksgam from China, which would have taken too long even if the political situation in Sinkiang had permitted it, there were three alternatives open to us: first, to cross from the Karakoram pass to the head waters of the Shaksgam and make our way down over the difficult glacier trunks which had defeated Mason's party in 1926; second, to cross the Shimshal pass and force our way up the lower gorge of the Shaksgam before the river became too high: and third, to cross the main Karakoram range from the Baltoro glacier. The first two alternatives would probably have involved considerable difficulties with the river even early in the year, and we might easily have been cut off before reaching a suitable base. Besides this the journey either to the Shimshal or to the Karakoram pass would have been very long and costly, particularly as early in the year as we would have had to tackle it. The third route was much more direct; moreover, the difficulties involved were of a purely mountaineering character, and though we were likely to have considerable trouble in transporting several tons of stores and equipment over a difficult glacier pass early in the year, this route seemed to offer the best chances of success.

The party had to be small, but not so small as to prevent us from taking adequate advantage of our opportunities. Above all, every man must be willing, whatever his other duties, to undertake his full share of load-carrying. Tilman was as keen as ever. Spender was the best man I knew to take charge of the survey, and I was very lucky in getting him to come with us again. Unfortunately the necessity of limiting our baggage to the barest essentials made it impossible for him to undertake any sterio-photogrametric work, and we had to resort to less elaborate methods. I also invited John Auden of the Geological Survey of India to accompany the expedition, and his department kindly seconded him for the purpose. Auden had done a good deal of climbing in Europe and had travelled widely in the Himalayas in the course of his work. In 1933 he had made an expedition to the Biafo glacier in the Karakoram and his knowledge of the first part of our route and of the people was a very great help. Seven Sherpas were engaged. I entrusted their selection to Angtharkay, and his choice proved admirable.

The question of finance was easier than it had been before. I estimated that the total cost of the expedition, including three return passages to India (Auden joined us from Calcutta) would amount to £855. The Royal Geographical Society, the Survey of India and the Royal Society each contributed generously towards the funds.

We assembled in Srinagar at the end of April. I had heard so much about the wonders of Kashmir that I was prepared to be disappointed. I expected to find a place in no way superior to the other Indian hill stations I had seen, and hideously disfigured by the horrors of excessive tourist traffic; in fact a kind of Himalayan Chamonix. I was wrong. The Vale of Kashmir is a lovely place. With its wide plains completely surrounded by mountains, its great lakes and placid rivers, its floating gardens, the strange, colourful life of its river-dwelling inhabitants, the peaceful sense of its isolation, the variety and soft friendliness of the side valleys it is quite unlike anything else I have seen. Even the racket of its exploited capital is remarkably unobtrusive, at least to the casual visitor. Admittedly we saw it through rose-tinted glasses, for we were the happy guests of Sir Peter and Lady Clutterbuck, whose kindness and hospitality made our work of preparation in Srinagar a most delightful experience.

The passes leading out of Kashmir to the north are not officially open until June; but by travelling at night it is possible to take a caravan of porters over them a good deal earlier in the year without undue risk from avalanches. We started up the Sind valley from Gangarbal with a caravan of twelve pack-ponies on the 5th of May. We changed to porter transport before reaching the foot of the Zoji La, which we crossed on the 9th. The pass marked a sudden change of scene. In the Sind valley we had been amongst pinewoods and pleasant meadows, above which stood shapely rock peaks draped with little glaciers of clean, blue ice; it was like an Alpine valley in the spring. Once across the pass, we found ourselves in bleak, colourless country of bare, shapeless hills, rendered more dreary by the untidy remains of winter snow. I thought that this was a gloomy foretaste of what we were in for during the whole season. But as we followed the rivers down into the maze of gorges forming the basin of the Indus, the country changed again. The steep mountain sides were still utterly barren, but the deep, twisting valleys and their sleek, powerful rivers had character and a grim beauty. Every few miles we came upon a stretch of intensive cultivation perched upon an ancient river terrace, and irrigated by the hardy ingenuity of the local population. The apricot trees were in full blossom, a pink mist above the fields of young corn climbing the hillside in steps of vivid green. It was like coming upon a corner of Kentish spring in the midst of the barren crags of Aden. Sometimes these belts of cultivation continued unbroken for several miles, and there our way would lie through shady orchards, the path flanked by broad ribbons of mauve and white iris. It was utterly unlike any country I had seen before, though typical of nearly all the great river valleys of the Western Himalayas and the Karakoram. I never lost my early delight in its bold contrast and extravagant grandeur. Later we found that many of the side nullahs, so stark and rugged where they joined the main valleys, held in their upper reaches little fairy combes of pinewood and flower-filled meadows.

After a fortnight we reached Skardu, the capital of Baltistan. From there we crossed the Indus by an ancient ferry, and made our way to the north along the Shigar river. The main stream of the Indus marks the boundary between the Himalayas and the Karakoram, though it seemed to me that the division was somewhat artificial. Five more days took us to Askole, the last outpost of habitation in Baltistan. The last two marches were over very difficult country. The route had frequently to be altered according to the state of the river. Sometimes long detours were necessary to avoid an impassable gorge, and in places rickety ladders propped against the rock solved the problem presented by a vertical precipice. More alarming still were the rope bridges across the river. These were made of three strands of thick rope, slung in the shape of a V, with one rope for one's feet, while the other two ropes served as hand-rails.

Many a hardened mountaineer has been known to blench while passing over these frail contraptions, swaying giddily over the raging flood. Most of the Sherpas were terrified of them, though each laughed immoderately at the craven performance of his fellows.

With our arrival at Askole we had reached the most critical stage of the expedition. Immediately ahead was the mighty barrier of the main Karakoram range, and everything depended on our being able to transport our equipment and about one and a half tons of food across it to the Shaksgam valley beyond. But besides this food, which was calculated to keep the party alive for three and a half months, we had to take with us food for the men who were carrying it, and also food for those who had to carry the porter's food. And not only had these men to be fed while they were with us, but they had also to be catered for on their return journey to Askole. It was the old problem which has to be faced whenever a journey is planned through country where no supplies are available, and where everything has to be carried: a party cannot travel for many days without the carriers being burdened with so much of their own food that they cannot carry anything else. In this respect a man is a very inefficient beast of burden, for he eats more in proportion to his carrying power than any of his four-legged rivals.

Until the middle of the nineteenth century there were a number of passes leading direct across the range from Baltistan to Hunza and to Sinkiang, which were used by travellers, traders and small bandit armies. But since then these passes have all been abandoned, and although we know from the records of early European explorers that they were in fact used by the native peoples, their existence is merely legendary as far as the present-day population is concerned. It is not quite clear why they fell into disuse, though it was probably due to a combination of several causes, one of which was the great changes which have taken place in the glaciers. Whatever the reason, it is now a difficult matter to persuade the Baltis to venture far above their normal summer grazing grounds.

Two of these passes led from Askole to Yarkand by way of the Shaksgam river. They were known as the Old and the New Mustagh passes. Of these only the Old Mustagh pass had been crossed by Europeans, once in 1887 by Younghusband and again in 1929 by the party detached from the Duke of Spoleto's expedition, under Professor Desio. From their accounts it appeared that the Old Mustagh pass was very difficult, and it seemed unlikely that it would be possible for us to cross it so early in the year and with so much baggage. The route over the New Mustagh pass was unknown and probably much longer. However, Desio had reported the probable existence of a practicable saddle west of the Old Mustagh pass, and we decided to gamble on that.

When we arrived at Askole on 24 May we opened negotiations with the local headmen for the recruiting of porters, and the collecting of 4,000 pounds of flour. There was no difficulty about the latter, and for the next thirty six hours a steady stream of flour came to our camp carried in sheepskin bags. It was then transferred to canvas bags we had brought for the purpose and was weighed up into sixty-pound loads.

The question of porters was much more delicate and had to be handled with considerable care. The inhabitants of the valley of Askole, for all their remoteness, were more accustomed to expeditions than those of any other part of the Karakoram. At first sight that fact might appear as an advantage; but this was very far from the case. Most of the expeditions had been bound for the head of the Baltoro glacier, which involved for the porters a straightforward journey with very little hardship. Several of the enterprises, notably the 1929 Italian Expedition, the 1934 International Expedition led by Professor Dyhrenfurth, and the French attempt to climb Gasherbrum in 1936, were run on a huge scale, quite regardless of cost. Upwards of six hundred men were employed. The porters were paid fabulous wages besides acquiring all kinds of perquisites and loot from abandoned equipment and stores. Naturally, the men of the Askole valley soon came to regard expeditions as heaven-sent opportunities of making small fortunes with very little trouble to themselves. Moreover, they had formed very definite ideas as to what an expedition should look like, and to them our Spartan outfit appeared laughable. We could neither inspire confidence by our appearance nor tempt with a bottomless purse. We had every reason to resent the methods of our plutocratic predecessors.

At first it was assumed that we were merely going up the Baltoro glacier, and things seemed to be going well. But when it dawned on the populace that something very much more arduous was expected of them we met with blank refusal. However, after many hours of apparently hopeless argument, we succeeded in winning them over, and quite suddenly we found that the entire multitude was clamouring to be enrolled. Our dramatic change of fortune was presumably due to the realisation of a few of the more thoughtful spirits that we would not employ the whole population and that they had better take what they could get while the going was good. Once a few had changed their attitude the rest followed with the speed of an avalanche. But so long as we retained our connection with the Baltis we were for ever hearing invidious comparisons between the bounty of the 'Dook Sahib' and our poverty.

We had reduced our equipment to the barest minimum, but even so we required a hundred local men. Of these about one-third were to carry the food and equipment to be used in the Shaksgam, the rest were needed to carry food which they ate themselves. We had brought seventeen men from Skardu. These were invaluable, for they were not imbued with the big ideas of the Askole men and were prepared to do a job of work in return for their pay. Moreover, they tended to despise the others and usually sided with us in the innumerable disputes and strikes that occurred when conditions became uncomfortable; or at least they remained neutral and so broke the otherwise united front against us. We had decided to retain four of them for the whole period of our stay, so as to increase the carrying power of our small party.

We set out from Askole soon after noon on 26 May. On the third day we reached Paiju, a pleasant patch of willow jungle near the snout of the Baltoro glacier. The weather was bad and our prospects looked gloomy. Everything depended upon our getting the loads across the range with the least possible delay. It would obviously be impossible to cross an unknown pass with such a large caravan in bad weather. Also it was clear that a great deal of new snow was falling on the high mountains to add to the masses of unmelted winter snow. Matters were still further complicated when Tilman and one of the Sherpas, Sen Tensing, became ill with fever. After much deliberation it was decided that they should remain at Paiju with Auden and two porters, while Spender and I and the other Sherpas went on with the main body. We could not afford to wait, for the whole caravan was now consuming 220 pounds of food a day.

The next few miles of our way led up the Baltoro. The size of the glacier was prodigious compared with those on Mount Everest and in Sikkim and Garhwal. It rose somewhere beyond our range of vision in a knot of giant peaks culminating in K2, the second highest mountain in the world. It was flanked throughout its course by countless spires, immense columns of granite standing six or eight thousand feet above their bases, supporting graceful summits, so remotely inaccessible that they seemed hardly to be part of the same colossal structure. Had we not known of the existence of the Mustagh pass and the saddle described by Desio, nothing would have persuaded us to look in this fantastic country for a way across the range.

After another day we turned to the north and entered the narrow valley of a tributary glacier known as the Trango. For a time the weather continued to be bad and snow fell. In these conditions the Baltis seemed to be entirely incapable of looking after themselves. They crumpled up at the end of the day's march and refused to do anything towards making themselves comfortable or protecting themselves from the weather. It was surprising to find this failing in people whose livelihood depended so much on their ability to use difficult country to the best advantage, and whose forefathers were accustomed to making arduous journeys across the glaciers. Much of their lives must have been spent in the open, herding their flocks in high mountain pastures, and yet they seemed to be ignorant of the simplest notions of outdoor comfort: camping in the most protected places, building walls for shelter, crowding together for mutual protection and making use of rock overhangs. But I must admit they were tough, and put up with more cold and discomfort than I had expected them to endure. Fortunately the weather changed at the critical moment, and we were able to avoid the disaster of a complete collapse before we had even found the pass.

The fact that no one had ever crossed Desio's saddle also had a bad moral effect upon the Baltis. They knew that the Italian party had been up the Trango glacier, and they assumed that they had returned because they had failed to find a pass at its head. We could not maintain for long the pretence that we knew the way, and each mistake made them more certain of our incompetence. Nor could we tell them how long it would take to reach the pass. What seemed to worry them most, however, was the fear that if we managed to cross the pass we would find ourselves in a country from which we could not return.

Farther up, the remains of the winter snow was leg-deep upon the glacier, and it only stayed firm until about the middle of the morning; after that the going was terribly laborious. We wasted most of one day reconnoitring a route up a valley which ended in a semi-circle of precipice crowned by a hanging glacier terrace. But at length we found a glacier rising gently to a saddle which we imagined must lie on the crest of the main watershed. By then the spirit of the Baltis was almost broken. For some days all except the seventeen Skardu men had been clamouring to be allowed to return. They certainly had plenty to complain about; the nights were bitterly cold, the camps, on little rock platforms dug out from beneath the snow, were bleak and comfortless and such fuel as we had been able to bring from below was most inadequate. Luckily the good weather held, and by pointing to the saddle and promising them that if they could reach it we would ask nothing more of them, we managed to persuade the men to stick it for just one more day. But when, the next morning, we reached the saddle we found to our dismay that it was not the crest of the pass we were seeking. Beyond, more than a mile away across a curving basin of snow, we saw another col a few hundred feet higher. The Askole men were still some way below, and before they had a chance to share this devastating discovery we plunged down into the basin and waded through soft snow until we were half-way across. The Skardu men followed without protest. The basin proved to be the top of the hanging-glacier terrace which we had seen at the head of the valley we had reconnoitred. Eventually most of the Askole men arrived, but it was clear that we could not induce them to go a step farther. They lay in the snow, holding their heads and groaning, though the altitude was only about 18,000 feet. Only the Skardu men were willing to come on with us. We paid off the rest, and after watching them safely back over the first saddle, we made a dump of their abandoned loads. Then we struggled with as much as we could carry. The second saddle proved to be the true pass, and soon after nightfall that evening we camped on a little rock outcrop in the upper basin of the Sarpo Laggo glacier, on the northern side of the main continental watershed.

The next few days were occupied in rescuing the remainder of the loads from the hanging-glacier terrace, and in bringing them across the pass. Then, while Spender began his survey, we started to relay the baggage down the glacier. In the meantime Tilman, Auden, Sen Tensing and their two porters arrived. The invalids had recovered from their fever, but they were still very weak and it had been a hard struggle to drag themselves across the pass. On 14 June we reached broad gravel flats below the Sarpo Laggo glacier, and here we established our main base, nine miles south of the Shaksgam river. Most of the Skardu men returned from there and left the fifteen of us – four Europeans, seven Sherpas and four Baltis – to our own devices.

In spite of the many vicissitudes, we had accomplished the journey over the range almost according to schedule. That evening I experienced a sense of profound relief, of delicious freedom and of happy expectation of good things in store. Warmed by the unaccustomed luxury of a blazing fire, its leaping flames fed with unstinted wood, untroubled by the cares of the preceding weeks, we could reflect upon the entrancing prospects of our position. East and west of us stretched an unexplored section, eighty miles long, of the greatest watershed in the world. To the north, close at hand, across the Shaksgam river, was the Aghil range, with its unknown peaks and valleys. We had food enough to last us for nearly three and a half months, and a party equipped and strong enough to meet the opportunity.

13   Shaksgam – 2

One of the most acute problems of expedition life is the difficulty of preserving harmony among the members of a party. In the sentimental days before the last war there was a tendency to hide or to gloss over this ugly factor in the otherwise romantic accounts of expeditions. But sufficient of the inner history of the classic expeditions has leaked out to show that they suffered at least as much from this particular form of human frailty as their humble successors. Today the bugbear is widely, though by no means universally, admitted.

All manner of things, great and small, are liable to promote discord. Garrulity is notoriously hard to bear; silence can be no less trying. Even an unconscious display of virtue can be as intolerable as any vice, gentlemanly poise as hasty temper, efficiency as clumsiness, knowledge as ignorance, energy as sloth. In conditions of boredom or of nervous strain one is quick to resent the way a man drinks his soup or wears his hat, or the silly manner in which his beard had grown, or a thousand other trifles that in normal circumstances would pass unnoticed. When one is on short rations it generally seems that one's companion has secured the larger portion of a meal; and he invariably occupies more than his share of the tent. Disagreement about the route is a common cause of open hostility. On occasions when this has occurred and we have each gone our own way, I have found myself hoping that my opponent will fall down a crevasse rather than that he should get there first. I remember once that someone became very angry when I playfully threw an egg at his face; it was not that there was at the time any scarcity of eggs, nor was the egg particularly bad. There is no limit to people's unreasonableness. I know several travellers, most delightful people, who admit quite frankly that they cannot stand having a companion on their journey. Very wisely they travel alone. Others, of course, are equally incapable of enduring their own exclusive company for long, though they quarrel with all who share it.

Admission of this universal weakness is the first step towards combating the evil. For only then can one recognise the phenomenon when it shows its ugly head, or see it retrospectively in its true light. Sometimes even at the time one can appreciate its comic side. But acceptance does not solve the problem, and the personal relations between the individual members of an expedition can, more than any other single factor, make or mar the success of the enterprise.

It is extremely hard to predict which men will get on with each other, though I suppose most of us imagine that we have a clear idea of the kind of people we can or cannot live with. Our particular likes and dislikes may or may not reflect our own characteristics. For example, I do not find self-centred people specially hard to bear; far worse, to my mind, is a man who continually talks platitudes. But this does not imply that I am not selfish myself, nor that I do not think always in clichés. I often find that I get on well with men who are given to making wild statements providing they support them with intelligent argument. I consider that people who never say anything unless they are perfectly sure of their ground become most irritating. But even for individuals there is no rule. Certainly few people will agree upon what constitutes the ideal companion.

It would be difficult to find two people less alike in their intellectual make-up then Tilman and Spender. Yet I regard each in his way as the best companion I could wish for. Their own relationship was a curious one. Neither appeared to take the other particularly seriously, though I detected a strong mutual esteem. Far more inflammable was the contact between the two scientists, and it was generally prudent to keep them separated as much as possible. This was odd in a way because each was untiring in his co-operation in the work of the other. Perhaps it was because they both had unusually hearty appetites, or perhaps because both had brothers who were celebrated poets. I find that scientists often are rather intolerant of one another.

But though without direct experiment it is almost impossible to tell which men can tolerate each other's company, there are certain conditions that can and must be observed when organising an expedition. The first essential, as I have said elsewhere, is that every man should feel that he has an important part to play. Nothing is more conducive to bloody-mindedness than the feeling, even for a short time, that one is superfluous or redundant. It is surprising how quick people are to feel this. For this reason the expedition should be divided as much as possible into small, self-contained units, each with its special task and responsibility. On an exploratory expedition the advantages of this method are obvious. But it is remarkable how much better men like each other after a few weeks' absence. The prospect of meeting 'old so-and-so's' party to-morrow, of hearing an account of his adventures and of recounting one's own, rarely fails to have a most stimulating and refreshing effect. The illusion of brotherly love may be short-lived, but it is well worth while.

The second essential condition for the achievement of harmony is interest. Each man must be capable of deriving a deep satisfaction from some aspect of his environment and of sustaining his enthusiasm. It is a capacity that can only be discovered by experience. It does not necessarily demand the pursuit of scientific study or even a hobby. Some men appear to derive a strong philosophical satisfaction from dragging a sledge across miles of arctic snow, or from mere existence in strange conditions. Many people have an intangible though profound feeling for certain types of country, and can be completely content doing any job which takes them into such places. Presumably for most mountaineers such a feeling for mountain country is their principal reason for climbing.

Thirdly, it is important that all the members of a party should be in agreement about the general policy and conduct of the expedition. I have suffered agonies of ennui and self-righteous disgust on an expedition that has appeared to me too large and clumsy, and I have made myself an infernal nuisance in consequence. No doubt the protagonist of large expeditions would be equally unhappy with the light expeditions that delight my heart.

In my opinion far too much emphasis has been laid on leadership in connection with mountaineering and exploratory expeditions, for this led to an exaggerated notion of the importance of the leader and the difficulty of his task. How often does one hear the word 'brilliant' applied in this connection, when in fact all that was called for was the exercise of a little tact and common sense? In ordinary mountaineering the man who has had most experience on the particular type of ground to be covered generally assumes tacit charge of the party; the more evenly experience and skill are distributed among the members, the less obvious is this assumption of charge. Anyone who tries to play the dictator in the lower valleys is likely to become very unpopular. As far as possible the same principle should be applied in the whole conduct of an expedition. A leader should make his position as inconspicuous as he can, and he should certainly avoid the appearance of taking his responsibilities too seriously. His primary task is the selection of his party. In the field his main function is to see that every man is placed in a position which gives him the widest scope for his particular job and for the use of his own initiative. Heavy military discipline, obviously necessary when vast armies are involved, is wholly out of place when dealing with a handful of carefully selected and thoroughly competent specialists. When it ceases to be laughable, it becomes intolerably irksome.

Travel in unexplored country is a curious mixture of freedom and cramping self-discipline, of careless abandon and rigid time schedule. Free from all the tiresome restraints of normal life, encircled by a boundless horizon, one is all the more a slave to the elementary considerations of time and distance, food and warmth, weather and season. The simple life is simple only in that it deals with direct fundamental things.

It was already the middle of June when we reached our base in the Sarpo Laggo valley. In less than a month the Aghil range would be almost encircled by an impassable barrier of flood, leaving only one line of escape, eastward, through a tremendous tangle of unexplored mountains to the country mapped by Mason's expedition, itself many weeks' journey from the nearest habitation.

To be caught beyond the Shaksgam by the summer floods would almost certainly be disastrous, for we could hardly survive there until the following winter when the melting of the glaciers would slacken and the rivers shrink. Days were precious and we had no time to waste in relaying supplies. Thus an automatic limit was set to our work in the Aghil range, for without relaying we could only carry with us enough food for three weeks.

The valley of the Shaksgam river was a weird place, shut in on both sides by great limestone cliffs, slashed across with twisted streaks of yellow, red and black strata which gave them a bizarre appearance. The bottom of the valley was composed of gravel and sand flats, often as much as a mile wide. Over these the river flowed, sometimes concentrated into one great body of water as it swirled round a bend in the valley, sometimes split up into a dozen streams which sprawled their independent courses across the flats. Spread out at intervals along the valley we found jungles of grass, willow and tamarisk, natural counterparts of the cultivated oases of the Indus valley. The main river was turoid, but, on each side of it, clear streams flowed through a chain of deep green and blue pools. Steep, glacier-filled corries split the vertical sides of the main valley, forming narrow openings into a dark forest of Dolomite spires.

At the foot of one such cleft we found a collection of ancient stone shelters which gave us a clue to the route through a narrow defile to the Aghil pass. Here we came upon a sudden change of scene. A wide grassy valley carpeted with drifts of mauve primulas, sloped gently away to the north, cradling a placid lake and backed by the rounded ice-caps of the Kuen Lun. Looking back across the Shaksgam valley, framed by vertical rock walls, we could see the full splendours of the Karakoram, rising to the mighty cone of K2.

The party was divided into three parts, and for a fortnight of perfect weather we worked upon our several tasks. Spender stayed in the vicinity of the pass, to fix its position and to map in detail two hundred square miles of the surrounding country. Auden journeyed north to the Yarkand river, and then worked his way back across the range by another route. Tilman and I went eastwards to find the Zug Shaksgam. We started by climbing a 20,000 foot peak, then we found a high pass across which we travelled to the basin of the river. It was already too swollen for us to attempt a crossing, but we were able to follow it up-stream until we were certain that it was in fact the Zug Shaksgam, and down-stream through deep canyons to its junction with the Yarkand. The country through which we travelled was extremely difficult and our short weeks were over-crowded with toil and interest, though the glaciers were relatively small and we were never beyond easy reach of fuel. This and the fine weather gave us a sense of freedom, for we were able to travel from dawn until nightfall, lying down to sleep wherever we happened to be. In the wide valleys north of the Aghil range, as in those of the Sarpo Laggo, we found enormous herds of wild sheep and countless snow-cock. Elsewhere that year, we met with foxes, wild asses and small mountain wolves. When we had time to stalk them, the wild sheep provided us with poor sport but a welcome change of diet.

The expedition reunited in a pleasant jungle in the Sarpo Laggo valley on July 8th. The following day Spender went off to complete the survey of the intricate system of glaciers coming down from the main Karakoram range west of K2, while Auden, Tilman and I set out to explore the country lying immediately to the north of the great mountain. From the summit of a peak 21,000 feet high, on a calm and cloudless day, our senses sharpened by a difficult climb, we looked into the heart of this wild and lovely region. Later we stood for one unforgettable hour in the midst of a wide amphitheatre at the foot of the north face of K2. A single buttress, straight and slender, rose from the level icy floor of the cirque in one prodigious sweep of 12,000 feet to the gleaming summit dome. We watched avalanches, involving perhaps hundreds of tons of ice, break from a hanging glacier nearly two miles above our heads. Long before the ice reached the foot of the precipice it was ground to a fine powder, slowly to vanish in a misty spray. Nor did any sound reach our ears.

When, towards the close of the last century, Sir Martin Conway travelled from the Hunza valley, up the Hispar glacier and across the Hispar pass at its head, he came upon a large basin of ice and snow. He named this the 'Snow Lake', and although he did not explore it, he estimated its area at three hundred square miles. Since then it had only been seen once, by the Workmans, who, following Conway's route, also did not explore the region. Something of a legend had grown up around the 'Snow Lake', which gave rise to a good deal of geographical speculation. It was suggested, for example, that it might form an ice-cap of a kind unknown outside arctic regions, in which many of the vast glaciers of the Karakoram had their origin. Its southern fringes, traversed by Conway and the Workmans, represented the limit of exploration in this part of the Karakoram, so that the map of the main continental watershed faded into the unknown with this intriguing enigma.

From our base in the Sarpo Laggo we looked to the west up a mighty ice stream which stretched away into a jagged horizon of far distant peaks. This was the Crevasse glacier up which, in 1889, Younghusband had tried to make his way in search of the Shimshal pass. On its lower reaches he had encountered a forest of ice pinnacles, so complicated that he had abandoned his attempt. From the size of the glacier and its general direction we calculated that one of its upper branches might lead us, if not into the 'Snow Lake', at least to its vicinity.

With food sufficient for nearly two months we started to work our way up the Crevasse glacier. It was a laborious task for the way was intricate and hard to travel, and though the Sherpas carried as much as 120 pounds each, our loads were more than we could transport in a single journey. But our slow progress enabled Spender to make a detailed map of the country through which we passed. After a fortnight of steady work we had penetrated the region of ice pinnacles and reached a point some twenty miles up the glacier. Beyond this the ice was smooth and easy to travel. The glacier divided into a number of branches. We went forward in several lightly laden detachments to explore the range ahead of us and to search for passes that would lead us into whatever country lay beyond.

After another ten days we had learned sufficient to enable us to form further plans. We had found many routes, each leading in a different direction, each with intriguing possibilities. To make the best use of our unique position we decided thenceforward to work in three independent parties, each with its separate objective to be pursued as circumstances and the nature of the country dictated. We did not meet again until we returned to England.

Auden and the four Baltis crossed a pass which took them to the south into the Panmah glacier system, and thence to Askole. Tilman and two Sherpas set off to the west in search of the 'Snow Lake'. Abandoning all but the barest necessities, they crossed a long series of passes, eighteen or nineteen thousand feet high, until they found the great basin, crossed it and connected Conway's explorations with our own. Finally they broke through the great rock wall to the south of the Hispar pass into the fertile valleys near Arandu in Baltistan. Meanwhile Spender and I, with the five remaining Sherpas carrying the heavy survey equipment, struck north, and, after wandering for a month through a maze of ranges reached habitation in the remote valleys of Shimshal.

It is hard to compare the experiences of life or to assess their relative value. Each is influenced by the mental impression left by its forerunners; none can stand quite alone. With each new view our standards alter, with each fresh endeavour our interests change. I cannot say which mountain venture or which mountain scene has afforded the deepest delight. Certainly no experience of mine has been fuller, no undertaking more richly rewarded than those few months among the unknown mountains beyond the crest of the Karakoram. The vast scale of the country, its complete isolation from any source of help or supply, demanded all our ingenuity and a wide range of mountaineering technique. Striving to traverse and understand such a world, and thus to absorb something of its peace and strength, was at once our task and our reward.

Our time was all too short, and we were sorely tempted to extend it into the winter. For with each phase of our journey new problems crowded in upon us. It was hard indeed to call a halt. But I had promised Tilman to return to England to help with the preparations for the 1938 Everest Expedition, and I had to remain content with a resolve to come back some day to this land of boundless promise with unlimited time before me.

The first people we met were salt-gatherers in the valleys beyond the Shimshal pass. Our sudden descent from an unknown country caused some consternation among these folk, who took us for a band of Chinese marauders. It was with difficulty that we reassured them, and when they had called up armed reinforcements we were escorted in a state of friendly arrest across the pass to Shimshal, where we succeeded in convincing the headman of our nationality and our innocent intentions.

There can be no denying that one of the great pleasures of an expedition lies in the return to normal things. This fact indicates no lack of appreciation of the life involved, no lessening of its value. It is a natural delight in contrast, in rest after toil, in soft living after austerity. I know few joys more poignant than the relaxation of walking along a path after months of mountaineering travel; there are few pleasures sweeter than the sight of abundant fertility, of flocks and fields and orchards, after the desolate splendour of high places.

Our journey back to Srinagar took four weeks. It was the most varied and the most impressive that I had then experienced in the inhabited regions of high Asia. First there was the passage through the monstrous gorge of conglomerate cliffs below Shimshal, astonishing and terrifying even to our practised eyes; then the slow climb up the moonlit precipice, parched and bare, to escape from its infernal depths to the crest of a pass 8,000 feet above; the descent on the other side into a gentle land of meadow and pinewood where we slaked raging thirsts and cushioned our tired limbs in beds of deep grass. Our way led through Hunza, that principality straight from the pages of legend with surely the most fantastic setting in the world; here, as guests of the old Mir, we reclined on couches in the shade of the palace garden, eating luscious grapes and pears and peaches and melons from an inexhaustible supply.

There is a peculiar quality about the western ranges of Central Asia, that I have since come to appreciate more fully, though I am no better able to account for or describe it. It is an atmosphere created, I fancy, partly by the country, its fantastic natural phenomena, its vastness and arid severity, and partly by the people, their vivid mode of living, their habit of wide travel, their kinship with the Western world, perhaps too their proximity to the cradle of civilisation. These two attributes of weird environment and peaceful culture blend together in an unusual harmony which makes travel in this region an unforgettable experience.

14 Karakoram, 1939

The vague plans that I had so timidly formulated in 1933 were developing with the most gratifying smoothness. The horizons of the 'untravelled world' had widened with each step along the enchanting road of exploration. The fascination of new country had deepened with each fresh experience. Each expedition, however successful in the achievement of its main purpose, left behind it a ragged fringe of unsatisfied desire which formed the nucleus of some new and more ambitious venture. I was constantly debating in my mind new ways of approach and better methods of travel and of living in uninhabited country, and I was continually aware of fresh and exciting possibilities. Luckily the question of finance had presented no great problem and I found it easier to raise money for expeditions of wider scope.

A severe limit has always been imposed upon expeditions in the high Himalayas by the shortness of the summer season and by the difficulty of crossing the southern passes until the winter snows have melted. These factors have restricted the actual work of an expedition to three or four months in the remoter districts and enormously increased its cost. I had often resented this limitation and had resolved at the first opportunity to break down the seasonal barrier. By providing suitable equipment, and arranging for the disposition of the expedition at points where they would be least affected by the rigours of winter and spring, it seemed that it would be possible to do useful and well-coordinated work throughout the year. Besides the enormous extension of opportunity and freedom of movement that such a plan would offer, one would gain a totally different view point and a far more intimate contact with the country that one was seeking to discover, by a leisurely and uninterrupted sojourn in it through all the seasons.

It is curious how time is affected by familiarity. The Kamet expedition, my first in the Himalayas, had lasted less than three months. It had seemed an eternity, as though I had spent half my life travelling among those vast and lovely valleys. Later, double that time seemed sadly insufficient, and I felt that I could not claim a real understanding of such places until I had lived a full year in their solitudes.

The frequently recurring expeditions to Mount Everest had made it impossible for me to embark upon this attractive experiment. In 1939, however, the opportunity came. The most obvious choice of country was the Karakoram, since its problems and its fascination were so fresh in my mind. The Shaksgam expedition of 1937 had fulfilled its main purpose in the fixing and detailed mapping of the country surrounding the Aghil Pass and the great glacier system lying immediately to the north of the main Karakoram watershed between K2 and the Shimshal pass. There still remained much of the Aghil range to be explored, as well as the mountains stretching to the north-east of the Shimshal pass across the Oprang river, before the map of the main features of the Great Karakoram could be completed. From the experience I had gained in 1937 it was clear to me that the task would best be tackled during the winter, when the river, instead of presenting the traveller with impassable barriers, might even be used as high roads by which to penetrate into the heart of the unexplored regions. I mentioned my plans to the Surveyor-General of India when I was in Calcutta in 1938, and he replied that he was anxious to straighten out the topographical confusion which existed in that part of the main range surrounding the basins of the Hispar, Biafo and Panmah glaciers. This was an obvious prelude to my winter plans. I submitted detailed proposals to the Surveyor-General, who at once offered me full support and encouragement.

This, then, was the outline of my plan. The party would consist of four Europeans equipped to spend some sixteen months in the field. We would spend the summer of 1939 in the region of the Hispar-Biafo watershed. The principal task here would be to make an accurate triangulation not only for the mapping of this country, but also to form a basis for our winter work. The winter of 1939-40 was to be spent in the country to the east of the Shimshal pass. As this was beyond the main range, the snow precipitation would be light. It would be extremely cold, but we would be provided with special arctic equipment, and I was not unduly worried on that score. During the spring of 1940 we would attempt a journey from Shimshal to Leh via the Shaksgam river, for which I proposed to acquire a small herd of yaks to be used both for transport and as a source of food supply. In the summer of 1940 I hoped to travel from Leh to the source of the Indus exploring the unknown Aling Kangri range on the way. Thence – well, who could tell?

Alas! the end of this way of life was at hand, and most of the lovely plans came to nothing. It was clear to most people that war must come sooner or later. But to me it seemed that little purpose would be served by anticipating it; and one hoped that it would be later rather than sooner. In any case, it did not seem to matter whether one were in the East or in Europe when the storm came. Spender and Tilman, whom I had hoped to have with me, thought differently. Spender had a scientific job of considerable importance: Tilman, who was on the reserve list of officers, did not wish to be away for so long. He went instead for a short trip to the mountains of Assam.

However, to share my plans I had excellent companions. Scott Russell, a practised mountaineer, came to help in the exploration, to make detailed botanical collections and surveys, and to continue some physiological researches which he had been making into the effect of cold climates upon plant growth. Eadric Fountaine came as doctor and general help, and also to make zoological collections, and to study certain medical and ethnological aspects of the people of Shimshal. Peter Mott came as chief surveyor. All these three had had experience of Arctic work, which would have been invaluable in the execution of our winter plans. The Surveyor-General lent the expedition the services of two Indian surveyors, Fazal Ellahi, who had already made a considerable reputation by his mountain surveys and his resource in difficult circumstances, and Inayat Khan. Nine Sherpas, under my old friend Angtharkay, were engaged. The expedition was financed by grants of money from the Royal Geographical Society, the Royal Society, the Percy Sladen Fund, the British Museum and the Royal Botanic Gardens, Kew. Mr R.W. Lloyd and Mr A. Courtauld also most kindly contributed towards the funds of the expedition.

We set off across the passes to Gilgit in the middle of June, and once again enjoyed the gentle progress through entrancing foothill valleys which is the prelude to all Himalayan expeditions. We crossed the Tragbal and the Kamri passes on fine mornings. The remains of the winter snow was still on the ground, and the huge cone of Nanga Parbat stood clear in the sparkling air. In the sunlit woods of the Gurais we forgot the ugly turmoil of the world we had left behind. In the lower valleys of the Indus basin the fruit was already ripe, and every few miles we stopped to gorge ourselves with mulberries and apricots.

From Gilgit we travelled on past the giant peak of Rakaposhi, which rose from a belt of pinewoods in the gorge of the Hunza river in one colossal sweep of 20,000 feet. It presents one of the most stupendous mountain faces in the world. At Nagir we were received with great courtesy by the old Mir who entertained us with exhibitions of polo and dancing. We began our work on 3 July. The party was divided into several groups, each with its allotted task – some to explore and map the giant glaciers of the Nagir district, some to work on the triangulation, some to cross the Nushik La to Baltistan in the south and some to establish a dump of food up the Hispar glacier at the foot of the Hispar pass. The glaciers of this region were flanked by wide ablation valleys formed by ancient lateral moraines, which offered easy and pleasant roads for travel. They were filled with willows and rose thickets and wild flowers. In July the roses were in full bloom and for miles along the glacier great banks of their gay blossom lined the ablation valleys. Our camping grounds were meadows carpeted with flowers of every colour.

Early in August the party reunited at a rendezvous on the Hispar glacier. While Fazal Ellahi was making a detailed plane-table map of the Hispar glacier and Mott was carrying forward his triangulation we relayed supplies across the Hispar pass, which formed a huge ice-plateau, to the 'Snow Lake'. Again the party was divided up, the better to cover the enormous area of country we had set ourselves to explore before winter set in. Fazal Ellahi worked from a base on the 'Snow Lake'. It was his task to survey this and then to work his way slowly down the Biafo glacier, which has a total length of some forty miles. Mott and Russell crossed a difficult pass to the south-west, and I did not see the former again until we met at Gilgit two months later. Fountaine and I made our way down the Biafo and then east to the Panmah, where we spent a busy three weeks mapping. In September we separated and each made his way by new passes back into the Snow Lake. Fountaine then set off on a long journey up the Chogo Lungma glacier and over a pass at its head, which led him eventually back to Gilgit.

I had arranged to meet Russell at a rendezvous on the 'Snow Lake'. I arrived first and waited for a few days of heavy snow-storm. Late one afternoon his party was seen approaching through the mist. I went out with Angtharkay to meet him. The approach to our camp was guarded by an intricate network of crevasses. With a deep covering of fresh snow it was a laborious and delicate task threading our way through this area, and the two parties approached each other slowly. When at last we were within earshot, Russell shouted out the shattering news that England was at war with Germany. He had heard it on the tiny wireless receiving set that we had brought to get time signals for our astronomical work.

It was a strange, dreamlike experience hearing such news in those surroundings. I felt for the moment as though one of the crevasses had opened and that I was dropping into a bottomless pit. I passed the news on to Angtharkay, and for a timeless moment we stood motionless. Then we went on to meet the other party, relieved them of some of their loads and made our way slowly back to camp, where I listened to such details as Russell was able to give. It was no dream, but a grim reality. I suppose we must have been expecting it, but that did not seem to lessen the shock. It was hard to realise the meaning of the disaster. Perhaps even now the London where we had planned this very venture was a chaos of destruction and terror. How fantastic, how supremely ridiculous it seemed in our remote and lovely world of snow and ice.

As if to point the contrast the mists cleared and for a moment the glacier was bathed in a sunset glow reflected from the high peaks. The great granite spires of the Biafo stood black against a deep blue sky. At least this mountain world, to which I owed so much of life and happiness, would stand above the ruin of human hopes, the heritage of a saner generation of men.

He is lucky who, in the full tide of life, has experienced a measure of the active environment that he most desires. In these days of upheaval and violent change, when the basic values of to-day are the vain and shattered dreams of tomorrow, there is much to be said for a philosophy which aims at living a full life while the opportunity offers. There are few treasures of more lasting worth than the experiences of a way of life that is in itself wholly satisfying. Such, after all, are the only possessions of which no fate, no cosmic catastrophe can deprive us; nothing can alter the fact if for one moment in eternity we have really lived.

A panoramic view across Snow Lake to the south and west from Khurdopin Pass.

A view east from the camp on Hispar Pass showing the Sim Gang Glacier section of Snow Lake with the icy walls of the Ogre on the right and Bobisghir on the left.

Michael Spender in rags after three months in the field.

Peter Mott surveying from above Snow Lake.

A crevasse on the edge of Snow Lake below Khurdopin Pass.

A 19,000-foot ice peak above the col linking the Chocktoi and Nobande Sobande glaciers. Peak 6960 of the Latok group is in the distance.

The Choktoi Glacier basin flanked by the Latok peaks and the Ogre (right). Shipton and Fontaine crossed cols at the head of the valley (*off picture, right of the Ogre*) to return to Snow Lake.

Shipton with his mother and Elie Richard in the Dauphiné in 1926.

Angtharkay descending an ice cliff to gain Nobande Sobande Glacier.

Leading Tryfan's Terrace Wall Variant in North Wales in 1928.

On the boat to Kenya, 1929.

Shipton and Lewa approach Kamet's summit (25,447 feet/7,758 metres) in 1931.

Batian from Point Piggott. This splendid vantage point enabled Shipton and Tilman to make an advance assessment of the difficulties of the west ridge which faces the camera. *(Inset)* Shipton and Wyn Harris on the summit of Nelion in 1929.

Everest seen from a 23,000-foot peak to the north that was climbed in 1935. The East Rongbuk Glacier curves round from the left into the cwm below the North Col. The route took the sunlit/shaded rib in the centre of the face.

A telephoto of the North-East Ridge and North Face of Everest from the summit of Khartaphu, a 23,000-foot peak first climbed by Shipton and Edwin Kempson in 1935. The pre-war route follows the spur rising from the bottom right and thence across the upper slopes towards the summit. The heavy, unconsolidated snow conditions seen here frustrated all attempts in the late thirties.

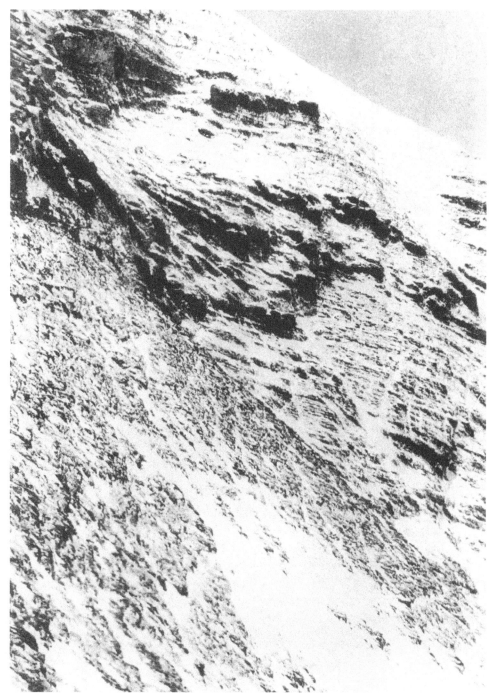

The upper slopes of Everest's North Face, cloaked with snow. The best pre-war attempts reached the rock bands beyond the diagonal line of the Great Couloir. In unconsolidated snow these slopes are very dangerous, but Reinhold Messner's solo ascent in 1982 and that of the Australian climbers in 1984 proved that in adequate snow conditions rapid progress is possible.

Frank Smythe and Shipton after their 1933 attempt.

Printed in the USA
CPSIA information can be obtained
at www.ICGtesting.com
JSHW012016140824
68134JS00025B/2446